Producing for \

Producing for Web 2.0 is a clear and practical guide to the planning, set up and management of a website. It gives readers an overview of the current technologies available for online communications and shows how to use them for maximum effect.

The third edition sets out the practical toolkit needed for web design and content management. It is supported by a regularly updated and comprehensive website at www.producingforweb2.com where readers can take part in blogs and forums, see examples of programming and demonstrations of concepts discussed in the book, as well as try things out themselves on the testing site.

Producing for Web 2.0 includes:

- illustrated examples of good page design and site content,
- comprehensive online support and testing areas,
- advice on content, maintenance and how to use sites effectively,
- ideas on how to maximise available programs and applications,
- tips on using multimedia, including video, audio, Flash and images,
- a glossary and a list of terminology,
- a chapter on ethics and internet regulations for journalists and writers,
- tutorials for the main applications used in website design,
- step-by-step guides to difficult areas with screenshots,
- guides to good practice for all those involved in journalism, broadcasting and media studies, and
- a list of resources including websites and guides to further reading.

It is the perfect guide for anyone coming to web design for the first time, or producing multimedia materials.

Jason Whittaker teaches on the Journalism programme at University College Falmouth, and is also Professor of English and Media Arts. He has more than 15 years' experience as a technology journalist and is the author of several books on new technologies, including *The Cyberspace Handbook* (2003) and *Web Production for Writers and Journalists* (2002), as well as several books on William Blake. His most recent publication is *Magazine Production* (2008).

Producing for Web 2.0

A student guide

Third edition

Jason Whittaker

Routledge
Taylor & Francis Group

LONDON AND NEW YORK

First published 2000 as *Producing for the Web*
by Routledge
2 Park Square, Milton Park, Abingdon, Oxon OX14 4RN

Simultaneously published in the USA and Canada
by Routledge
270 Madison Ave, New York, NY 10016

Second edition published 2002 as *Web Production for Writers and Journalists*

Routledge is an imprint of the Taylor & Francis Group, an informa business

© 2000, 2002, 2009 Jason Whittaker

Typeset in Scala and Scala Sans by The Running Head Limited, www.therunninghead.com
Printed and bound in Great Britain by CPI Antony Rowe, Chippenham, Wiltshire

British Library Cataloguing in Publication Data
A catalogue record for this book is available from the British Library

Library of Congress Cataloging in Publication Data
Whittaker, Jason, 1969–
Producing for Web 2.0: a student guide / Jason Whittaker. — 3rd ed.
    p.   cm.
Rev. ed. of: Web production for writers and journalists. 2002
Includes bibliographical references and index.
1. Web sites—Design. 2. English language—Composition and exercises. 3. Web site
development. 4. Authorship. 5. Web publishing. I. Whittaker, Jason, 1969– Web production
for writers and journalists. II. Title.
TK5105.888.W48 2009
006.7—dc22

                                                                        2008053200

ISBN 10: 0–415–48621–1 (hbk)
ISBN 10: 0–415–48622-x (pbk)
ISBN 10: 0–203–88203–2 (ebk)

ISBN 13: 978–0–415–48621–7 (hbk)
ISBN 13: 978–0–415–48622–4 (pbk)
ISBN 13: 978–0–203–88203–0 (ebk)

For Sam, for her patience

Contents

Walkthroughs

Preface to the third edition

When *Producing for the Web* was first published in 2000, the world of web design was very different from that of today. The first dotcom boom had taken place (shortly to be followed by a dotcom bust), and while a number of the key technologies had already been established, the transformation in web publishing that has come to be known as **Web 2.0** was still to occur.

That first book concentrated principally on HTML and general principles of design. By the time it was revised, as *Web Production for Writers and Journalists* in 2002, Dreamweaver was being accepted by many as the industry-standard application for web design. That edition concentrated much more on creating websites using Dreamweaver, as well as introducing more substantial sections on providing content for the web.

In the intervening six years, online publication has changed dramatically. Blogs, while not entirely new in 2002, were rarely used, and many of the most popular sites on the web today, such as Wikipedia, Facebook and YouTube did not exist or had only just been founded. Even Google, far and away the most successful of the 'new' new media companies at the time of writing, was little more than a humble search engine, without a host of add-on utilities such as maps, email and even an office suite.

A big difference between *Web Production for Writers and Journalists* and *Producing for Web 2.0* is the status of Dreamweaver – and,

indeed, any other web design application. Steve Hill, citing both Khoi Vinh, the design director for NYTimes.com, and Dave Lee, at UKPG, summed up the situation on his blog (srh.typepad.com/blog/2008/04/index.html) with a very simple question: 'Who's using Dreamweaver?'

These and other commentators have drawn up a wish list of the various skills that the ideal recruit would have (note: terms below and others elsewhere that appear in bold are explained in the glossary at the end of the book):

- an extensive knowledge of **XHTML** and **CSS** (cascading style sheets), the fundamental technology for creating web pages and determining their appearance,
- a sound knowledge of a scripting language such as JavaScript, to provide greater interactivity,
- an understanding of Flash, the main way for developing 'rich' applications online,
- a 'comfort' level with database and application programming languages such as MySQL and PHP being used to drive many dynamic sites online,
- multimedia skills with image, audio and video,
- last but not least, a solid foundation in news values – that is, knowing how to write in a way that will attract readers and convey information quickly.

The one skill that is rarely – if ever – required is a knowledge of Dreamweaver. And yet, as Hill points out, for a majority of students engaged in media studies, and some teachers too, activities such as online journalism are the same as creating websites, which amounts to learning Dreamweaver. The advantage of Dreamweaver as an 'industry app' (or, at least, that is how Adobe would like to see it) is that teaching the package provides a clear rationale for having something to teach – something that also costs money and is thus of value to the 'industry' (as with other sectors, such as page layout with InDesign, image editing with Photoshop, video editing with Avid, or computer aided design with AutoCAD).

But the vast majority of web production simply does not work that way these days. Not only was the original web built on open standards (such as **HTML**), but many of the most dynamic and useful systems for getting content online – **wikis**, **blogs**, **content management systems** (**CMSs**) – are also available as free, open-source products. Such applications can teach much more valuable transferable skills than learning one particular interface: despite the fact that very often one particular site or system such as Joomla! or Blogger may have superficial differences to the next, underlying principles are frequently the same. Despite this, I am not completely sceptical about the value of using Dreamweaver for certain tasks, and throughout this book the reader will encounter various examples of how to achieve particular aims using that program.

The ideal web producer, then, would be a coder with a solid understanding of XHTML and CSS in particular, but also familiar with other programming and scripting languages as well as database design. Furthermore, he or

she would be very competent with a wide range of multimedia formats, and an expert writer to match. The list sounds formidable – and in many ways it is. In practice, there are plenty of very successful web producers who only touch the most essential elements of design and concentrate instead on producing content, whether in the form of text or other media. What is more, the various platforms covered in this book make it easier than ever to get material online, so it is more than possible to publish your work without ever understanding a single line of code.

Despite this, for those who wish to move beyond the basics, a core knowledge of the technologies involved in online publishing is immensely valuable. What is more, while the media landscape for web production has changed immensely since the publication of *Web Production for Writers and Journalists*, an emphasis on key writing skills remains very important, and this title is in some ways a return to the grounding in design and underlying programming techniques similar to that covered in the first edition of *Producing for the Web*.

After introducing the reader to the principles of Web 2.0 in chapter 1, what makes it different to web production during the 1990s, chapter 2 will look at what is required to plan and prepare before you begin to build a site. Chapter 3 covers the core skills for web design, both in terms of general design and navigation as well as using XHTML and CSS. These skills are expanded into client- and server-side scripting in chapter 4, before moving onto how to use multimedia in chapter 5. *Producing for Web 2.0* assumes a certain degree of continuity between core web design skills and publishing platforms which can be considered as closer to Web 2.0 models, these being covered in chapter 6. Chapter 7

> The ideal skills for web production include a knowledge of XHTML and CSS for creating and formatting web content, as well as dynamic scripting, multimedia skills, database design and knowing how to write in a way that will attract readers and convey information quickly.

covers content management systems, specifically Joomla! Writing, which still remains central to most of the content that appears online, is the subject of chapter 8, while the final chapter on post-production considers the testing and promotion of your site, with particular emphasis on new requirements for modern web production, such as optimising a site for search engines.

THE *PRODUCING FOR WEB 2.0* SITE

To accompany this book, the companion site includes extended examples of coding included in the text, as well as technology updates and a blog with extended articles on new developments in the web world.

You can find the site at http://www.producingforweb2.com.

CHAPTER 1

Introduction

Since its invention by Tim Berners-Lee in 1990, the web has rapidly transformed the means by which information can be published and disseminated. Central to the original ideal of the web was the ability to transfer data regardless of the platform on which it was viewed: so long as a visitor had a browser, it did not matter which hardware or operating system he or she used to get online.

Since about 2004, however, the ease and capabilities of the web have undergone considerable changes – what is commonly referred to as Web 2.0. This chapter will begin with an outline of the principles of Web 2.0 publishing, as well as the various options open to web producers.

THE INTERNET AND WEB 2.0

Web 1.0

There are plenty of books that have appeared in recent years on the history of the internet. As the focus of this title is recent developments that have been bundled together under the title 'Web 2.0', the context of web development throughout the 1990s can be dealt with very quickly.

The beginnings of the internet, as opposed to the world wide web, lie in the Cold War and plans to build a communications structure that could withstand a strategic nuclear attack.

DARPANET (the US Department of Defense Advanced Research Projects Agency) launched the first network in 1968, and through the 1970s and 1980s various research and military institutions connected to this backbone.

Until 1990, however, the internet was still very much an esoteric and restricted concern. What changed this was the work by Tim Berners-Lee, a consultant at the European Centre for Nuclear Research (CERN), who wrote a short program, Enquire-Within-Upon-Everything, or ENQUIRE, that enabled electronic documents to be linked more easily. A year later, he developed the first text web browser, NeXT, and so launched the world wide web.

CERN continued to develop the web as an academic tool, but by the end of 1992 only 26 hosts were serving websites, growing slowly to 1,500 by 1994. The boom in web (and internet) usage came that year when Marc Andreessen, at the National Center for Supercomputing Applications, developed a graphical web browser, Mosaic, and then left to form a new company, which was to become Netscape Communications.

At the same time, developments in personal computing, such as the decline in price of PCs and the launch of a new operating system, Windows 95, meant that more people than ever before were starting to use computers as part of their daily lives. While Microsoft had originally been dismissive of the internet, by

1997, with the launch of Internet Explorer 4 as part of the Windows operating system, they began to pursue this new market much more aggressively (too aggressively according to the US Department of Justice).

The late 1990s saw the dotcom bubble expand – and then burst. Paper millionaires appeared and disappeared in the space of a few months, and a post-millennium malaise set in when it seemed for a few years that nothing good could come out of the overvalued medium.

Yet the investment and innovation that took place in those years did have some incredibly important consequences. While many half-baked websites (quite rightly) disappeared without trace, some such as Amazon, eBay and Google became household names. Internet usage generally, and the web in particular, had become completely normalised in many instances, for some users displacing traditional media altogether as faster broadband connections rolled out in different parts of the world. At the same time, the often difficult process of getting content online was becoming increasingly simplified through such things as blogs, wikis and **social networking** sites, leading some commentators to remark on a new phase of web publishing – Web 2.0.

What is Web 2.0?

Web 2.0 is a term coined by Dale Dougherty of O'Reilly Media and Craig Cline of MediaLive prior to a conference of that name which took place in 2004. It is a rather loose term that refers to a collection of platforms, technologies and methodologies that represent new developments in web development.

The term itself has generated a considerable amount of controversy, most notably from Tim Berners-Lee, the inventor of the world wide web, who, in an interview

> Core principles of Web 2.0 include using the web as a platform to run applications, rather than relying on the operating system, allowing users to take control of their content, and employing new methods to share that content more easily.

for IBM in 2006, remarked that 'nobody even knows what it means'. Berners-Lee pointed out that the innovations implemented by Web 2.0 applications, for example simplifying the sharing of data and making online media much more inclusive, were actually pioneered as part of the development of the supposedly outdated Web 1.0. Likewise, Steve Perlman (the man behind **QuickTime** as well as many other innovations) more recently observed that many so-called Web 2.0 sites were really very static in their approach to content and lacked real multimedia support; many such applications, he observed in an interview with CNET, currently touted as cutting edge will be obsolete in only a few years.

In addition to such criticism, a more general observation is that certainly much Web 2.0 commentary is little more than internet marketing hype familiar from the dotcom bubble at the end of the 1990s. Despite these reservations (all of which are extremely valid), Web 2.0 is a convenient label to distinguish some real innovations that have taken place since the turn of the century. More than this, however, it recognises that recent years have seen a remarkable change in the applications of new technologies driven (among other things) by revolutions in computer usability and bandwidth.

In a blog entry in September 2005, Tim O'Reilly offered a succinct overview of what Web 2.0 was meant to achieve, observing that 'like many important concepts, Web 2.0 doesn't have a hard boundary, but rather, a gravitational core. You can visualise Web 2.0 as a set of principles and practices that tie together a veritable solar system of sites that demonstrate some or all of those principles, at a varying distance from that core' (O'Reilly, 2005).

Key elements of this 'gravitational core' include:

- using the web as an applications platform,
- democratising the web, and
- employing new methods to distribute information.

The implications behind a 'democratisation' of the web are contentious to say the least, and this idea is better limited to considerations of usability and participation rather than any implied political process (although that is often invoked), but these three bullet points in some shape or form do identify the nucleus of what Web 2.0 is meant to achieve with regard to platforms, participation, and data as the focus.

The web as platform

O'Reilly observes that the notion of the web as platform was not new to Web 2.0 thinking but actually began with Netscape in the mid-1990s when it took on Microsoft with the assertion that online applications and the web would replace Windows as the key operating system (OS). As long as users could access programs and data through a browser, it did not really matter what OS or other software was running on their desktop computer.

Several factors indicate the difference between online services in the 1990s and those currently labelled as Web 2.0, and also indicate why Netscape failed at the time:

- Limited bandwidth: for processing and delivering data, online services simply lagged behind and/or were too expensive in comparison to desktop applications at the time.
- Limitations of the 'webtop': Netscape's alternative to the desktop, the 'webtop', was much closer to Microsoft's core model than it assumed; achieving dominance by giving away a free web browser was meant to drive consumers to expensive Netscape server

products rather than allowing them to plug into a range of services. The software application had to succeed for Netscape to be viable.

O'Reilly contrasts this approach to that of Google's, which began life as a web service: the ultimate difference, argues O'Reilly, is that with Google the core service is combined with the delivery of data: 'Without the data, the tools are useless; without the software, the data is unmanageable' (2005). Software does not need to be sold and licensing of applications is irrelevant, because its only function is to manage data, without which it is redundant: that is, it 'performs' rather than is distributed. As such, 'the value of the software is proportional to the scale and dynamism of the data it helps to manage'. Furthermore, data should be as easily exchanged as possible between different applications and sites.

Rather than simply providing static information as was common to many (but by no means all) Web 1.0 sites, Web 2.0 services make much greater use of **applets** to use that data dynamically, for example to send messages to large numbers of users via a simple interface (Twitter) or share favourite links (delicious). Simplicity of use to the end user often belies very complex technology behind the scenes, and core technologies include server software, content syndication, messaging **protocols**, standards-based browsers (non-standard **plug-ins** are to be avoided as they cannot necessarily be installed on different devices) and client applications accessed through the browser.

The important features of the web as platform are as follows:

- to make data accessible from any platform connected to the internet, regardless of its location or the operating system,

> Web 2.0 platforms are designed to make data accessible, regardless of its location, so that it can be exchanged as seamlessly as possible, providing services previously carried out on the desktop.

delicious.com, one of the new generation of social bookmarking sites.

- to exchange that data as seamlessly as possible between different sites and applications, without the need for proprietary plug-ins,
- to carry out tasks previously carried out on the desktop via an online service and thus make them more easily shared,
- to use applets to provide a 'user rich experience'.

An architecture of participation

The 'democratisation of the web' is a phrase often used in conjunction with Web 2.0, but one that *Producing for Web 2.0* will avoid because of the assumptions it makes about democratic processes as ultimately being tied too often to consumption (this is not to deny a link between the two, but rather to draw attention to the limitation of such connections, a full analysis of which is beyond the scope of this book).

Rather, here we will use a more neutral term, again first used widely by Tim O'Reilly but with its roots in open-source software development and the ideas of Lawrence Lessig – an 'architecture of participation'. Such participation builds upon the interactivity that was an early part of web design, in contrast to other media which tend to emphasise passive consumers (not necessarily in interpretation, but certainly in terms of production) versus active producers. Despite the fact that Berners-Lee believed that early users would be authors as well as readers, and nearly every site had pages that required users to click hyperlinks to navigate a site, most such pages were very static.

In the mid-1990s, however, companies such as Amazon were actively encouraging visitors to post reviews of books, and of course there had long existed interactivity on such things as bulletin boards which started to transfer to mainstream sites. The development of audience interactivity, then, can be seen as an evolution of early forms of connecting people

Wikipedia is one of the most remarkable Web 2.0 sites to have emerged in recent years.

(as pointed out by Berners-Lee), emphasising the interaction of users with a site to a lesser or greater degree. At its most developed, this involves a much greater degree of trust in users so that, for example, with a wiki the process of editing and contributing is much more decentralised.

O'Reilly has spoken of the ability of sites such as Wikipedia to 'harness collective intelligence', although a consequence of this letting go of centralised control makes it much easier for users to enter incorrect information accidentally or deliberately. An important outcome of this simple fact is that for this to function correctly, it depends upon a community of informed and interested users to constantly monitor and moderate activity.

Attwell and Elferink (2007: 2) point out:

the Architecture of Participation is not a software system as such – or even a collection of software tools – but rather a bringing together of various technologies and activities designed to facilitate and promote participation, communication and the active construction of meanings and knowledge.

Core to this is trust, that a site is not a 'walled garden' but something that should be as easy to enter and leave as possible (which in turn relates to issues of usability) and, to maintain this trust, that users' data belongs to them. In turn, this has drawn attention to the relationship between sites that involve some form of social networking or communal activity and ownership of intellectual property, with trends established by the development of open-source software and the role of organisations such as the Creative Commons (creativecommons.org) being important in developing new attitudes towards copyright, drawing a middle line between anarchic piracy that damages trust and over-restrictive regulations that stifle innovation.

The social impact of these architectures of participation is already proving itself to be immensely important, for example in the rise of the blogosphere (which encapsulates the successes and irritations of much of Web 2.0 capabilities). The combination of community and architecture draws attention to the main capability of Web 2.0 development: technology provides the framework to exchange data (the architecture) that should be as simple and seamless as possible, but without a community of users to produce that data in the first place the technology itself is redundant.

Data as focus

Web 1.0 was as much about information as Web 2.0, but the means for distributing data has changed significantly. One important consequence of creating participative architectures has been the growth of

user-generated content (**UGC**), or consumer-generated media, referring to publicly available content produced by end users rather than the producers or administrators of a site.

Often UGC is only part of a site but in some cases, as with Flickr or YouTube, it constitutes the entire process (with attendant problems in terms of copyright with YouTube, for example). Some media organisations are therefore switching from being the providers of content to being the providers of frameworks and facilities where content can be shared.

The OECD (Organisation for Economic Co-operation and Development) emphasises that genuine UGC involves creative effort on the part of the contributor, rather than simply being material such as video or audio digitised from another source, and that it is produced outside the normal professional routines and practices.

In addition, whereas most sites until the dotcom crash tended to produce static

Flickr was one of the first sites to make sharing user content its core activity.

HTML pages that were relatively cumbersome to update, after this event many began to experiment with new ways to make data more interactive. One important development, which was initiated in the 1990s, was syndication or web feeds, whereby content on one site could be made available to multiple external sites or newsreaders on a user's computer. While the technology available for 'push' syndication (streaming data to subscribers) began to be developed around 1995, it was only from 2001 onwards that formats such as **RSS** (Really Simple Syndication, or RDF Site Summary) started to win widespread acceptance. The effect of syndication is that users can receive updates of changes to rapidly updated content, such as news feeds, blogs or forums, without the need to visit a site.

> **Really Simple Syndication (RSS) is an important way in which data can be shared and updated between multiple sites.**

Two important foci, then, of Web 2.0 technologies are simplifying the process of creating information so that many people may contribute (sometimes referred to as crowdsourcing), and simplifying how data is shared. Blogs and wikis are good examples of the former, whereby users with minimal technical experience may enter or upload media much more quickly than was required when creating a personal home page. As well as syndication, a number of other methodologies have emerged for the sharing of data: tags are a means by which visitors may enter opinions and information about an article or piece of media which, in turn, will be picked up by search engines thus attracting other visitors.

In contrast to what O'Reilly distinguished as the Web 1.0 method of organising data – directories or taxonomies, which would require some form of centralised administration – Web 2.0 methods such as tagging create a **folksonomy** (also known as social indexing or tagging) whereby users apply their own categories to identify material of interest. Of course, the lack of control over terminology can create inefficient indexing (with plenty of synonyms – what is know as polysemy), but

folksonomies have arisen due to the perceived inefficiencies of traditional web indexing or searches. In addition, the introduction of the **permalink**, a **URL** to point to a blog or forum entry after it has passed from the front page to an archive and which does not change, allows data to remain in circulation.

Another phenomenon associated with Web 2.0 is the long tail. Coined by Chris Anderson, editor in chief of *Wired* magazine, 2004, the long tail defines the process of focusing on less popular information or resources that previously were unviable because of some physical limitation. Also referred to as niche marketing, the long tail works by making available data to fragmentary audiences, in contrast to hit marketing, the process of constructing a few large-grossing hits because there is only so much space to show movies at the cinema, or carry DVDs, CDs or books on shelves. Anderson gives examples of the 1.7 million Indians living in the US who could only see Hindi films on a handful of screens, or the lack of documentaries available in Blockbuster. As Anderson points out, 'The average Barnes & Noble carries 130,000 titles. Yet more than half of Amazon's book sales come from outside its top 130,000 titles' (2006: 83). Digital distribution makes it possible to provide relatively obscure back-catalogues and, via search engines and other forms of organisation of data, connect that material to users on a wider scale – thus making them viable.

Always in beta

The adoption of the internet as a means for distributing software has resulted in new models that contrast greatly to previous cycles and which have consequences for distribution of other media.

Traditionally, a software concept would be proposed and written in alpha form, then distributed as a beta for testing and, after a release candidate was developed the final version would be distributed for sale. As applications became more complex, it became quite clear that bugs and improvements not picked up at the beta stage would need further patches to fix. By contrast, a great deal of software used by Web 2.0 sites is always in beta, drawing on the fact that open-source software in particular can be modified by a much wider range of developers and programmers than in traditional companies. The continuous development cycle for this new type of production process is often referred to as 'always in beta', with updates being released as and when they are created and/or tested, rather than waiting for a convenient date in the schedule.

> **The continuous cyle of development on new sites means that they are never final but 'always in beta', with users playing an important role in co-developing how they perform.**

Another effect of this approach is to treat users as co-developers: just because a feature is available does not mean that it should be used. Overloading a site with additional abilities can simply make it confusing, while elements that are popular can be rolled out on a wider basis.

Simplicity is often key, and this also applies to development and distribution of data: as O'Reilly remarks, the best way to think of information is via syndication not co-ordination – that is to make information available as quickly and cleanly as possible rather than attempting to control what use of it is made at the other end. Likewise, data of all kinds should be designed to be hacked and remixed into new forms – with 'some rights reserved' becoming a useful contrast to 'all rights reserved'.

The always in beta model for content has had its greatest impact in areas such as rolling news, which in some senses may be said to have predated software development: hourly bulletins offering new information as and when it became available (although, in pre-Web formats, still dictated by a schedule). In regard to this, Paul Bradshaw (2007) has suggested a publishing model that although really devoted to online news has some crossovers to other types of new

media publishing. Bradshaw identifies the speed with which online publishing can take place, with an alert allowing an author to produce a speedy response in terms of a blog entry or article identified as an initial response (such as a news story). More than this, however, online publishing can also emphasise depth as stories are returned to and more detailed accounts presented, through multimedia or – and this is where Web 2.0 tools become useful – interactive responses from multiple users.

What is particularly appealing about this model is the fact that it also indicates the different styles of discourse which users and producers (terms that become increasingly blurred in this format) are starting to respond to: we expect a blog to be more informal than, say, a video package, and so may assess and evaluate it accordingly. In addition, the genesis for stories and information does not necessarily begin with the producer but may instead originate with the end user who identifies a particular event.

Distributed applications

A consequence of the focus on the web as platform is that software increasingly needs to be written above the level of a single device. This is certainly not new to Web 2.0, and was fundamental to Berners-Lee's original idea for data interchange between a number of different computing platforms. However, with the proliferation of devices that can now connect to a network, such as TVs, mobile phones and media players (such as the iPod), the ability to create services that can serve data to multiple end users with different applications, some of them probably not conceived of at the time of design, reinforces the importance of creating open rather than proprietary standards for data exchange. This was the problem for Netscape's webtop model, which ultimately wished to lock users into a vertical market from their browsers up to their servers.

As with content, so the principles of being able to hack and remix data is important to software, the new model for which is to create applications via 'snap-ins' or plug-ins, taking source material distributed elsewhere on the web and presenting it in an innovative fashion. Key to this has been the development and distribution of open **APIs**, or application programming interfaces. An API is a standard set of instructions (the interface) to allow different elements to communicate, for example a website and a remote service provided by a third party. An important element of Web 2.0 design has been that certain companies, such as Google, Facebook and Flickr, have made their APIs freely available for non-commercial use so that, for example, web designers can call on Google Maps, friends lists in Facebook or photo albums in Flickr to make them available on their own websites.

The API usually works seamlessly, so a visitor to a site is not even aware that content is being provided from another domain. APIs are usually employed to create **mashups**, web applications that combine data from more than one source to create a single tool, for example by combining data from Google Maps with data from estate agents, thus creating a service that was not imagined by either party. Mashups editors also often make use of RSS feeds to source data from other sources, something that is made possible by the fact that information is increasingly separated from presentation, allowing it to be re-used in novel forms.

As Jesse James Garrett (2005) says, **Ajax** is a good example of this new approach to producing software: 'Ajax isn't a technology. It's really several technologies, each flourishing in its own right, coming together in powerful new ways'. It incorporates **XHTML** and **CSS** for presentation, dynamic interaction and data exchange via

Facebook is one of many sites that has made its API available to third-party developers.

XML, **XSLT** and the document object model (**DOM**), and asynchronous data retrieval via **XMLHttpRequest**; and binds everything together with **JavaScript** (all these are technologies that will be explained in the next chapter). What appears to be one piece of software is in fact a hybrid of many other forms that can be customised and re-adapted much more quickly.

WEB PRODUCTION SKILLS

The skills required to produce a website can be incredibly varied. A lot of talk in media industries in recent years has focused on the notion of convergence, that different production techniques as well as the means for consuming media will come together in a single platform. The internet and computing are obviously the most important technological driving forces behind this phenomenon, although economic, social, cultural and even political factors have an important role to play.

The complexity of setting up a site should not be overemphasised. If you need a quick and easy route into publishing your ideas and thoughts, then a blog can be as easy as using a word processor – with the ability to embed multimedia instantly. However, for a complex, multi-user content management system a raft of programming, design and content production skills can be called into play, nearly all of which will be covered to a lesser or greater extent in this book.

How to plan for a website

Before creating anything technical, a web producer needs to think ahead with regard to planning for their site. What content will it contain? Who will use it? Will you need multimedia? How will it be tested and maintained?

As part of the pre-production process

covered in the next chapter, we will outline some of the ways in which you can prepare for your website in order to manage it effectively from the initial idea to final testing and deployment. Project management can be a slightly daunting term for small-scale developments, but having clear ideas and objectives about what you wish to achieve will help you when it comes to the design stage.

For the first stage of planning, it is important to know what you want – perhaps a blog for fast and easy publishing or a Facebook group if you want interaction from lots of users. In some cases, designing a website from scratch may be the least efficient way of reaching your target audience.

Knowledge of core technologies

Even if you are planning to take advantage of the many Web 2.0 publishing options available online, an understanding of at least some of the core technologies will be immensely useful in customising what is on offer. While there are, for example, plenty of templates available on sites such as Blogger, knowing how to modify that template's HTML structure and its appearance via CSS (cascading style sheets) will provide you much more scope in getting your message across. One of the ironies of Web 2.0, noted in the preface, is that the simplicity of publishing online has made a knowledge of underlying code much more important in many ways than learning a complex web design application. Throughout this book we will return repeatedly to the essentials of code needed to customise as well as build a site.

The most important core skills are a knowledge of HTML (or, rather, XHTML, rewritten in accordance with XML principles) and CSS, but you will also be introduced to client- and server-side **scripting**, in the form of JavaScript and PHP, as well as XML, the

> A knowledge of core technologies such as HTML and CSS will enable you to modify and customise many of the free services that are provided to users online.

database programming language **SQL** and some other new technologies such as Ajax that draw together these languages. In some cases, what is offered is a taster of such languages rather than a comprehensive overview, but just about anyone should be able to modify an existing platform or begin to create dynamic sites from scratch.

Web design skills

An understanding of the underlying code is immensely important to being able to create and fix websites. Indeed, one of the key skills that is required for design is the ability to identify and solve problems, debugging your site when things go wrong and do not work quite as you intended.

Knowing how to code, however, is not the same as being able to create an efficient design. How will users navigate around your site and find the information they need? What is the structure of the site and how do pages relate to each other? What will those individual pages look like, and where will content go? Paying attention to such things, as well as knowing how to work with colour, typefaces and design layout, will make a huge difference to how your site is received.

In addition, while the emphasis in this book lies with knowing core web coding languages (at least enough to customise and modify a pre-existing template), there will be plenty of examples of using a visual web editor such as Dreamweaver to create your own site. Such editors should never be used as a simple replacement for any knowledge of HTML in particular, but can be a very handy supplement for creating your own sites.

Multimedia skills

One of the effects of convergence is that the web is becoming the ideal platform for publishing a wide range of media. Although the very first web pages were purely text, within a couple of years the inclusion of images had transformed the presentation of online documents, enabling them to use magazine-style layouts. For most of the 1990s, this was the standard form for web design, music (in the form of **MP3** especially) being added to the mix by the end of the decade. Sound was available to designers prior to this, but bandwidth did not really support high-quality audio and the less said about the horrors of embedded midi files in pages in the mid-1990s the better. It was not really until about 2004–5 that broadband access to the web became widely enough available for video to be added to the mix, but since then visuals have become an important part of any web producer's repertoire.

One of the consequences of this is the impact that has been felt in a number of established disciplines and professions, such as journalism. Where once it was enough for a journalist to master a pen (followed by the typewriter and word processor), increasingly he or she will also need to be familiar with at least basic skills in handling a camera, audio recorder and video camera to succeed. It should be noted, however, that there is often a considerable difference between the quality and skills of audio and video work required for many sites compared to high-definition radio and television broadcasts. This is not an excuse to be shoddy, but in practice people listen to or watch short clips online when embedded as part of a website (video on-demand and online radio being two exceptions of course) in contrast to the ways in which they consume more traditional media.

News values and writing skills

The reference to journalism draws attention to the final vital skill for an effective website: video, audio and interactive technologies such as Flash may have made the web a much more exciting place, but the fact remains that a great deal of what we do online is read copy – from captions and comments to full-blown articles. Many professional websites can be let down by spelling mistakes and solecisms – or simply by containing content that is far too dull.

The ability to spot a story and craft copy is an essential skill for the producer of a successful site, one which should never be underestimated. In many respects, the traditional skills for writing news – compressing as much information as possible into the first paragraph, ordering it by relevance and using the inverted pyramid – are eminently suitable for the web. Readers typically scan only the first few lines of an article before deciding to continue or move on, and so being able to convey what a page is about immediately and vividly is extremely important.

What this all means is that the ideal candidate for a web producer is an impossible figure: one who knows how to code, can handle multimedia equipment, has an eye for design and can also craft the perfect story. In practice, for all the talk of convergence and multi-skilling, large professional sites still rely on some division of labour where writers write, photographers take pictures, broadcasters produce audio-visual materials and web designers code and handle layout. And yet the ability to work across these different areas can enhance and improve the core area that you, as an individual, decide to focus on. If you are a writer, a good understanding of web design will make you appreciate why certain types of copy work better online than in print, while good literacy will improve the professionalism of your designs.

> **The ability to spot and craft good news copy is in many ways more important than ever as readers scan only the first few lines or words of a story before deciding whether to read on.**

CHAPTER 2

Pre-production

In this chapter, we will look in more detail at the decisions that need to be made before you begin to construct a website, including selecting the right platform for your content, whether it's a personal website or a multi-user content management system (CMS). We also outline the relevant technologies that go into making the web producer's 'online toolkit', and give advice on selecting and setting up a web server.

PLANNING A WEBSITE

The temptation when creating a website is to jump straight in, but if a site is to be a success some planning ahead will make a significant difference. Resources must be allocated, deadlines observed and tasks established. What this consists of will obviously vary from project to project: if you are a student engaged in a college project, there will be specific outcomes that you have to achieve, of course, while it may be that you are setting up a site that will be used by multiple content managers as part of a business or company project.

Managing a project

Anyone involved in project management will be presented with a job for which they have limited workers, time and resources. Even if this is a sole project, for example to be submitted as college work, you must plan ahead to determine what you will need to do in a particular timescale. The first step in managing more effectively is to divide a complex project into essential tasks that can be assigned deadlines and set in order.

In addition to ensuring that time and workers are allocated to meet a deadline, effective management should consider the consequences on deadlines if budgetary constraints are applied, for example how much work can be achieved if a certain amount of money is cut or moved elsewhere, or which tasks will have to be prioritised if deadlines are changed.

To make the process easier, a project can be divided into four distinct sections: defining the project, creating a project plan, tracking the project and then closing it. In this part of the chapter, we are most concerned with the information that feeds into the first two areas. A project plan that maps out tasks and deadlines can be an indispensable tool for defining clearly the scope and resources available. The first step is to ensure that these are assessed realistically, ensuring that assumptions can be met. To help with this, a project plan breaks down the project into tasks that can be assigned different resources and workers, having identified who or what will fulfil each task.

A project plan can proceed by one of two ways: you can enter a start date and schedule the plan forward to determine the best deadline, or enter the completion date and schedule the tasks backwards. Once people and resources are assigned to tasks the essential building blocks, resources, need to be tracked, both to ensure that work is spread as evenly as possible and also to plan for eventualities such as ill-health or other work.

Closing a project is, typically, the successful delivery of a website. However, one of the main mistakes made when creating such a site is failing to provide for its running costs, such as for time and maintenance. Closing a particular project may in fact consist of completing the first stage, but should also look forward to requirements and allocations for updates and future maintenance.

> **Planning a project is an important skill in determining what time and resources you will need to complete your tasks.**

define the function of the site, its purpose and audience. This draws attention to an important point: web developers may not be the final users of a site, and so the developer should get feedback from those users wherever possible. But this also requires negotiation: a person or group who commissions a site may build an ever larger wish list that becomes nigh on impossible to achieve, so having a clear idea of what is achievable or even desirable is also important.

Much has been written about 'user-centred design': the ideal or average user does not really exist, but there are some fundamentals that affect nearly all web production. First of all, speed is key: most users expect pages to load almost instantly, and as a rule of thumb any page that takes more than ten seconds to load will lose visitors. Second, because the end user's browser cannot be guaranteed, it is important to test a site in multiple browsers. Finally, a site's audience does not wish to appreciate aesthetic appearance in any abstract sense, but wants to find information as quickly as possible, making navigation immensely important.

Planning the workflow

Before even beginning planning that will determine the structure and content of a website, the first step is to process a model by which work will develop. Rather than including pages and content on an ad hoc basis, one simple development model is often referred to as a 'waterfall model' whereby the function of a site is established, a prototype is built and tested before the full site is released, with feedback occurring at each stage.

At this the initial stage, it is important to

The waterfall model describes how each stage of planning flows down to the next and then informs the previous one.

Once the audience for a site is determined, it is important to work out the functionality of a site. Thus, testing is essential in order to determine that the overall form of a site is *useful*, that its audience can find what they require with the minimum of effort. This is not something that can always be done before web design begins, and so we shall return to this subject in the final chapter on post-production, but such testing is not simply part of the final stage of web production; it should be done at every stage of the process.

Defining goals and audience

The first step in analysing requirements is to determine the purpose of your site and who will use it. Here is a checklist of the types of questions you will need to ask for different projects:

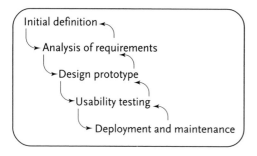

- Are there specific criteria that the site has to fulfil? For example, if it is a student project, are there specific requirements that you have to demonstrate (an understanding of XHTML, graphic design, clear communication) as part of the project brief? While *Producing for Web 2.0* is a student guide, in fact the criteria for a well-designed student project will seek to emulate many (although not necessarily all) the conditions of a more commercial brief, and so will be expanded on below.
- Is the site to be maintained by you as, essentially, the sole content manager, or is it to be used by multiple contributors?
- Will the site need to be updated on a regular basis, and what are the technical capabilities of those who will be adding material if this is not restricted to you?
- If this is part of a commercial or corporate website, are there already established workflows and procedures that need to be emulated by the site? For example, if information is gathered from members of a college via Word (or similar) documents that are then emailed back to be processed at a later date, this step may be considerably simplified by using a dynamic scripting language such as PHP to process forms and output the information directly to a site.
- Will there be multiple levels of access to a site? This may consist of allowing certain users to add content, but restricting the roles of others to being readers. Alternatively, certain sections of information on a site may need to be restricted to certain categories of visitors, regardless of whether they are to be authors.
- What type of content needs to appear on the site? Is it important to have relatively large articles or shorter news stories? Will the site better fulfil its aims by allowing for shorter comments or postings, as on a bulletin board? Do you want to allow users to communicate with each other via the site? Do they need to be able to upload multimedia content easily?
- Does content need to be organised into logical sections, such as news or reviews, to make it easier for visitors to browse?

The last bullet point does raise an important consideration: most web producers tend to consider articles as the be-all and end-all of web content, whereas in fact a more hands-off approach that can encourage communication between users is to allow the space and architecture for a bulletin board or comments on materials posted by other users (such as the comments appended to videos on YouTube). If you are going to concentrate on articles, the following are some of the typical elements that you will need to include to allow visitors to navigate your content:

- **A unique identity**   This allows articles to be located more easily.
- **A headline**   Fairly straightforward – the title of an article.
- **An author**   Again, it may be important to allow visitors to navigate via author names (or by-lines).
- **Short descriptor**   A brief account of an article's contents.
- **Publication and/or editing dates**   When an article was published and dates of when it has been changed or modified.
- **Keyword listings/searches**   Visitors will probably have key terms they are thinking of when looking for material, such as 'car sales' or 'dynamic web design' rather than the specific titles or authors that are assigned to particular articles.
- **Article status**   Some sites will distinguish, for example, between content that is current and that which has been archived but not removed from the site.

This type of information is known as metadata. We shall deal with this in more detail in later chapters on dynamic web design and post-production, but it is information about information – that is it tells us the contexts in which an article was created or operates (who its author was, when it was published) rather than telling us explicitly what the article is: to discover that, the visitor can read the article itself.

Such rather specific requirements should also be considered more generally through a series of questions. Who will use your site? What do they hope to achieve when they visit your site, and what information do they need for that? What similar sites currently exist, and what do they do that is helpful or a hindrance?

Site architecture and platforms

After considering the general audience and aims for your site, the next step is to consider the site platform and architecture. XHTML and CSS will be fundamental to your site, and the next section of this chapter will consider different web technologies in much more detail. For example, if your site needs to collect data from visitors through a series of forms, then you should really employ a dynamic scripting language such as PHP to process that data. Likewise, if you wish to build quite a complex site for multiple users, it will probably be simpler to use third-party software such as a content management system.

Even if you wish to create a site that is largely restricted to your own content, creating a static XHTML site may be far from the best option. For example, if you have only a relatively limited interested in customising graphic elements of your site, but want something that allows you to get content up as quickly and as regularly as possible, a blog may be a much better alternative. Likewise, if you wish to connect to a large number of users across popular sites such as Facebook and MySpace, then considering how to engage with elements of these may be a much better way to attract visitors than creating your own site from scratch.

Once you have decided which web technologies you wish to use, the next step of the planning process is to outline a site structure, how information is to be distributed across pages. The structure of a site is important: like

chapters in a book or a storyboard, it serves a practical function, both for the producer and the visitor to a site. For the producer, having a clear idea of the site's structure can establish the parameters for the most important information, whether there should be a link to a particular area (information about a company or individual, for example) that is accessible from every part of the site. For the visitor, a clear site structure is useful in navigating through a site and for orientation.

The first page is typically referred to as the home page, or it may be a portal for a larger site or intranet, having very little unique content itself in such cases but largely consisting of links to other parts of the site. If the first page is to be quick loading, a 'flag page', then this should have clearly definable links to the rest of the site. A common mistake is to provide a series of pages with minimal information (and probably loaded with adverts) before reaching the important parts of the site; while the temptation may be to keep visitors in situ for as long as possible, the likelihood is that they will simply hit the back button on their browser.

> **Before creating your site, you should determine a basic structure which will help you determine how different sections will link together.**

Another potential problem for developers is that as a site becomes established, the majority of visitors are likely to come to pages via a search engine. While a site structure offers a way of organising content, it cannot – and should not – impose a means of reading through pages. Unlike much other media, such as most books or video, websites are intrinsically non-linear and non-sequential. Having a clear idea of the underlying organisation of your content instead provides you with the basis for clear navigation to any other part of your site, regardless of where the visitor enters it. The tried and tested way is a menu of top-level links that lead to those sections you have identified as the most important.

These top level links can be mapped as a hierarchical tree structure, indicating the most

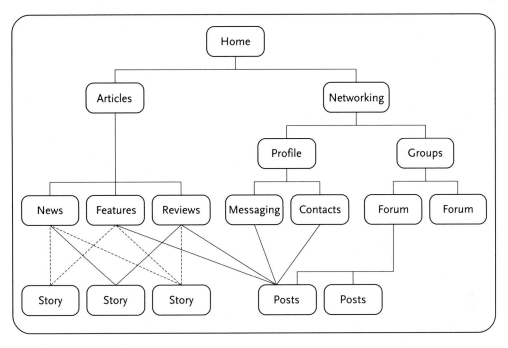

Mapping out your website is a useful step for organising content.

logical layout of site sections. For example, a commercial website may divide products into categories for sales, as well as provide services and contacts. Top level links should be available throughout the site.

Beyond this top level, other categories may become important as the tiers of information cascade down. For example, in a sports section, identifying different activities such as football, athletics or rugby becomes important in a way that it is not for someone reading the current affairs pages.

Designing templates

Although we shall deal with the various elements that go into a web page in more detail in the following chapter, an essential part of pre-production is planning how your pages will look. Across any well-designed site, there will be a degree of consistency across all the pages, including such things as a standard header for branding, a main navigation menu or menus, and a standard area where new content is

displayed. Setting up a template means that whichever page is visited, it will feel part of a larger whole, and although larger sites may have slightly different layouts for different sections they should be inter-related.

Similar to the metadata or types of content that you need to plan for on your site, it is important to work out the general areas that will be included in a template, for example:

- **A masthead**   Typically containing the site title and/or a logo, this is the main element that provides consistent branding across your site. Other information that could be included in the masthead includes a strapline, offering a snappy description of your site, and possibly contact information about your business.

- **Navigation toolbar**   As your visitors need to find their way about a site, there should be a coherent means of navigation, with standard links found from one page to the next. In most cases, this will consist of a navigation toolbar, or navbar, either on the left-hand side or above the main content. Although common, this is by no means the only way to provide a navbar but it is important to be consistent.

- **A page title** Individual pages will need some space to indicate the title of that particular page. This may, if relevant, also include a by-line or author's name.
- **Main content area** The title leads into the main content, on most sites usually located beneath the masthead and to the right of the main navigation bar. This is the section of the template that will vary most from page to page, but again there should be a degree of consistency which is typically provided via CSS.
- **Footer** Many sites offer a small area at the bottom of the page that does not change – offering regular links to ancillary content, for example, or a copyright statement.

These are the types of elements that would go into the *structure* of a page template, and how they appear on the page will be affected by its design. Rather than launching into CSS and HTML coding, or adding elements in a web editor, it is much better to get a sheet of paper and start sketching different versions of how you would like the page to appear. Once you have fixed on a version you like, then use an image editor such as Photoshop to create what is known as a mock-up or composite (comps for short); this can give a much better sense of how the page will look without committing to any markup in XHTML or CSS.

An important consideration when preparing a template is whether to go for a fixed or a fluid design: a fixed design assigns a very definite area to content (such as 700 pixels wide), and although this is preferred by many designers because it offers greater control over the look and feel of a template, it can waste a great deal of white space on larger resolution monitors. Fluid designs, on the other hand, scale up or down depending on the size of the browser window.

Web browsers

Fluid design draws attention to an important fact for web developers – that it is impossible to guarantee how a visitor will be viewing a page. Monitor resolutions can vary wildly from small sub-notebook screens to massive desktop

Templates provide consistency to a site in terms of layout and design.

Mozilla Firefox is one of the most popular browsers for surfing the web.

monitors, and different visitors may be using different web browsers, such as Safari on a Mac, Internet Explorer running on Windows or Firefox on **Linux**.

The disparities between web browsers are not as bad as they used to be. During the mid- to late 1990s, Microsoft and Netscape introduced proprietary tags into HTML so that pages designed for Internet Explorer (IE) often would not appear correctly in Navigator, or vice versa. Today, the push towards open standards has removed the worst of these abuses, but there can still be annoying surprises which makes it worthwhile to test your site in as many browsers as possible. Internet Explorer is by far the most popular as it is the default browser in Microsoft Windows, but there are alternatives you should be aware of:

- **Mozilla Firefox** The most popular browser after IE and managed by the Mozilla Corporation, Firefox is currently on version 3.0. Its code is open source and free, meaning that many developers have created third-party plug-ins such as media players and ad blockers (www.mozilla.com/en-US/firefox/).

- **Safari** Developed by Apple, Safari is the default browser for the MacOS, as well as other Apple products such as the iPhone. The current stable release is version 3, and since 2007 it has also been available for Windows. Safari offers a high level of compliance with internet standards, including CSS 3 (www.apple.com/safari/).

- **Opera** The fourth most popular browser, but with a much lower market share after IE, Firefox and Safari, Opera is free for personal use on PCs but not for other devices. Currently on version 9.5, Opera has often introduced features such as extra security or tabbed browsing that have been picked up at a later date by competitors (www.opera.com).

WEB TECHNOLOGIES

This section is not exhaustive, but outlines the most commonly employed technologies used in websites.

HTML

Hypertext Markup Language is the core language used to create web pages. It is a simple system that describes the structure of text within a document, denoting such things as paragraphs, headings, links and images, as a series of tags that are interpreted, or parsed, by the browser with the content then displayed in the browser window accordingly.

The first HTML prototype specification appeared in 1991, consisting of 22 elements, and quickly went through a number of revisions. The complete specification for version 1.0 was published in 1993, followed by HTML 2.0 in 1995 and HTML 3.2 (the first to be standardised by the World Wide Web Consortium) in 1997. HTML 4.0 and 4.01, what were to be the final versions of HTML before it was replaced by XHTML, appeared in 1998 and 1999, although a draft specification for HTML 5.0 was published early in 2008.

The early versions of HTML were not always followed as closely as they should have been: the commercial struggles between Netscape and Microsoft in the mid- to late 1990s in particular saw the introduction of proprietary tags that were incompatible with other browsers – hence the importance of **W3C** standardisation. The latest draft of HTML is intended to provide clear criteria to 'user agents', that is applications such as browsers, so that information coded in HTML can be passed as easily as possible between programs.

While HTML employs tags such as <head>, these are actually part of what is referred to as an element, which also includes the content between an opening and closing tag.

<h1 class="greeting">Hello, world!</h1>

The entire example above is a level 1 heading element, with opening and closing tags <h1> and </h1>. The content appears between these two tags, and within the opening tag, class="greeting" forms what is known as an attribute, that is a piece of code that modifies the element. The attribute itself divides into two parts: here class is the name of the attribute, and 'greeting' is its value.

XHTML

Since 2000, the preferred standard for coding pages has been XHTML, or eXtensible Hypertext Markup Language, which rewrote HTML in accordance with XML specifications (see the section on XML later in this chapter). The main difference between the two is that rules now matter: HTML was fairly forgiving of mistakes made in the HTML coding, so that even if elements were not correctly presented there was still a good chance that most if not all the page would display. The downside of this is that HTML was developed to enable users with different computer platforms to share information as easily as possible: as the ways for viewing the web via different devices, such as mobile phones, proliferate, so sloppy coding can result in information being lost or misinterpreted.

In addition, as we shall see in the next chapter, the division of the content, structure and presentation of a web page has resulted in some other major changes to HTML. Throughout the 1990s, the presentation of content – for example the colour of a background or the style of a font on a page – was handled within HTML. However, as presentation is now increasingly handled by cascading style sheets (CSS), many elements and attributes have been 'deprecated', that is their status has been downgraded. The <font>

> **XHTML is the preferred standard for coding pages and provides stricter rules regarding the formatting and presentation of hypertext markup.**

element is a good example of this. Previously, if you wished to change the colour and typeface of a font, you would do so as follows:

<font face="arial" size="3" color="red">Text here</font>

With multiple changes to fonts within an HTML document, incorporating multiple <font> elements would bloat the code of a page and become extremely unwieldy to edit at a later date. The tag was therefore deprecated in HTML 4.01 and is not supported at all in the strict implementation of XHTML.

As well as not using deprecated elements, XHTML documents must have a closing tag, unlike earlier versions of HTML. For those elements which do not normally have a closing tag, such as <img> and <br>, which insert an image and line break respectively, a space and forward slash should be inserted before the final angled bracket, as in <br />.

XHTML 1.0 can be implemented in one of three ways: Strict mode requires no deprecated elements or attributes; Transitionalmode allows for the use of presentational elements in HTML such as center and font; Frameset allows for the use of frames, which were common in web pages designed during the 1990s, but because of the difficulties they pose for search engines in particular are not commonly employed any more and will not be dealt with in this book. In addition, browsers sometimes employ what is known as 'quirks mode': as older web pages did not properly implement either CSS or Strict HTML 4.01 or XHTML, so browsers will attempt to emulate older browser standards to render these legacy pages as accurately as possible.

Examples throughout later chapters in this book will largely refer to XHTML 1.0 standards in Transitional mode. Shortly after the original standard was implemented, work began on a modular version, XHTML 1.1, which could be customised and extended for further web-enabled devices. It has not received widespread support, however, and, like XHTML 1.2 and 2.0, will not be discussed particularly in this book.

XHTML and the doctype

An XHTML document must begin with a document type declaration (**DTD**), or doctype. This declares what type of document the page is and corresponds to the different forms of XHTML:

- **Strict** <!DOCTYPE html PUBLIC "-//W3C//DTD XHTML 1.0 Strict//EN" "http://www.w3.org/TR/xhtml1/DTD/xhtml1-strict.dtd">
- **Transitional** <!DOCTYPE html PUBLIC "-//W3C//DTD XHTML 1.0 Transitional//EN" "http://www.w3.org/TR/xhtml1/DTD/xhtml1-transitional.dtd">
- **Frameset** <!DOCTYPE html PUBLIC "-//W3C//DTD XHTML 1.0 Frameset//EN" "http://www.w3.org/TR/xhtml1/DTD/xhtml1-frameset.dtd">

Although it looks like an element, the doctype does not have a closing tag but simply conveys information to the browser so it knows how to display a page according to proper rules. The doctype has to be displayed as shown above, complete with capitalisation and quotes (although it may be on one line). There are also doctypes for older versions of HTML.

The document tree

An XHTML document can be considered as an inverted tree, with various elements extended as branches from the root element <html>. A parent element can have child elements, that is tags that can be nested within the parent. For example, all elements that display content on a page, such as image or heading tags, will be nested within the <body> element, which is their parent.

Child elements are nested within parent elements. In the diagram on page 22, elements for emphasis (em) and an anchor (a) are located between paragraph tags (p) which, alongside a top level heading (h1), must be placed between body tags.

Standard attributes

At the end of this book, you will find a list of common XHTML elements and their attributes,

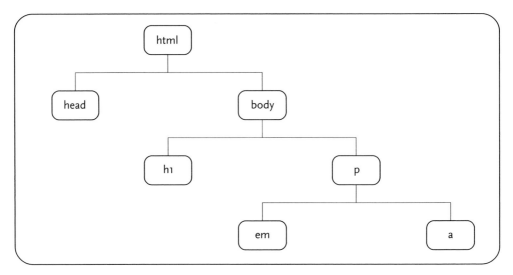

In an HTML document, elements are nested inside parent elements, creating what is known as the document tree.

but there is a series of attributes that can be included in just about any opening element. These are as follows:

- **class** Indicates the class to which an element belongs, and is often used for presentation and client-side scripting, such as with JavaScript. For example, defining a paragraph using the attribute class ="introduction" would change its formatting according to the rules specified for the class introduction in a CSS document.
- **id** Provides a unique identifier for an element and must be a unique text label within a document (ids cannot be shared between elements). An id is often called upon by scripts to make changes within a web page. Its first character must be a letter, although, as with a class name, the remaining characters can be numbers or a hyphen (-) or underscore (_).
- **style** This specifies CSS properties for an element. Although valid, presentation of a document is better handled via an external style sheet.
- **title** Provides a title for an element.
- **dir** Sets the direction in which text should be written, either ltr (left to right) or rtl (right to left), and is important for internationalisation.
- **lang** Specifies the language in which content is written according to an abbreviated code, such as en for English, es for Spanish, and jp for Japanese.
- **xml: lang** Also specifies the language.

CSS (cascading style sheets)

While HTML and XHTML deal with the structure of content, how text is defined as headings or paragraphs, or where images are placed, for example, CSS control the presentation of a web page. CSS level 1 was defined as a W3C standard in 1996, and work began on CSS level 2 in 1998. While we shall draw on some elements of CSS 2 in the next chapter, the fact that it is – after all this time – still a working draft means that most examples will be drawn from CSS 1. There is a new version, level 3, currently under development.

While the fundamental building block of HTML is the element, in CSS it is the rule which tells HTML elements how they are to be formatted on the page. For example, the following is a simple rule for text:

body {font-size: 12px;}

The rule is the entire statement above, and splits into two parts. First of all, there is the selector which indicates the element of a page to be formatted. Next, within the curly brackets, comes what is known as the declaration. This in turn is divided into two parts: the first a property, the aspect of an element such as font, colour, width and so on that is to be modified, and the second is the value. A declaration must always be followed by a semi-colon. In the above example, the default font for all pages that appears in the browser window is to be 12 points in size.

> An understanding of CSS is extremely important for anyone who wishes to produce well-designed web pages.

In addition to HTML elements such as body, p and h1, CSS rules can be applied to classes. A class can be assigned to just about any element in HTML and carries a rule or series of rules that will format that element in a different way. A class is indicated by a point before a name assigned by the web designer. For example:

.boxout {color: red;}

The significance of using classes is that the same element can have multiple formats applied to it in a single style sheet by using different classes. If the default colour of your paragraph text is to be dark grey, for example, you would include the rule:

p {color: darkgray;}

But if you wanted to format a paragraph as red in a boxout, you would set up its class as:

p.boxout {color: red;}

In the HTML document, the change in style would be indicated using the class attribute, as in:

<p class="boxout">Red text here.</p>

There is also a pseudo class selector, which begins with a semi-colon. Unlike classes, which can be specified for any element by the designer, there are only a few pseudo classes for hyperlinks, including :link, :visited and :hover, and these will be dealt with in the next chapter in the section on rollover links.

Finally, there is also the ID selector. This is preceded by a hash sign (#). Whereas a class can be assigned to multiple elements on a page, the ID attribute cannot be assigned to more than one element and so is much more specific than a class.

Cascading and attaching styles

The reason why CSS is referred to as *cascading* style sheets is because multiple style declarations can be assigned to elements, either within an HTML file itself, as multiple declarations in the same style sheet, or as multiple style sheets attached to the web page.

Consider three styles for a heading, for example, which are attached to the web page in different ways:

h1 {color: red;} – as part of a linked style sheet
h1 {color: blue;} – as part of an embedded style sheet
h1 {color: green;} – as part of an inline style.

In these examples, the last style takes precedence over the other two in the hierarchy of the cascade, while an embedded style takes precedence over a linked style sheet. Therefore the heading would be green in colour, but if the final style was removed, then it would appear blue. It would only appear red if both the embedded and inline styles were removed.

Similarly, cascading works according to the greater degree of specificity of a style:

h1 {color: green;} – as part of the general element selector
h1.intro {color: red;} – as part of the class "intro"
#introduction {color: blue;} – the specific ID "introduction".

If the HTML code was simply <h1>Heading</h1>, then its colour would be green, but if it is assigned a class, as in <h1 class="intro"> then this overrides the general h1 style. Finally, giving a particular heading the ID "introduction", as in <h1 class="intro" id="introduction">, then it would be blue in colour. The virtue of this approach is that you may have several properties for headings, such as typefaces or sizes, but you only wish to change one or two of these at particular points in your document. Setting up a class or an ID allows you to modify specific values for a selector while still inheriting the overall general values.

How to use style sheets within a web page will be considered in more detail in the next chapter, but it is worth noting the difference between linked, embedded and inline styles. In general, the linked style using the element <link> is preferable because this means you can control the appearance of multiple pages simply by editing one style sheet that is linked to them. However, if you wish to over-ride the style sheet for certain selectors, then you can embed a style sheet within a page by using the <style> element within the header of a page, as with:

```
<style>
<!--
body {
background: black;
}
p {
color: white;
}
-->
</style>
```

The lines <!-- and --> simply comment out the style so that it will be ignored by older browsers that do not support CSS.

As noted above, an embedded style sheet such as this would take preference over a linked style sheet, but if you wished one paragraph to be in a different colour, then you could override the embedded style with an inline one, for example:

```
<p style="color: red">Red text here.</p>
```

The particular paragraph this style was attached to would appear with red text, while all the others would be white. It is not recommended to use inline or embedded styles too frequently as they are not as convenient for formatting the presentation of an entire site in that you must edit every HTML document in which they appear, but they can be useful if you want a particular style for one web page or part of a page.

XML

XML stands for eXtensible Markup Language and is a specification that allows users to create their own markup languages. Devised throughout 1996 and 1997, it became a W3C standard in 1998.

Development began on XML because some users were beginning to be aware of the limitations that HTML and the web would face in future. In particular, because HTML could describe documents for display in a web browser but little else, it would become difficult to transfer to another device such as a mobile phone. Likewise, translating a document from one language into another for multi-lingual sites would be extremely difficult.

XML was designed to share information between a number of formats and platforms. The most difficult concept for new users to understand is probably that XML does nothing by itself. Rather, it is a markup language that allows users to define their own tags (hence it is extensible) to define data so that it may be shared more easily – particularly between computers and applications. Humans are good at deriving meanings from words and phrases (that is they can fairly easily understand semantics) but computers are not.

If you had a product listing, for example, in HTML the code might look something like the following:

```
<body>
<h1>The Gadget Store</h1>

<h2>Gadget One</h2>
```

```
<p>Gadget One is the late must-have
   item!</p>
<p><em>Price: £19.99</em></p>
<p><em>Post and packaging: £1.99</
   em><p>

<h2>Gadget Two</h2>
<p>How can you live without Gadget
   Two?</p>
<p><em>Price: £15.99</em></p>
<p><em>Post and packaging: £1.99</
   em><p>
</body>
```

A person could probably make sense of this quite quickly. The <h1> tag defines a company, <h2> defines an item, and the lines in bold (<em>) indicate prices, but a computer is unable to make sense of this. Where the problem arises is if you need to transfer this information from a web page to another program, say a spreadsheet, to analyse sales for example. To a browser, <h1> and <h2> simply indicate headings, that is the structure of the web page, not items.

What XML does is it provides structure for meaning, so the above example in XML code might look like this:

```
<?xml version="1.0"?>
<companyProduct title="The Gadget Store">

<item>
<name>Gadget One</name>
<description>Gadget One is the late must-
   have item!</description>
<price>£19.99</price>
<postage>£1.99</postage>
</item>

<item>
<name>Gadget Two</name>
<description> How can you live without
   Gadget Two?</description>
<price>£15.99</price>
<postage>£1.99</postage>
</item>

</companyProduct>
```

If you opened this file up in a browser capable of parsing (reading) XML, it would simply display the text as above – remember, XML itself does not do anything, rather it describes the meaning of data. To work with that data in a web page, you need to use CSS or XSLT (see below) to format the information. However, what this XML code does do is to tell another computer application such as a browser what that information means – it is quite clear, for example, that £1.99 for postage is different from the two prices of £19.99 and £15.99, whereas in the HTML code both were indicated simply with the tag <em> for emphasis. As such, an XML document is said to be self-describing.

XML looks like HTML, then, in that both use the same angular brackets to indicate elements, and it can also make use of attributes to modify tags – we could distinguish <price type="wholesale"> from <price type="retail"> in our example above. The fundamental difference is because XML allows you to define what these tags are, until you specify how they are to be used in XSLT the browser will not know what to do with them, in contrast to HTML where tags are clearly defined in terms of their effects. In fact, as has been mentioned previously in this chapter, it is better to think of XHTML as a very specific set of defined elements that the W3C and browser developers have agreed how to use.

Well-formed versus valid XML
The top of our sample XML file in the previous section begins with the line <?xml version="1.0"?>. Strictly speaking, this is not necessary, but it is good practice to include it because it makes clear that this is an XML

> **XML is an important technology for many Web 2.0 sites because it allows producers to define types of information that can then be shared between different sites and applications.**

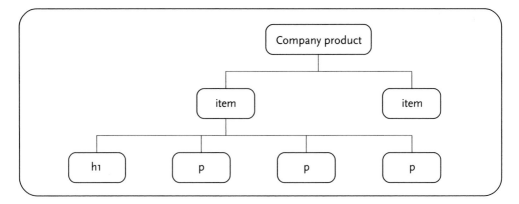

As with HTML, elements in XML are nested, with a parent element passing information about a document's structure down to a child element.

document and what type is being used (there is also version 1.1, but some features of this are contentious, so we shall stick to version 1.0 in this book).

An XML document is more than simply a sequence of elements: they are, in fact, hierarchically nested. Similar to the document tree for XHTML, there is a root element that contains all the others. Children elements may be nested within a parent, and this structure enables information to be passed up and down the tree.

How information is passed up and down this tree leads onto the next point, which is that there are two types of XML document: those which are well-formed, and those which are valid. Well-formed documents are the simplest to work with: they must contain a single root element that contains all other elements, they must have a closing as well as opening tag, or a self-closing 'empty' tag such as <br />, all attribute values must appear in quotation marks, and they must be nested properly. Thus the sequence <item><description></description></item> would be a correct nested order, but <item><description></item></description> would not.

A valid XML document is more complex. All the above rules must apply to it, but in addition it follows a set of rules set out in the document's DTD (document type declaration). Creating

valid documents is a complex process and the examples in this book will generally restrict themselves to those which are well-formed, but it is important to understand the principles behind the DTD which we have already encountered in relation to XHTML (itself written according to the rules of XML). XML allows you to create any kind of language you want, but if you wish a document to be able to pass information to other applications then it must be consistent. There are two ways to achieve this: via DTDs, which we shall consider here, and XML Schema, which we shall not deal with.

If a DTD is supplied with a document, the XML parser compares the document to the rules laid out in the DTD. If the document does not match those rules, the parser gives an error message and refuses to decode the rest of the document. This looks like creating a great deal of effort and complexity, and is the reason we shall concentrate on well-formed XML in later chapters. By declaring such things as the proper sequence of elements, however, a DTD can be extremely useful for ensuring that documents are formatted correctly, which is important when passing information between applications. For example, a website may handle documents where there has to be an identification number; if that number is not present, the document will be invalid, but at least you will know as soon as you try to load it in the browser, rather than having it hanging around on a server for months, storing problems for the future.

XSLT

As has been mentioned previously, XML documents by themselves do not do anything in the browser, but rather they structure information so that it can be interpreted by an application such as a browser. To transform XML into HTML so that it can be displayed in the browser, you must either use CSS or XSLT (eXtensible Stylesheet Language Transformations): the latter can also transform XML into plain text (useful for other applications) or other types of XML or even do such things as pulling out multi-lingual tags to create foreign-language versions of a document.

As with creating valid XML documents, this is a more complex process than using CSS, so in this book we will concentrate on the latter when working with well-formed XML documents. However, it is worth understanding the principles behind XSLT.

XSL files are XML documents and so must follow the rules of XML, and begin with a stylesheet element:

```
<xsl:stylesheet version="1.0"
    xmlns:xsl="http://www.w3.org/1999/
    XSL/Transform">
```

Version 1.0 is the most widely supported at the moment, and this is followed by an output element, which can be formats such as text, html and xml, and the template and apply-template elements. These look for root elements in the input xml file and, when located, apply the various styles contained in the XSL file.

PHP

PHP, which was developed by Rasmus Lerdorf in 1994 as a kit called Personal Home Page

Tools is now referred to as PHP: Hypertext Preprocessor. It is a server-side scripting language, that is the code is handled by the web server which hosts the page. The server processes all instructions and then outputs the results as static HTML. Since its initial development, PHP has gone through several versions, each becoming more sophisticated, and the current release – version 5 – came out in 2004.

Because it is available for free, and also works very well with the database **MySQL**, PHP has become an extremely popular language for developing dynamic sites. It is relatively easy to learn, and as a mature language certainly compares well with alternatives. It can even be used to create desktop applications, although we shall concentrate on web development in this book.

> PHP has become one of the most popular scripting languages on the web, and even a basic knowledge enables users to create much more dynamic and interactive sites.

Just about any web server that supports dynamic sites will support PHP in conjunction with MySQL, and you need a server to test your work. However, if you wish to develop a PHP site on your desktop computer, an easy way to set up a test environment is to install WAMP, which installs the server **Apache**, along with PHP and MySQL and will be covered later in this chapter.

PHP files are indicated with the extension .php, and instructions are indicated by using angular brackets with question marks, for example:

```
<?
echo "Hello World!" ;
?>
```

This very simple piece of code will be output as the line of text 'Hello World!' using the command echo. PHP code can be mixed freely with HTML (a more efficient way of writing pages as you do not need to use the echo command), and like most programming languages it makes use of a number of core concepts:

- **Functions**   A function is the command that performs certain actions within PHP code, and PHP 5 has over 140 groups of functions for such things as manipulating strings of text. It is also possible to create a user defined function using the function command, which follows the syntax: function myfunction_name ($argument) {action to be executed ;}. These functions are then called in the code of a dynamic page to run the action defined in the curly brackets.

- **Variables**   A variable, which is indicated by the dollar prefix, is effectively a container for values in code. If you set an image to be 100 pixels wide in HTML, it would always be that size. However, if you assigned it the variable $imgSize then the image could be made to change its size according to various conditions. A variable is assigned using the equals sign, for example $imgSize=100, and variables are extremely easy to use in PHP. Those with a knowledge of other programming languages may know of variable types such as strings (a series of letters or words), integers (numerical values) and Boolean (true/false) that have to be declared. PHP does not require the variable type to be declared, but will recognise, for example, that '10' is a string value while 10 is an integer.

- **Constants**   Not as useful as variables (and so not as widely used), it is also possible to define a value that remains constant throughout a piece of code.

- **Arrays**   An array is a set of values linked together for a common purpose, for example a set of physical descriptors, and is defined using the function array () with or without named 'keys', as in $phys_descr=array("gender" => "male", "age" => 45, "height" => 175, "weight" => 85, "hair_colour" => "blonde").

- **Operators**   These compare information such as that found in variables so that certain functions can be performed, with common operators being < (less than), > (more than), == (equal), === (identical) and !== (not equal).

- **Control structures**   A control structure is a means of enabling PHP code to look at a variable at a common point and make it perform certain tasks depending on what that variable is. The most common control structure is If . . . Else . . . whereby if a certain value is found one task is performed, but something else is done if it is not. Other control structures (which we shall look at in greater detail in chapter 4) include Do . . .While . . . which repeats a loop while a certain condition is true and Foreach, which is used with arrays to perform the same function on each value in turn.

SQL and MySQL

SQL, or Structured Query Language, is a standard language for retrieving information from and modifying information in databases. It was originally developed by IBM in the 1970s, and a wide variety of SQL programming languages exist but the one we shall refer to in this book is MySQL, released in 1995 and currently on version 5. MySQL is free for most uses and, because it is so closely integrated with PHP, is one of the most widely used database languages on the web.

With PHP, the database language MySQL is one of the main technologies driving dynamic websites online today.

MySQL is a relational database, that is information is stored in a table or multiple tables containing fields and records. The advantage of this approach is that, for example, if you are compiling a bibliographic database, one table could store author records with information in fields such as age, nationality and so on, which could then be linked to another table storing records about books such as title, date, publisher and so on. For those authors who had published multiple titles, you would not need to enter repeat details each time you wished to make a new record for a book.

By convention, SQL command words are written in capitals and each statement, like PHP, ends with a semi-colon. The language is fairly easy to understand, as in the following example:

SELECT name FROM authors WHERE category="non-fiction";

As the statement suggests, this will find the name of all non-fiction writers in the table authors. One thing to note is that any good database table should have what is known as a primary key, which is the column that uniquely identifies any record (usually called something like ID): this allows you to specify very particular records – there may be two or more John Does in your database, but there will only be one primary key that is number 124, for example.

For a web page to communicate with a database using a server-side language such as PHP, the page must specify the host name of the database server, a username, a password, and the name of the database to work with. If this is on your desktop PC using a test server, the server name will be localhost and the PHP command would be as follows, using the variable $link which would be called by other elements in the page:

$link = mysqli_connect('localhost','userna me','password','database_name')

This command opens the database, while the function mysqli_close($link) would close the database. PHP can then be used to query the database and return results based on those queries, or insert information into the database.

JavaScript and DOM

While PHP is a server-side scripting language, JavaScript is a client-side language, that is one that runs in the browser on the user's local

computer to process instructions contained in the web document. Developed in 1995 and called Livescript, it was originally bundled as part of the Netscape browser (Microsoft developed a variant called JScript in the mid- to late 1990s) and is now supported in some form by most browsers. It was standardised as ECMAScript from 1996 onwards.

JavaScript is used to write functions that can interact with the browser, for example by opening pop-up windows or validating the content of forms, and because it runs locally in the user's browser it can respond more quickly than server-side languages. The downside of this is that it has fewer features than a language such as PHP, and certainly is not sufficient for such things as connecting to a database.

One of the oldest and most popular scripting languages employed by websites, JavaScript has developed considerably since its early years and now drives a range of dynamic effects.

There are several ways in which JavaScript can interact with elements of a page. By using built-in events such as mouseup and onload, the simplest way is to use what is referred to as the inline model. This creates a simple function linked to an event and output that is listed in the <head> of an HTML document, and then includes a reference to that event and function in the <body> element, for example <body onload="myFunction"()> will cause the script to execute.

A more flexible way of linking scripts is to use the Document Object Model (DOM): although not technically part of the JavaScript standard, DOM linking is widely supported by browsers and will be the format used in this book when JavaScript examples are presented.

The Document Object Model is useful because it allows JavaScript to modify a page dynamically, although its support in Internet Explorer (as opposed to Firefox or other browsers) is incomplete. The basis for thinking about DOM is the document tree, already referred to in the section on XHTML, which can be thought of as having parent, child and sibling nodes:

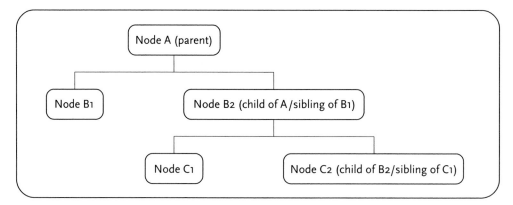

The DOM (Document Object Model) works as a tree with parent, child and sibling nodes.

This tree reflects the structure of a page's HTML code, with <html> as the root or parent node, <head> and <body> as its child nodes, and then various other elements as children of these two nodes. Using JavaScript, it is possible to navigate through the various nodes of this document tree and edit, delete or add nodes and their attributes. Consider, for example, this script:

```
<script type="text/javascript">
document.getElementByID("header").
    innerHTML= "New text for the header";
</script>
```

This short instruction will use the DOM set of instructions (document) to find an element which has been assigned the ID 'header' and then change its content to write the line 'New text for the header'. Similarly, you can change images on a page by running a script:

```
<img id="myImage01" src="landscape.
    jpg">
<script type="text/javascript">
document.getElementById("myImage01").
    src="portrait.jpg";
</script>
```

The code between the <script> tags could be attached to a button: when pressed, it would find the image with the ID 'myImage01'

and substitute a portrait picture for one of a landscape. As such, the DOM model is extremely useful for creating dynamic web pages with JavaScript.

Ajax

As will have been gathered throughout this chapter, most of the web technologies considered so far are fairly mature, with standards extending back a decade or more and very much precursors to Web 2.0 technologies (although changes and modifications to them in recent years have made them more flexible and powerful). The new kid on the block, and one that is leading to an increasing number of online innovations, is Ajax, or asynchronous JavaScript and XML. Actually, although the term Ajax was only coined in 2005 (followed by a W3C draft specification in 2006), the fact that it draws heavily on JavaScript and XML already indicates that it is not completely new, and draws on techniques going back to the mid-1990s.

Although we shall not deal with Ajax directly in this book in terms of programming skills, in fact most of the elements will be dealt with indirectly through other technologies addressed in this book. In addition, particularly in the chapters on Web 2.0 tools and content management systems, Ajax frequently has an important role to play in enabling more sophisticated features.

Ajax is not really one technology, but rather a collection of techniques for creating web applications. It can retrieve information asynchronously in the background from a server: that is, a page loads and continues to function while data is called up to provide new functions, leading to improved performance: for example, pages may share a great deal of content, and only the new content is requested when a new page loads. Likewise, an Ajax application may only reload part of a page when a request is made, giving a faster response.

Originally, the techniques brought together by Ajax included:

> One of the most exciting new technologies to emerge recently, Ajax typically combines JavaScript and XML to dynamically update sites in real time and provide greater interactivity.

- XHTML and CSS for web page structure and presentation,
- XML and XSLT for the interchange and presentation of data,
- the Document Object Model for dynamic interactivity with that data,
- XMLHttpRequest for asynchronous communication and
- JavaScript to bind these technologies together.

Ironically, current Ajax development does not require XML, JavaScript nor even asynchronous communication, but the above list gives a good idea of the core technologies – most of which have already been covered in this chapter and will be explored in more detail later in the book.

Although by no means the only technology in this area, Ajax has been particularly important in the development of what are known as rich internet applications (RIAs), that is, websites that have the features of traditional desktop programs (although there is some debate as to whether Ajax is, strictly speaking, an RIA technology). Examples of sites using Ajax to deliver web apps include BlinkList.com, Google Calendar and Orkut.com.

Java

For a few years, **Java** was one of the key technologies for web development. In recent years, it has fallen behind other tools such as Ajax and Flash – so much so that, early in 2007, Steve Jobs commented that 'nobody uses Java anymore', referring to it as a 'heavyweight ball and chain' as far as the iPhone was concerned.

Certainly Java is processor intensive and, for certain devices such as mobile phones, can be cumbersome to deploy, yet its principles were extremely important for future development of web applications and it is still widely used. Originally called Oak and created in 1991, the first public implementation of Java came in 1995. Because it was platform independent, allowing programmers to write code for an application once and run it anywhere that included what is known as a runtime engine, Java became very popular in browsers and extended the capabilities of websites in the late 1990s.

In addition, Java was very secure compared to other network applications at the time, running code in a 'sandbox' that made it impossible for downloaded code to perform certain actions, such as reading or writing to the local disk, or making a network connection to a host other than that from which the Java applet came. As applets would be downloaded automatically, and more often than not from sites that were not indicated as trusted by the user, this was important for preventing the spread of computer viruses.

Java has a very rich set of APIs (application programming interfaces) that handle such things as graphics and user interfaces. The syntax of the programming language is similar to C and C++, and some commentators have compared it to a platform in its own right, rather like the Windows or Apple Mac operating systems. We shall not cover the application of Java in any detail in this book, but you may encounter applets from third-party sources that are useful and easy enough to incorporate into your own website.

Flash

While Java may not be quite as ubiquitous as it once was, another means of adding interactivity to web pages, Flash, has gone from strength to strength and is an important addition to a professional web developer's toolkit.

Having acquired an animation package, SmartSketch, in 1995, Macromedia released the first version of Flash in 1996, and it is now part of the Adobe Creative Suite. The main function of the original version of Flash was to create **vector**-based animations with a fairly limited amount of interactivity. Over the next decade its programming language **ActionScript** developed to provide media rich applications, and the ability for Flash to produce high-quality video and audio has made it the streaming software of choice for many websites.

The widespread adoption of the Flash player (with Adobe claiming that over 99 per cent of internet users have this software installed, although these figures must be treated with a little scepticism) has resulted in its extensive use on websites. Despite this, or even because of it, the usability expert Jakob Nielsen wrote a polemic denouncing Flash content as '99% bad' in 2000, and while Nielsen overstated his case it cannot be denied that there were – and still are – plenty of useless Flash websites out there.

Flash files are developed in an authoring environment where developers can create animation, video and even full-blown applications. These are then distributed using the free Flash player (usually installed as part of a browser, but also available as a standalone

device), and there are a number of third-party programs such as SWiSH that are capable of creating Flash compatible (.swf) files or Flash video (.FLV).

ActionScript is based on ECMAScript, the same language that is used for JavaScript and JScript, evolving out of the limited actions available in early versions of Flash that performed functions such as playing and stopping files. ActionScript 3.0, the current version, made fundamental changes to the language (Flash Player 9.0 has to run two runtime engines, one for scripts written in ActionScript 1 and 2, and one for those written in version 3), making it more suitable for RIAs (rich internet applications). There is also a version called Flash Lite for use on mobile phones.

Flash tends to divide developers to some degree. There are many, particularly those with a stronger visual background in the arts or design, who swear by its abilities – it is, effectively, one of the premier programming languages for building online applications. However, while many improvements have been made since Nielsen's criticisms (he was later hired by Macromedia to enhance Flash), Flash-heavy sites can still cause problems for people with motor or visual disabilities, particularly if they need to use screen-reading software, and run into trouble on certain platforms. Adobe's remark that over 99 per cent of browsers worldwide have Flash installed disguises the fact that only about half run the latest version, and in some cases (on corporate computers, for example) plug-ins such as Flash may be disabled for security reasons. Relying on Flash to convey information is therefore not a good tactic: it has made the web a richer place, but a good developer always ensures they have an alternative for those who cannot use it.

> **Despite its popularity, Flash tends to divide developers into those who want to make full use of its interactive capabilities and those who tend to see it as less flexible and accessible than plain HTML.**

ONLINE MEDIA TOOLKIT

Strictly speaking, the tools required to create a website are very simple: aside from a server to host and test your files (which will be covered in the next section), to create a site using most of the technologies outlined in the previous section all that is required is a text editor. It is possible to create sophisticated sites this way, using XHTML, CSS, and XML, as well as scripting languages, and many textbooks on designing sites emphasise the benefits of hand-coding your own site. If you include an image editor as well, then the vast majority of what you need to achieve online can be done inexpensively and simply.

However, and even bearing in mind the comments made in the preface to this book about the problems with teaching software such as Dreamweaver, *Producing for Web 2.0* is not puritanical about creating sites. It is important to understand the principles behind such things as XHTML – interfaces tend to change quickly with fashions, but the underlying code evolves much more slowly – but in the real world, where many people want to get a website up fast and do not have the time or inclination to memorise hundreds of commands, a web editor is extremely useful.

Likewise, for adding multimedia elements such as audio and video, having a decent program to edit and work on your clips is extremely important. For those wishing to use Flash, this simply cannot be done in a standalone text editor – although there are alternatives, as we shall see, to Adobe's flagship application.

Web editors

Before considering web editing programs in any detail, it is worth commenting a little more on which text editor to use. Nearly every computer user will be familiar with a word processor such as Word, but despite the fact that these programs have handy little web editing toolbars in place, they are entirely unsuitable for hand-coding your own pages. The tendency for such programs is to insert a great deal of rather spurious code into a page, and they also generally fail to separate HTML structural code from the CSS rules used to govern presentation.

If you want to use readily available text editors on your computer, then a program such as Notepad on Windows is far better. This way you will have complete control over your code.

Web editors may be divided into two main groups: the first group consists of code editors, which work with lines of code and are generally chosen because they offer handy devices to designers such as colour-tagging for different types of code, as well as ready-made libraries for complex elements; the second is **WYSIWYG** (what you see is what you get) editors which tend to be preferred by novice designers because it is easier to see how a page is developing. Some applications such as Dreamweaver offer both. Professionals nearly always tend to prefer code editing because, unfortunately, what you see nearly always covers a great deal of surplus (and, subsequently, difficult to manage) code behind the scenes.

However, when choosing a web editor it is best to fix on what your requirements are. A purist approach will concentrate on elegant hand-coding every time – and with good reason. But if you are producing a website for a specific task, such as a college project or to set up a personal home page, and simply do not have hundreds of hours spare to master every aspect of XHTML and CSS, then there are plenty of decent web editors that will serve you well, covering a range of prices and expectations. Here are a few sample editors:

> While it is possible to create a site with nothing more than a text editor, the web producer will almost certainly need to gather a range of tools to help him, including visual web design software, image editors and multimedia applications.

- **Dreamweaver**   Formerly owned by Macromedia and now part of the Adobe Creative Suite, Dreamweaver is the nearest thing in web design to industry standard software. It provides both WYSIWYG and code design environments, and has a host of tools and extensions for handling just about everything you would wish to do on a site. The fact that it also integrates with other Adobe products such as Photoshop also makes it the program of choice for many designers.

  However, before rushing out to get a copy of Dreamweaver, there are a few things to take into account, not least of all its price (currently around £250 for a full version at the time of writing, although students are able to buy it at discount). More than this, however, is the fact that Dreamweaver is an incredibly complex piece of software and can be very time-consuming to learn for more than the basics. If all you wish to do is create simple sites, there are better options available. By the same token, if you do want to devote lots of time to learning web design but are not sure you will use Dreamweaver in future (say, when you leave a course), then your time may be better devoted to understanding XHTML and other technologies. Dreamweaver is the best web design application there is, but it should not be approached lightly (www.adobe.com/products/dreamweaver).

- **Expression Web**   Part of Microsoft's new suite of creative tools, which include media encoding and page design applications, Expression effectively replaces Microsoft's old web design software, FrontPage (although the 2003 version of this software is still available as part of the Office live suite at office.microsoft.com). As a competitor to Dreamweaver and the Adobe CS range, its main attraction is for those users who wish to integrate with other Office products. Strong on CSS, it is another application that offers both WYSIWYG and code views of pages (www.microsoft.com/expression).

- **Fusion**   If you wish to create a website with the minimum of fuss, this program from NetObjects is probably the best web editor available today. It is not really suitable for those who wish to understand all elements of XHTML and hand-coding in that its simplicity of use comes at the price of hiding away a great deal of coding behind a very elegant interface. This is not really the best application to learn about the underlying principles of web design, therefore, but it is very good for quickly creating fairly complex sites (www.netobjects.com).

- **Nvu**   At the opposite end to Dreamweaver, at least in terms of price, Nvu (pronounced 'en-view') is a free WYSIWYG editor that runs in Windows, MacOS and Linux. It also provides a code view of HTML pages and, although basic in terms of its capabilities, is perfectly adequate if you require a free WYSIWYG editor (nvudev.com).

- **Coffeecup**   There are many shareware HTML code editors available on the web and Coffeecup is one of the longest-running and most used. Later versions have added a WYSIWYG interface, but the reason this editor has been used by most people is because it offers a highly developed code editor at a low price (www.coffeecup.com).

> There are plenty of web editors available on the market today, with prices and features to match different types of budget and capability.

Image editors

While it is possible to create web pages using no more than Notepad, and multimedia may be of no interest to you, every web designer requires some form of graphics software. The standard applications that come with computers such as Paint for Windows are unsuitable for more than the most basic tasks, and at some point you will find their capabilities limited. Most image editors are **bitmap**, or raster, image editors, that is they work with images pixel by pixel and are best suited for photographic editing. Others are vector editors that allow you to create your own drawings and illustrations.

There are more image editors than even web editors, and while we shall list a couple of sample applications it is more useful to think of what you will need from a graphics program:

> While you can get by creating a site without access to a WYSIWYG web editor, for all but the most basic HTML pages a decent image editor is a necessity.

- At the very least it should offer the ability to preview images as you edit and optimise them for the web.
- You will need to determine whether you will need vector editing tools or will a bitmap editor be sufficient?
- Will you require an editor that has more advanced features such as animation?

The following are some sample applications:

- **Photoshop and Illustrator**   The industry standard image editors and part of Adobe's Creative Suite, Photoshop and Illustrator are, respectively, a raster and vector editing package. Neither is really suitable for the casual user, and both have features for print that are not particularly relevant for the vast majority of web producers. For a student wishing to work in design, however, knowledge of each of these applications is crucial. For occasional users, Photoshop Elements is a much simpler (and cheaper) program (www.adobe.com/products/creativesuite).
- **GIMP**   The GNU Image Manipulation Program has come a long way since its original release and now offers a great many professional level features, particularly for a free application. Its interface is not dissimilar to Photoshop's, and if you do not have an image editor

installed this is worth downloading (www.gimp.org).

- **CorelDRAW!**   Although looked down on a little in the graphics community (mainly because it was designed for PC rather than Mac, but also because Corel's aggressive upgrade path did often result in buggy releases), CorelDRAW! is definitely worth considering if you require an advanced raster and vector editor for about the same price as Photoshop (www.corel.com).
- **Paint Shop Pro**   For a long time the only decent low-cost alternative to Photoshop, Paint Shop Pro offers many of the same features to Adobe's program. Easier to use than GIMP, it has lost ground to that application as a Photoshop substitute (www.corel.com).

Audio

While the early days of the web were restricted largely to text and image, this was followed fairly quickly by audio. The suitability of the medium for such things as internet radio, even across narrowband modem connections, was one of the first important developments in media streaming. This was followed by the popularity of MP3 for filesharing and distributing music, and then podcasting, whereby digital audio files are not simply shared on a site but can be syndicated by an RSS feed, so that material is made available to other sites or devices (such as portable players).

With the rise in popularity of MP3, audio editing software has greatly increased and ranges from high-end professional studio packages to some extremely competent free applications.

- **Pro Tools**   The industry standard application owned by Avid, this will be overkill for most users, especially as much of the software is designed to be used with particular hardware. Although cut down versions are available (the free release of Pro Tools for PC and Mac has been discontinued), this is really software aimed at those working in a studio who require a very high level of control over all aspects of audio (www.digidesign.com).

- **Audacity**   Although not a standard for the music industry, the free audio program Audacity is becoming something of a de facto standard for users who want an effective editor for such things as internet projects. If you do not have access to professional packages, this is highly recommended as a means for modifying your clips (audacity.sourceforge.net).
- **WavePad**   Again aimed at people such as web editors rather than music recorders, WavePad will service most requirements at a fraction of the cost of Pro Tools. It is easy to use, although Audacity (despite a somewhat less user-friendly interface) has the edge (www.nch.com.au/wavepad).
- **Sound Forge**   This application comes in two forms: Sound Forge itself which is designed for professional users and is probably the application which most closely rivals Pro Tools, and Sound Forge Audio Studio for casual users (www.sonycreativesoftware.com).

Video

Although video was slower to take off on the internet, mainly because of the relatively slow bandwidth available to most users, that has changed dramatically in the past five years or so – as is evidenced by the YouTube phenomenon among other things. In contrast to audio, where MP3 tends to dominate with a few other formats such as Real Player or Ogg cropping up occasionally, there is a fairly diverse range of video formats that can be encountered, such as **MPEG**, QuickTime and Flash video.

> In recent years, advances in video and audio compression mean that online multimedia has at last become a viable component for many websites.

The main tools that will be required by a web producer are a decent video editor as well as an encoder to compress video into a suitable format for online distribution. In most cases, a video editing package will do both of these, but it also possible to compose the video sequence as you want it on your desktop and then use encoding software – online, or on the desktop – to convert it into the type of file you require. We shall deal with this in more detail in the chapter on multimedia. As with music editors, the following is just a small sample of the many applications available today:

- **Avid**   The industry standard that is used in many broadcasting companies, its high-end products such as Media Composer and Symphony are expensive and very complex. Unless you are working within a company or educational establishment that has invested in these, it is unlikely that these are the tools you will be using. Avid Xpress is considerably cheaper and offers a way into learning this software (www.avid.com).
- **Final Cut Pro**   Final Cut is Apple's highly respected video editing software for the Mac and the main competitor to Avid (it is particularly popular in the film industry as opposed to broadcasting). As with the professional versions of Avid, it is rather expensive but also extremely versatile (www.apple.com).
- **Premiere**   Because of its integration with other Creative Suite products such as Photoshop and Dreamweaver, Adobe Premiere is a fairly popular choice although it tends to fall slightly between high-end professional software and cheaper products aimed at more casual users. For the latter, however, Premiere Elements is a good choice (www.adobe.com).
- **Ulead**   Owned by Corel, Ulead is responsible for a number of video editing

and multimedia packages of which the most important are Media Studio with support for such things as High Definition TV (less important on the web at the moment), and its entry level package VideoStudio (www.ulead.com).

- **Pinnacle**   Pinnacle produces budget-level video capture hardware and software that comes in two forms (as with Ulead's software). Liquid is a semi-professional suite of tools, while Studio is an inexpensive video editing package (www.pinnaclesys.com).

- **iMovie/Windows Movie Maker**   If you are only a very casual video user, then you may have all you need for basic video editing already in the form of iMovie for the Mac and Windows Movie Maker. Although they lack many of the features of high-end products, for creating a simple movie and exporting it in a suitable file format they are perfectly adequate.

Flash

Flash has already been discussed in the previous section on web technologies, and this section will simply point out some of the ways in which you can work with Flash files for your own site. As well as the general editing packages here, in chapter 5 we will look at some of the free or shareware tools available that are tailored to specific features, such as adding a video player or image gallery to your site.

- **Flash CS Pro**   The main application for professionals wishing to develop Flash applications and part of the Adobe Suite, Flash CS Pro (currently version 3) is effectively a programming environment. It is by far the most complete and also the most expensive product in this category, and not at all for casual users (www.adobe.com).

- **SWiSH**   One of the better Flash alternatives, SWiSH does not have the flexibility and versatility of Adobe Flash itself but is considerably easier to use if

you wish to produce animation, is much cheaper, and also has some ActionScript support for creating small-scale applications (www.swishzone.com).

- **OpenLaszlo**   A new, open-source program that is free to download, OpenLaszlo is actually a rich media development tool that is compatible in part with some Flash formats. It uses XML, PHP and other web standards to produce quite sophisticated applications (www.openlaszlo.org).

Acrobat and PDF

Although it will not be dealt with in any great detail, being more important for print than the web, nonetheless the Adobe **PDF** format does allow multimedia development including hyperlinks, multimedia embedding and forms. We would not recommend developing PDF sites, but the file format itself can be useful for distributing documents where formatting is important and needs to be preserved. Acrobat itself, available from adobe.com, is rather expensive if you intend merely to use it for this task, but there are plenty of cheaper applications such as Pdf955 (www.pdf955.com) and Jaws PDF Creator (www.pdfsoftware.com) which install as drivers that 'print' documents to the PDF format. There are also online converters, such as www.freepdfconvert.com and www.pdfonline.com, which can turn such things as Word documents into PDFs.

SETTING UP A SERVER

Before creating your site, it is obviously important to have somewhere to host your pages so that they can be viewed by others. The range of options available to web producers is extensive, ranging from free space included as part of an **ISP** package or supported by online advertising, to maintaining your own server, either as part of your company's infrastructure (beyond the scope of this book) or, more commonly, as a co-hosting deal with a large web hosting company.

Selecting a server

When looking for a host for your site, the following are the general types of hosting deals that are available:

- **Free space**   For a student wishing to set up their own site, this is often a tempting consideration. An ISP will often provide a limited amount of free web space with the package that connects users to the internet. Alternatively, sites such as Tripod (www.tripod. lycos.com) or Geocities (geocities.yahoo.com) provide free space. One thing to be aware of when using such space is that it is often funded by advertising, will be limited in terms of bandwidth, and may not allow access to more advanced features such as scripting.
- **Personal hosting packages**   Generally a much better option for creating a small-scale site, these paid options are widely available for less than £10 (or even $10) per month. They do not often provide a huge amount of space, but will give better bandwidth (usually around 30 or 40 gigabytes a month, depending on the option). There is also better support (if only via email/online support), as well as additional services such as access to dynamic features, software for website design and other tools, such as site analysis, email forwarding and even a domain name. The very cheapest packages are unlikely to offer database support for MySQL, but plenty of providers do include this.
- **Virtual and dedicated servers**   One problem with personal packages can arise due to the fact that one server (the actual hardware storing files) could be hosting a very large number of sites. This can make intense demands on the server if those sites are accessed continuously, so an alternative

> There are plenty of different types of hosting options that allow developers to set up low-cost or high-end secure sites for their content.

is to go for a virtual or dedicated server. The latter, as the name suggests, is a box dedicated to a particular site, so it does not share memory or processing power with other users. This is the most expensive option, typically between £50 and £100 per month for a basic server, and (with a few legal provisos regarding content and licences) the person or company hiring it can install whatever software they like.

A virtual server will be a box that hosts a smaller number of sites compared to shared packages, but guarantees that a certain degree of RAM and space is allocated to each site it supports. These will usually be about half the price of a dedicated server.

While prices can be very competitive for selecting a server, it is much better not to allow your choice to be dictated by this alone. Performance and availability is often much more important – it is a false economy to save a few pounds or dollars each month, only to find that your site is down more often than not or it does not have a backup plan to save your data in the event of a disaster.

Creating a test server

The server that you select to host your site will be stored in a warehouse with fast connections to the internet and, ideally, plenty of additional hardware to back up all your data and restore it quickly. In the meantime, however, you may wish to create a test server on your own computer to try out your designs before you commit them to the real world.

While Microsoft's Windows Server is slowly becoming much more widely accepted as a platform for delivering websites, particularly for corporate intranet and internet development, it is an expensive option for the casual user. Apache (apache.org) remains the most popular server and is a free, open-source product that works on multiple platforms. Until very recently,

Tripod is one of several services offering free web space to consumers.

however, it required considerable skill to install and, more importantly, configure to work with other elements such as PHP and SQL databases.

This changed greatly with the release of XAMPP (www.apachefriends.org/en/xampp.html) in 2002. XAMPP, which stands for cross-platform (X) software that includes Apache, MySQL, PHP and **Perl**, in recent years has created a one-click installation procedure to set up and configure these packages on Windows, MacOS and other operating systems as well as Linux and UNIX (for which Apache was originally developed). It should be pointed out that, to aid this installation, by default XAMPP leaves many security options open – it is not suitable for running a live server that is to be connected to online, and it should never be run without **firewall** protection. However, for

development this can reduce the once painful process of configuring these important packages to something that lasts about half an hour.

Once XAMPP is installed, you can test it by running a file called apache_start.bat (usually found in a directory called xampp or xampplite). Next, open a browser window and type http://localhost/ into the address bar: if installed correctly, this will display the XAMPP splash screen. Both the full version of XAMPP and XAMPP Lite include an application called phpMyAdmin, which can be used to check the MySQL and PHP installations. Enter the address http://localhost/phpMyAdmin/ which will display the home page with information about versions of these applications installed on your computer.

> **XAMPP is one of the best and easiest ways to set up a test server on your desktop so that you can try out your pages before hosting them live.**

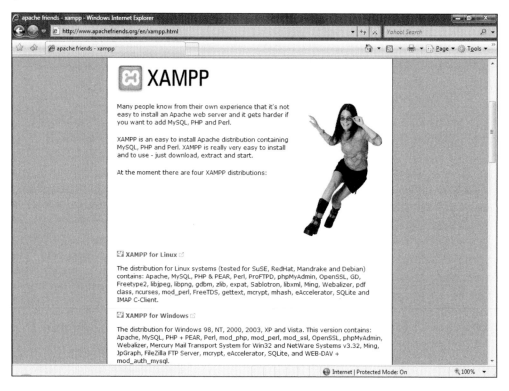

XAMPP is an extremely simple way to set up your own test server.

Registering a domain name

If you have a hosted package, the chances are that you will be able to register a domain name with the company storing your pages as part of the initial setup. However, it may be that you require additional domain names or, for example, you are using an alternative Web 2.0 publishing platform such as Blogger that you wish to bind to your own domain.

Domain names are ultimately registered and maintained by NICs (network information centres), such as InterNIC, set up by the US government in 1993, and Nominet UK, responsible for .co.uk addresses. In the US, InterNIC works through a company, Network Solutions, to register all domains, but in practice it is ISPs and other subsidiaries that will feed through customers who select a name (whether mywebsite.com, mywebsite.co.uk, mywebsite. org or other variations).

Once a domain is chosen, it must be bound to the DNS (domain name server) used by your web hosting company. In the registration details sent to you when you sign up, this will include a domain name such as ns.myhostcompany. com, which must be entered in a form on the site where you registered for a domain. If this is done by the same hosting company, it is extremely straightforward, but if you are using a third-party registration service it is vital to have the address for your host DNS.

A final point to bear in mind is that if a domain is likely to become very important to you, it could be worthwhile registering related top level domains such as .co.uk, .org, .eu and so on, as well as the main .com name. While there is a degree of protection available regarding the use of protected trademarks as domain names, at the very least you could face confusion if someone enters your web address wrongly and ends up on the site of a competitor.

Ready for design

With server space and a domain name for your site, as well as the necessary online toolkit and an understanding of what you wish to achieve, the next step is to begin designing your site. The next chapter will concentrate on the fundamentals of web design, focusing in particular on using XHTML and CSS to create and layout your web pages.

For more information and updates on pre-production, visit www.producingforweb2.com/pre-production.

CHAPTER 3

Designing for the web

Having considered the various components and technologies that can go into the creation of a website, now it is time to turn to the actual construction of a site. As well as specific practice, this chapter will also consider the underlying guidelines for using such things as text, graphics, multimedia and navigation on your site. Although there are examples of doing this using Dreamweaver as a sample application, it is important to understand the underlying code involved (XHTML and CSS) that controls the structure and appearance of content on a site.

This chapter does not, however, provide a comprehensive manual for XHTML or CSS, although plenty of examples will be given. It is important that you understand the basics of the code you are using, but general principles are much more important especially if, later, you intend to customise other sites.

DESIGN PRINCIPLES

Design is frequently thought of purely in terms of the appearance of the site, its aesthetics and how it looks. While this is important and contributes greatly to the success or failure of a site, design is also a question of usability. Just as a chair may look great but be impossible to sit on for extended periods of time, or a car may blow away the competition in terms of its sleek lines but guzzle enough gas to fuel a small economy, so a website that appears serene and sublime on the screen may leave visitors fuming with suppressed rage at best, indifference at worst, if they cannot find what they want.

During the 1990s, the early stages of web design were such that HTML did everything. A page would largely contain text content, perhaps with some images, and markup sent instructions to the browser telling it how to display such things as fonts, paragraph breaks, image sizes and other elements, as well as where the browser would display those elements on the page.

It would be wrong to describe what follows in this chapter as somehow unique to Web 2.0 design, in that this would imply that Web 1.0 gurus such as Tim Berners-Lee have had little to do with the development of important design principles. In fact, the basis of contemporary web design, which seeks (not always successfully) to separate the content, structure and presentation of a web page, has largely been driven by the W3C, and has evolved out of the earlier stages of web development. As designers and producers encountered problems and limitations with HTML, so the W3C has produced a range of specifications to guide developers.

This fundamental principle – the separation of content, structure and presentation – is then an evolution rather than a radical revolution. Nonetheless, without it many of the major changes that have been possible in Web 2.0 design would not have happened. While this chapter will concentrate on fairly straightforward web design, an understanding of the techniques and principles outlined here will be important when moving onto more complex projects such as those outlined in chapters 5 and 6.

When discussing the notion of this separation, it should be pointed out here that structure in this instance refers to where elements are placed on a page, rather than the structure of the site as a whole (which will be discussed later in the chapter). Content obviously refers to what is loaded onto the page, while presentation is how it appears, for example the use of colour and typographical styles. While HTML and XHTML tell the browser how to display a page (its structure), modern web design makes use of cascading style sheets (CSS) to control presentation, content is usually stored in a database and loaded into the page as required. The full implications of this last point will only be covered fairly briefly in this chapter: rather than building a dynamic, database-driven website from scratch, it is much easier to customise a content management system (CMS).

The virtue of separation is that content providers can concentrate on that, providing content, while all elements of the design of a page are done by professional web designers. Because all aspects of presentation are handled by separate CSS files,

> **The most important principle for modern web design is the separation of content, the structure of where it appears on the page, and the presentation and formatting of that content.**

Separating out structure, content and design can help to create elegant websites.

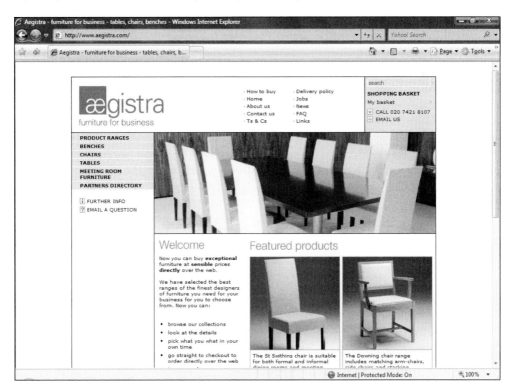

this means that changing the overall look and feel of a site requires a designer only to modify a single file, or group of files, rather than having to edit every single page. In addition, the same content can be repurposed for different visitors, for example those visiting from a mobile WAP browser or those who have visual impairments.

However, while there is much that is written on this separation, it is often easier to conceive theoretically than in practice. As Michael Cohen (2004) observes, even the semantic structural coding of simple text (such as headings and paragraph elements) involves some crossover as the presentation of an h1 heading will be determined by a style sheet; likewise, that h1 tag is part of the structure of the page, identifying one part of the text as separate from the main body copy. For structure, the crossover can be much more confusing if we are trying to maintain a strict separation: the structure of a menu, for example, will include ID tags that can be modified by a CSS file.

So this core principle is something of an illusion, in that content, structure and presentation always tend to be mixed up a little. However, it is still a useful ideal to strive for, and in practice it tends not to be confusing: the majority of presentation elements are controlled by CSS, structure is handled by HTML, and separate (mainly text) content can be called from a database.

Using HTML and XHTML

A detailed discussion of the underlying principles of HTML and XHTML can be found in chapter 2. This section will instead look at some of the implications of the differences between the two markup languages. Throughout this chapter, most of the examples will be XHTML compliant, but it should be noted that certain attributes of HTML that have been deprecated (that is they are not compliant with Strict XHTML) are still very commonly used, particularly when working with a web editor rather than by hand-coding, and as such attention will occasionally be drawn to them. It is probably most accurate to say that the examples included in this chapter are suitable for the Transitional version of XHTML 1.0 rather than the Strict version.

HTML, currently at version 4.1, is more forgiving than XHTML, but as the latter is becoming more important for well-formed documents it is a good habit for a student to get used to the additional requirements placed on coding a web page. Important points to remember are:

- XHTML elements must always be in lower case.
- XHTML tags must either include an opening and closing tag, for example <p> </p> or, where there is not an associated closing tag, include a final forward slash, for example <br />.

As has been stated in the introduction, it is not essential to know how to code a page to create a website, and when creating a complex page from scratch this would be a frustrating and confusing experience. However, if you wish to have any expertise in web design a good working knowledge of HTML/XHTML is a valuable skill: sometimes a WYSIWYG editor will throw up errors that are difficult to fix in a graphical interface but can be tracked down much more quickly when scanning lines of code. In addition, you will be able to work much better with the various components of web design that will be covered in this chapter, such as links, images, forms and tables, if you understand the principles behind them. Each section of this chapter will include brief examples of code which are designed to outline the principles of markup.

> **Although it is not essential to know HTML to create a website, some understanding of the underlying code is extremely useful when modifying a range of Web 2.0 sites and services.**

Consider, for example, the following piece of XHTML code, which would create the simplest possible web page but can still tell us a considerable amount about how the markup language operates:

```
<!DOCTYPE html
PUBLIC "-//W3C//DTD XHTML 1.0
    Transitional //EN"
"http://www.w3.org/TR/xhtml1/DTD/
    xhtml1-transitional.dtd">
<html>
    <head>
        <title>My first web page</title>
    </head>
<body>
</body>
</html>
```

If you typed this code into a text editor, saved it and loaded it into a browser, all you would see is a blank page with the title 'My first web page' displayed in the bar at the top of the browser. The DOCTYPE statement has already been dealt with in chapter 2, but let's consider the rest of this document.

First of all, note that the three elements used here – <html>, <head> and <body> – are accompanied by a closing tag – </html>, </head> and </body>. Also, for the page to display correctly (even with nothing in it), the tags must be nested correctly, that is when one pair of tags (such as <head> </head>) is included within another (such as <html> </html>), the closing tag of the nested element must appear before that of the nesting one.

These three tags provide the most basic structure for any web document. In HTML, as opposed to XHTML, the <html> </html> tags are not necessary in the sense that the page would still load in the browser without them; in pages that are strictly XHTML compliant, however, this element is necessary to tell the browser what type of document this is – there being the possibility of defining a range of other markup document types in future.

Of the following two tags, these are as much sections of the page as elements. The <body> tag will be dealt with only briefly here, as in many ways it is developed throughout this chapter, providing the canvas into which text, images and multimedia features are loaded. The <head> section, while not as rich in content as the body, is still important: it tells us about the document, such as links to external scripts and CSS files that control presentation. It will also be important in chapter 9 when turning to such things as metadata for search engine optimisation.

Styles and CSS

The main principles of cascading style sheets (CSS) have already been covered in the previous chapter; as with the discussion of HTML and XHTML above, the main purpose here is to consider the practicalities of using style sheets in your own web pages.

As with HTML, a basic understanding of CSS can be extremely useful in modifying different websites and services and is important to master if you want to fine tune your pages.

Different HTML elements that govern text formatting, such as headings (h1 to h6) or paragraph (p), are defined in a style sheet according to their selector, with different values attached to the properties indicated between curly brackets (property and value together comprise a declaration), according to the basic syntax:

```
selector {property: value}
```

Any style element can be used in two ways: either as what is referred to as an inline feature using the <style> </style> element, or as a link to one or more external style sheets using the <link> element. The latter is preferable because it means that you can change the look and feel of an entire site by editing the style sheet, rather than having to make changes to multiple

HTML pages. Such style sheets are plain text documents with the extension .css.

An example of using an inline style would be as follows:

```
<h2 style="color: red;">The default colour
    for my subheading</h2>
<p style="color: gray;">The default colour
    for body copy</p>
```

For an external style sheet, the link would be placed in the <head> element of the HTML file:

```
<head>
<title>A web page linked to an external
    style sheet</title>
<link rel="stylesheet" type="text/css"
    href="mystyle.css" />
</head>
```

The external style sheet, mystyle.css, would then contain the following rules:

```
h2 {color: red;}
p {color: gray;}
```

Changing the colour values in mystyle.css would then modify the properties for any level 2 headings and paragraph copy in all web pages that were linked to that file. Throughout this chapter we will consider how CSS can be used to modify the presentation of various HTML elements such as text, images, colour and tables.

Effective navigation

A well-designed website does not simply consist of an aesthetically pleasing interface, but is also easy to navigate: or rather, the creation of an aesthetically pleasing interface includes paying attention to navigation as well as text, images, and other design elements.

Good navigation depends on techniques for accessing the website – interface design – as well as how the site looks. For example, users with a visual impairment may have problems using a site that relies heavily on icons for navigation, so text alternatives have to be in place (using the ALT attribute in the image element for example, or providing text links alongside graphic ones).

Navigation tools should, ideally, be consistent in terms of position and overall look and feel, as well as providing feedback to visitors. If you change where a link appears from one page to the next those visitors may become disorientated. Likewise, visually consistent navigation tools play an important part in constructing the brand image of your site. Regarding feedback, there are several simple and common techniques that are useful in providing information to users, such as rollover graphics for icon-based menus, or hover links that are defined in CSS so when a visitor moves the mouse over a link it changes colour.

While the types of site may vary considerably on the web, many share some common features. First of all, most sites open with a home page or front page: like the title page of a book, it should provide some sort of overview as to the different sections of a site, with navigation links offering a content menu. Mapping your site, and thus having a sense of its overall structure, is an important basic principle for successful navigation.

> Good navigation depends on interface design as well as looks so that users can access information as easily as possible.

A common mistake when setting out these divisions is to lay out various sections in radically different ways, which can only serve to confuse visitors. A more successful technique is to implement the same common design with some minor changes for sections, for example different header graphics, or perhaps some colour changes across the top of a page. This can help rather than hinder visitors to a site, letting them know that they are in the news section rather than reading a review, for example, without unnecessarily perplexing them.

Navigation does not have to be dull to be effective, but it should always be straightforward.

TEXT AND LINKS

When Tim Berners-Lee devised HTML in 1990, it was originally conceived as a means to link together text documents. Despite the fact that since then the web has evolved into a fully multimedia environment, text remains core to most pages that are found online, and HTML includes a number of options for formatting text that, in conjunction with CSS, can be extremely useful for presenting your copy.

If text is one fundamental component of a web page, hyperlinks are the other. While it is easy enough to envisage pages without multimedia and even images (for all that it would look rather dull), a page of text without links would really be a text file rather than an HTML document.

Working with text

While a considerable amount of time and energy will be spent on such things as creating graphics for your site and ensuring compatibility across browsers, text remains at the heart of most web pages. Indeed, in the long term, once a site is up and running and demonstrated to be usable, creating the content for your site will demand most of your effort. Preparing suitable multimedia is the subject of a following chapter, while later we shall look in more detail at styles of writing suitable for the web. Here, however, we shall concentrate on the fundamentals that relate to using text for design.

At its simplest, text is fast: back in the days when users connected to bulletin boards at 300 bits per second rather than the multi megabit connections common today, all they could reasonably be expected to view was text. For modern designers, using text in terms of visual aesthetics can be frustrating: not only can users change the size of fonts (and, indeed, should be able to if they cannot read small text), certain typefaces may not be available on a local computer, causing the page to reflow in unexpected or unwanted ways.

Typography in print has a long and rich history, and by comparison web design can be very meagre. CSS has gone a long way to improving this, but in most cases the vast majority of fonts and typefaces that are available to print designers are not suitable for web pages. The reason for this is that web pages usually can only work with those fonts that are installed on a user's computer. Because of this, web design applications such as Dreamweaver tend to restrict available typefaces to a few font families that can be more or less guaranteed to be included on any visitor's PC. Downloadable and embedded fonts, as we shall see, do provide some workaround to this, but are not without their own problems.

The early HTML specifications included a number of elements to modify the format of text, such as the <b> </b> and <i> </i> tags for bold and italic. While it is still possible to use these within an HTML document, a much better way of controlling the presentation of text, as we shall see later in this chapter, is to use CSS.

Typography

Throughout this book, the term font will be used to refer to both the font and typeface (as it tends to be used when installing fonts on a computer), but strictly speaking the typeface is the style of type, such as Arial or Garamond, while a font is its size, usually measured in points.

Fonts are distinguished as serif or sans serif, and proportional and monospaced. A serif font has a short start or finish stroke, while a sans serif font does not; proportional fonts use

characters that take up only as much space as they require, while monospaced fonts use the same fixed width for all characters.

> Times   proportional serif font,
> **Arial**   proportional sans serif font, and
> `Courier New  monospaced serif font.`

Typically, serif fonts, by providing a little extra information, are easier to read for larger chunks of text, while sans serif fonts make bolder headlines. Monospaced text is not usually encountered – its principal use seems to be when designers wish to emulate typed pages or distinguish instructions within a web page.

In HTML, changes used to be made using the <font> element, but it is a much better idea to handle such things as font styles, colour and sizes using CSS, which will be dealt with in the next section. In fact, it is strongly recommended that you do not use the <font> tag at all to format your text: in official terms, it has been 'deprecated', that is its status has been downgraded and will not work in documents formatted according to the requirements of Strict XHTML. In any case, making changes throughout a document by modifying sections of text using multiple font tags means that it is a nightmare to change the presentation of a site at a later date, and CSS is much more convenient.

While the general fonts available to a web designer are rather restricted, there are ways to include more unusual typefaces in a particular design. The usual workaround is to include these in a graphic such as a **GIF**. While this works for a short heading it will not be appropriate for longer pieces of copy. Much more useful is the ability to embed fonts in a page. Microsoft's web embedding fonts tool (**WEFT**) is a free download (www.microsoft.com/ typography/web/embedding/weft3) that allows

> **Although web typography can appear very meagre compared to that for print, it has improved considerably. You will still be usually restricted, however, by the fonts available on a person's computer.**

you to create an embedded OpenType (**EOT**) file for each font you wish to include.

This process requires you to locate the font you wish to use, create an embedded, EOT font file, and then attach it to the style sheet associated with that page. The first part is easy enough, and the second is fairly simple using a tool such as WEFT, though you must remember to upload the .eot file to your server. The CSS code will look something like the following:

```
<style type="text/css">
<--!
@font-face {
    font-family: goudy;
    font-style: normal;
    font-weight: normal;
    src:url(http://www.mysite.com/
    EOTfilename.eot);
}
-->
</style>
```

While embedded fonts can seem like the answer to a web designer's dream in terms of using unusual typefaces on a website, there are a couple of downsides. First of all, they may slow down performance of a site: typical .eot file sizes are 20–25 kilobytes in size, not itself a huge amount but enough to make a noticeable difference as a page is downloaded. More significantly, visitors may receive a security warning when they load a page as the browser tells them it wishes to run a file. With the prevalence of scare stories (many of them justified) about the dangers of visiting various sites, this could result in visitors staying away from your site.

Lists

One important way in which text can be used on a page is via lists which come in three main types: ordered lists, unordered lists, and definition lists.

An ordered list is numbered (1, 2, 3 and so on), and uses the element <ol> </ol>, while unordered lists display bullet points and use

the element <ul> </ul>. Each item that appears within a list has to be displayed between the tags <li> </li> in both ordered and unordered lists. For example, a recipe would be formatted as follows in an ordered list:

```
<ol>
<li>Flour</li>
<li>Water</li>
<li>Eggs</li>
<li>Sugar</li>
</ol>
```

This would be presented as:

1 Flour
2 Water
3 Eggs
4 Sugar

An unordered list is marked up in nearly the same way:

```
<ul>
<li>Flour</li>
<li>Water</li>
<li>Eggs</li>
<li>Sugar</li>
</ul>
```

This is presented as:

- Flour
- Water
- Eggs
- Sugar

A definition list contains a term and its definition, and has three tags as part of the element: <dl> </dl> begins and ends the definition list; <dt> indicates the term to be defined; and <dd> provides the definition itself. For example:

```
<dl>
<dt>HTML</dt>
<dd>Hypertext Markup Language</dd>
<dt>XML</dt>
```

```
<dd>eXtensible Markup Language</dd>
</dl>
```

Ordered and unordered lists can be nested inside each other, simply by repeating the <ol> or <ul> elements. For example:

```
<ul>
    <li>Drinks</li>
<ul>
        <li>Coffee</li>
        <li>Tea</li>
    </ul>
</ul>
<ul>
    <li>Snacks</li>
<ul>
        <li>Biscuits</li>
        <li>Cakes</li>
    </ul>
</ul>
```

This would be presented in the browser as follows:

Drinks
- Coffee
- Tea
Snacks
- Biscuits
- Cakes

As with other elements of text, the presentation of lists can be controlled via CSS, and you will find some of the properties that can be modified in the CSS reference at the end of the book.

Hyperlinks

As text is essential to the majority of web pages, so just about every web page that you will encounter online will also have hyperlinks to link to other pages and documents. Hyperlinks can be attached to images (or other media such as video), but we shall concentrate here on linking to text: the principles largely remain the same with other types of hyperlink.

Links are the basic building block for

interactivity, allowing a visitor to navigate from page to page, and are employed in HTML using the <a> </a>, or anchor, element, which must also include the property href (for **hypertext** reference). The basic syntax for a link is as follows:

```
<a href="http://www.mysite.com">Link to
mysite.com</a>
```

Links may be absolute or relative. An absolute link, as in the example above, is an address to a specific page on a specific server (in this case the index page on the site mysite.com), and is necessary when creating links to pages on external sites. A relative link, by contrast, is defined in relation to the current page. For example, if you are editing a page in a folder called stories, and wish to link to another page, dailynews.htm, stored in a folder called news, both of these folders located in the directory public_html, then a relative link would look something like the following:

> **Hypertext links are the basic building block for interactivity, connecting documents and files across the web.**

```
<a href="../news/dailynews.html">Daily
News link</a>
```

The two full stops at the beginning of the href property indicate to the browser that it must go up a directory to look for a folder called news, in which is located the relevant file. It is best to use relative links wherever possible to all pages and documents on your local site; this way, if the site is moved to another server or domain name, all the internal links should continue to work correctly.

Hyperlinks can also be used to jump to anchors contained in the same page – what are referred to as bookmarks. This is done by giving a name to a section of the page (the bookmark) and then creating a link beginning with the hash sign (#) in the href property. For example, supposing that a section of your page has a heading called 'My Bookmark'. To create a bookmark for this page you would add the following code:

```
<h2><a name="bookmark">My
    Bookmark</a></h2>
```

To link to this anchor point, the following HTML would be used:

```
<a href="#bookmark">Link to bookmark</
    a>
```

In addition, using the instruction mailto will create an email link that opens an email program (if one is installed) rather than a new browser window, for example

```
<a href="mailto:someone@mydomain.
    com">.
```

Pop-up windows

By default, links open a new page in the same browser window as the old document, but it is also possible to launch a pop-up window to display content, which can be particularly useful if you are linking to a page on an external site but don't want the visitor to leave yours. To do this, use the attribute target="_blank", which opens the URL specified in the href property in a new browser window, for example <a href="http://www.externalsite.com/newpage.htm" target="_blank">.

If you wish to specify the size of the target window, you cannot do this using HTML alone but must use some JavaScript to set such things as the window height and width. The JavaScript function window.open by itself achieves more or less the same as the "_blank" attribute for an anchor tag, and its basic syntax is as follows:

```
<script>
function windowPopup(pageURL,title,w,h) {
var left = (screen.width/2)-(w/2);
var top = (screen.height/2)-(h/2);
var targetWin = window.open (pageURL,
    title, 'toolbar=no, location=no,
```

```
directories=no, status=no, menubar=no,
scrollbars=no, resizable=no,
copyhistory=no, width='+w+',
height='+h+', top='+top+', left='+left);
}
</script>
```

```
<a href="javascript:void(0);"
    onclick="windowPopup('http://
    www.externalsite.
    com','mypopup',499,100);">Link to
    external site</a>
```

This looks an awful lot of coding compared to the brief change to an attribute in HTML. However, the window.open function can be very useful because it can take a number of arguments to define how the pop-up window appears, including height, width, how far the window is offset from the left or top of the page, whether it is fullscreen or resizable, and whether the status bar is displayed.

Text and CSS

The example on the next page shows that one of the main uses for CSS is handling text. This section will not cover all elements of using CSS to format text (there is a more extensive list of values in the CSS reference in Appendix 2), but will give some examples of how a style sheet can be used to change the appearance of your text using the font and text properties.

> A common use for CSS is to provide sophisticated formatting options for text within web pages.

Using these properties, body copy formatted so that it is laid out in a standard way using the HTML <p> element could look something like the following.

```
p {
    text-align: left;
    color: black;
    font-family: arial;
    }
```

WALKTHROUGH ▶

Adding and formatting text in Dreamweaver

1 Using Dreamweaver in WYSIWYG mode is very similar to working with a word processor. The main difference is that, once you add text, formatting is carried out using the Properties palette at the bottom of the screen. Simply type the text you wish to add in the main workspace.

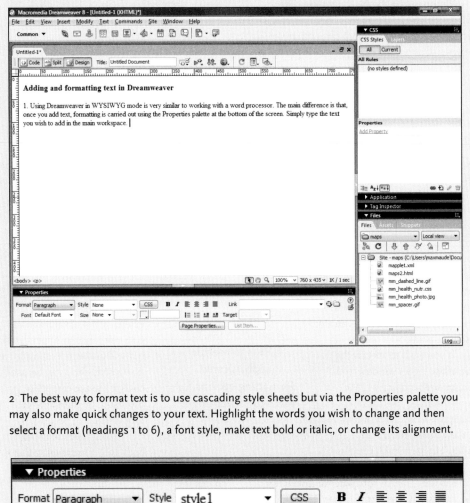

2 The best way to format text is to use cascading style sheets but via the Properties palette you may also make quick changes to your text. Highlight the words you wish to change and then select a format (headings 1 to 6), a font style, make text bold or italic, or change its alignment.

3 To add a pop-up link without using JavaScript, select the text where the link is to be embedded and enter a URL in the field titled Link in the right-hand side of the Properties palette. Alternatively, select a file to link to by clicking the yellow folder next to this field. Beneath this, in the Target drop-down menu, select _blank for your link to appear in a new window.

The style sheet entry could also be written out as follows:

```
p {text-align: left; color: black; font-family:
     arial;}
```

Some of the essential properties that regulate how text is formatted are shown in Table 3.1 on the next page.

Using some of the properties outlined above, this is a more complex example of the CSS formatting for our paragraph element outlined above.

```
p {
     text-align: left;
     color: black;
     font-family: arial;
     font-size: 12;
     line-height: 15;
     text-indent: 5;
}
```

Any text placed between the <p> </p> tags in an HTML page with this style sheet attached to it would display an Arial font, 12 points in size, black in colour with 15 points between each line; it would also be aligned to the left and the first line of each paragraph would be indented 5 points.

But what if you wanted some paragraphs to appear in a different format – for example text to be set in bold or capitalised? This is where classes come into play. The style outlined above, for example, could be defined as the standard text formatting for a page, and with a small modification – p.standard – would remain as it is in the style sheet. Then another class could be

Table 3.1

Property	Description	Values	Property	Description	Values
color	Sets text colour.	*HTML colours* (see page 63)	line-height	Sets the distance between lines.	normal *number* %
direction	Sets text direction.	ltr, rtl	text-align	Aligns text in an element.	left right center justify
font-family	Sets generic typeface.	*typeface name* (e.g. arial, times, garamond, etc.)	text-decoration	Adds decoration to text in an element.	None underline overline line-through blink
font-size	Sets the size of a font.	*number* or following values: xx-small x-small small medium large x-large xx-large smaller larger	text-indent	Indents the first line of text in an element.	*number* %
font-style	Sets the style of a font.	italic normal oblique	text-shadow	Adds a shadow to text in a specified colour and set distance.	none *colour* *number*
font-weight	Sets the weight of a font.	normal bold bolder lighter 100 200 . . . 900	text-transform	Controls how letters appear in an element.	none capitalise lowercase uppercase

defined with a new selector, say p.formatted, and its properties and values changed as follows:

```
p.formatted {
    text-align: left;
    color: black;
    font-family: arial;
    font-size: smaller;
    font-weight: bold
    line-height: 13;
}
```

In the HTML page, these classes would be used as follows:

<p class="standard">
This is a standard paragraph with 12 point arial text, 15 point line height and an indent of 5 points at the start of each paragraph.
</p>

<p class="formatted">
This is a formatted paragraph with arial text

in a smaller, bold font, a 13 point line height and no indent for the first line.
</p>

Rollover links and pseudo classes

One very common use of CSS with text is to format links so that they change colour and appearance when the mouse rolls over them. This requires properties to be set for the anchor class ('a' in CSS) that is tied to a series of common pseudo classes which are introduced with a colon. These are link, visited, hover, active and focus. Link defines the properties for a hyperlink in normal circumstances, visited for when a link has been clicked on, hover when the mouse is over it, active for properties when the user actually clicks the link, and focus for when a keyboard shortcut is used. An example of this in a style sheet would be as follows:

```
a:link {color: blue; text-decoration: none;}
a:visited {color: purple; text-decoration:
   none;}
a:hover {color: red; text-decoration:
   underline;}
a:active {color: black; text-decoration:
   underline;}
a:focus {color: green; text-decoration:
   underline;}
```

With this example, a link would be blue with no underline, and purple once it had been visited. When the user's mouse hovered over it, the link would change colour to red and be underlined, and when the mouse button was pressed its colour would turn black. Finally, someone using the keyboard to access the link would see the link change colour to green.

It is also possible to use other properties to create a much more dynamic menu using CSS, such as links in coloured boxes that change colour as the user moves a mouse over them as in this example:

```
a {color: blue;
font: 11px arial,helvetica,sans-serif;
text-decoration: none;
border: 1px solid black;
display: block;
width: 150px;
padding: 3px 5px;
background: gray;}
a:hover, a:active, a:focus {
color: red;
background: black;
font-weight: bold;}
```

This script creates a grey box, 150 pixels wide with blue text, in which the link text changes to red and the background colour changes to black when the mouse hovers over it.

WORKING WITH IMAGES AND COLOUR

So far we have covered the essentials for creating a web page, which is adding text and hyperlinks. Without these, you don't really have a web page (as opposed to a text document such as something that might be produced in Word or Notepad). At the same time, even taking into account the sophistication that CSS provides in terms of formatting text, any page that restricts itself to just words and links is going to look fairly dull. The next series of building blocks, then, is to incorporate images into our pages, as well as work with colour to improve the visual appearance.

Pseudo classes are popular on the web in formatting hypertext links so that they change colour when the mouse rolls over them.

Graphics and formats

After the web browser was invented at the beginning of the 1990s, the next great leap forward came with one simple addition coded by Marc Andreessen for the first graphical browser, Mosaic. The inclusion of the <img> tag meant that for the first time graphics could be included in pages, and the internet

Formatting text CSS with Dreamweaver

1 CSS formatting in Dreamweaver is handled via the Design pane, clicking on which shows tabs for CSS Styles and Layers. At the bottom of the pane are buttons to attach an existing style sheet or create a new one. Clicking the latter displays a dialog box which will ask you to provide a name for the class and either create a separate style sheet or embed it in the current page.

2 The Style Definition dialog controls CSS properties for a wide range of elements in HTML, including boxes and backgrounds, but here we shall concentrate on text properties only. Here, a number of elements can be set such as font, size, weight, colour and decoration. Once selected, click on OK or Apply to make these changes to the text style.

3 As different CSS styles are created, they can be edited from the Rules pane: as each property is selected, so a drop-down menu allows you to make changes to each variable. When a style has been created to your satisfaction, highlight the text that it should be applied to and, in the Design pane, right click the appropriate class then select Apply from the menu that appears.

almost immediately became a more visually appealing place.

The <img> element includes a number of attributes, but is useless in HTML (although not, in certain circumstances, with scripting languages such as PHP) if it does not include at least one src. This tells the element where to find the source of an image, and a sample of this essential syntax would look something like this:

<img src="../images/myimage.jpg" />

This element is one of the very few in XHTML that does not require a closing tag, and although it can theoretically support any graphical file format, to display inline images – that is graphics that appear in a set place in the browser window – you are restricted to the following formats:

JPEG

These make use of what is known as lossy compression, that is extraneous information that the eye cannot see is discarded, in order to compress an image as aggressively as possible. **JPEGs** support a colour range of 16.7 million shades, which makes them very useful for displaying photographic images with as low a file size as possible. In addition, they are extremely well supported by any graphical browser, making their adoption fairly ubiquitous. The downside is that compression can result in poor-quality images, whereby blocks of colour, known as artifacts, appear and degrade the image.

GIF

Another commonly used image file format, GIF images use lossless compression, whereby redundant areas of colour are calculated mathematically to produce smaller file sizes. GIF images are restricted to 256 colours, and the compression algorithm used tends to make them larger than JPEGs, so they are not as commonly found online although, again, any graphical browser can display them. However, for areas that involve large blocks of colour such as logos, GIF compression does not introduce artifacts and they can also be animated.

PNG (portable network graphics)

PNGs were introduced from 1995 onwards as a replacement to GIFs. Like them, they use lossless compression, and like them support transparency via what is known as an alpha channel. However, like JPEGs they also support the full colour gamut of over 16 million colours, although (very rarely) they sometimes will not display as inline images in older browsers.

Until not very long ago, the principal rule for using images was compression above all things. This is probably less important in the days of broadband connections, but is still a significant issue: overloading a page with graphics, particularly ones that are hundreds of kilobytes in size, will take valuable seconds to display in a page. When the average time a visitor spends on a particular page before they make a decision to stay or move on is estimated to be approximately eight seconds, anything that slows down loading times is to be avoided. Image optimisation therefore remains an important skill, and while the Preparing images in Photoshop walkthrough (page 100) shows how to optimise a graphic in Photoshop, the principles remain the same for most image editing packages.

Some of the other attributes that can be employed with the <img> tag are as shown in Table 3.2.

Table 3.2

Attribute required	Description	Values
src	Defines the source of the image file.	path name
alt	Alternate text – this is an attribute that should always be included as it will help visually impaired visitors who use screen reader software.	descriptive text
Optional		
width	Sets the width of the image.	number
height	Sets the height of the image.	number
Deprecated		
align	Sets the alignment of text around the image, with left or right being the most useful values.	top middle bottom left right
border	Sets a border in number of pixels around the image.	number
hspace	The horizontal space or gutter around an image.	number
vspace	The vertical space or gutter around an image.	number

This does not exhaust the list of attributes for the <img> element, but some of the others, such as usemap and ismap for creating image maps, are better dealt with via web editing programs than in raw HTML. Note that align, border, hspace and vspace have been deprecated, and thus are not recognised by Strict XHTML. It is now recommended that image spacing is handled via style sheets, although there are plenty of contemporary sites that use this as a convenient way to create a gutter around a picture.

Using some of the above, the code for an inline graphic in a web page could look something like this:

```
<img src="../images/
   myimage.jpg"
   alt="This is my
   image" width="300"
   height="150" />
```

Rollover images

A simple way to provide feedback to a visitor is to use a rollover image, which works by substituting one image with another using JavaScript. When the mouse moves over an image, the replacement is substituted, and when it moves out the original image returns to position, each step using the instructions onMouseOver and onMouseOut.

A rollover JavaScript would look something like the following:

```
<a href="pagetolinkto.html"
onmouseover="document.sub_but.
   src='rolloverimage.gif'"
onmouseout="document.sub_but.
   src='originalimage.gif'">

<img src="originalimage.gif" width="143"
   height="39" border="0"
alt="a rollover button" name="sub_but">
</a>
```

The rollover button must be attached to an anchor, though it is possible to use the hash (#) sign to simply provide an empty anchor that does not go anywhere. The original image source is identified in the <img> element, and this must also include the name attribute for the JavaScript to work.

Image maps

An image map is an alternative means of creating navigation around the site. Rather than using individual links or buttons, an image is divided into set areas, each of which can be linked to a different URL. There are two main methods for creating an image map: the original version was devised for HTML 2.0 and is usually referred to as a server-side image map; there is also a client-side image map, which is simpler to encode as it is handled by the browser rather than a **CGI** script on the server.

The code for an image map is a series of x and y co-ordinates that specify the areas around an image, along with the href links to other pages. It is possible to hand-code such maps, but generally the complexity of doing this means that creating an image map is something that is much better done in a web editor. Nonetheless, the important elements are <map> and <area>, and the HTML code for an image map would look something like the following:

```
<map name="myImageMap">
<area shape=rect coords="50,50 100,100"
   href="page1.htm" alt="page 1">
<area shape=circle coords="90,90
   250,250" href="page2.htm" alt="page
   2">
<area shape=poly coords="105,115 10,60
   90,120 200,200" href="page 3.htm"
   alt="page 3">
</map>
```

The important attributes for the map and area elements are shape (a rectangle, circle or irregular polygon) and coords (the x, y co-ordinates for upper and lower points in the

> **Image maps make use of graphics to provide another way to navigate through a site through clickable sections of an image.**

WALKTHROUGH▶

Images, image maps and rollovers in Dreamweaver

1 Inserting images in Dreamweaver is extremely simple: click the Images button on the Common toolbar and select Image. In the dialog box that appears, browse to your file and select OK to insert it. In the Properties palette, it is important to enter text in the Alt field, while Link allows you to provide a hyperlink to the image.

2 For larger images that are to be used for navigation, the bottom left of the Properties palette includes tools to create image maps. These four tools, a pointer, and buttons to create rectangular, elliptical and polygonal shapes, are used to select or draw hotspots on the image. After drawing on the image, the Properties palette changes to provide a field to enter a URL: when that is entered, different hotspots will link to different locations.

3 Rollover images work in a fashion very similar to normal images. Go to the Images button and select Rollover Image. The main difference is that the dialog box which appears has two fields for two images (the original and the second which will replace it when a mouse moves over it). Select your files, enter a URL for the hyperlink, and click OK.

Insert Rollover Image

Image name: navbutton

Original image: Browse...   OK

Rollover image: Browse...   Cancel

☑ Preload rollover image   Help

Alternate text:

When clicked, Go to URL: Browse...

case of circles and rectangles, or each point for a polygon). While the sample image map we shall create will be done using Dreamweaver, if your own web editor does not support image maps a useful little application is Mapedit (www.boutell.com/mapedit/).

Images and CSS

Because working with a web editor will still tend to insert HTML code into the <img> element, we have concentrated so far on working with the basics of formatting graphics on your page using HTML. However, attributes such as border, vspace and hspace are deprecated, that is they are unlikely to be supported by future versions of HTML, with presentation of images – as with text – now being handled via CSS.

As with text, styles for images can be inserted directly into html using the <style> element or (a better approach) linked to a separate style sheet. By creating a series of classes with different styles, you can then attach these to your various images. For example, to create a single pixel black border around graphics could be done by setting up a class called .imgborder:

```
.imgborder {
border-width: 1px;
border-style: solid;
border-color: #000000;
}
```

This class is then linked to an image in HTML using the class attribute:

```
< img src="myimage.jpg" alt="My image"
    class="imgborder" />
```

If you establish a class to be used with your images, such as .illustration, you can create a CSS rule using the float and margin-right/margin-bottom properties:

```
.illustration {
float: left;
margin-right: 5px;
margin-bottom: 5px;
}
```

The class is linked in as with the imgborder example above:

```
< img src="myimage.jpg" alt="My image"
    class="illustration" />
```

With this class, the image would appear to the left of any text with a five pixel border on the right and bottom. Changing the values of float and using margin-left and margin-top properties would create different types of margin and place the image elsewhere, for example to the right of the text.

CSS can also be used to provide greater control over background images by creating rules for the body selector that employ the properties background-image and background-repeat. Consider the following examples:

```
body {
background-image: url(../images/
    background.jpg};
background-repeat: repeat;
}

body {
background-image: url(../images/
    background.jpg};
background-repeat: repeat-y;
}

body {
background-image: url(../images/
    background.jpg};
background-repeat: no-repeat;
}
```

Each of these three styles loads an image called background.jpg from the folder images. The first example repeats it across the page and is very similar to the old HTML attribute for the <body> element, background, and tiles an image across a page; the second, however, simply repeats it vertically, while the latter loads one image only onto the page. It is also possible to place a background image precisely using the property background-position with x and y co-ordinates. Thus background-position: 200px 150px would place an image 200 pixels from the left and 150 pixels from the top of the browser window.

Colour

Simple but dramatic graphical effects are often achieved not by employing complex graphics but by the accomplished use of colour. Many colours are said to be complementary – for example blue and yellow or green and magenta – and a rather bland page can be improved greatly by placing a colour logo or small graphic in a noticeable position. By contrast, using too many different colours, or colours that clash, usually makes a page look tawdry and difficult to use. Also, bear in mind that colour-blind visitors may have a problem distinguishing certain colours, such as red and green.

Colours on a screen are produced by mixing different values of the three primary colours, red, green and blue. When mixed at full value, these produce white light, and black when the pixels emit no light. This RGB colour model is what is known as additive colour, that is light is emitted, rather than the subtractive colour of print, where certain wavelengths of light are absorbed by a pigment and the rest are reflected back to present a certain colour. So-called secondary colours are achieved by mixing each of the primary colours in equal amounts: thus blue and green produce yellow, green and blue produce cyan, and blue and red produce magenta.

A concern of older web developers was to ensure that all colours on a web page could be displayed in any monitor, including those that had very low memory. A palette of web-safe colours, consisting of just 216 different hues, was therefore developed. However, this is much less of a problem today than the simple fact that different monitors and graphic cards will be set up in such a way as to display various colours in slightly different ways. While a professional developer can calibrate their monitor to ensure consistent values for colours there is, unfortunately, no way to ensure that visitors to your site will do the same.

> Colour is incredibly important when designing pages, transforming the ways in which users interact with your site.

As every colour is defined as a combination of red, green and blue values, so each spot of colour has a value assigned to it for RGB ranging from 0 (no colour) to 255 (full colour). Thus black is set at 0 for each RGB value and white is 255. In HTML, while it is possible to assign colours via names for common hues, such as red, brown, gray, lightgray, this palette is limited and it is more common to determine colours using a hexadecimal number. Hexadecimal comprises 16 digits (as opposed to the two of binary or ten of decimal), from 0 to 9 and A to F representing the numbers 10 to 15. HTML uses this hexadecimal code in pairs to create over 16 million possible shades, with a hash sign (#) before the code. Thus black is #000000, white is #ffffff, and unmixed red is #ff0000.

Sometimes you will see three instead of six digits: this offers fewer shades of colour, with just one digit representing each RGB value, but is still useful for a wide range of colours. Red, for example, would be written #f00 in this scheme.

> Modern web design principally works with colour through CSS, using these formatting instructions to handle everything from shades of text to the border colour of any borders or margins on the page.

Colour and CSS

Colours can be assigned to just about any part of a page. Obviously, photographs or graphics created in an image editor such as Photoshop will be modified within an application external to a web editor, but when modifying colours that relate to different parts of your web page, such as text or a background, this is an aspect of presentation and thus better handled via CSS.

Unsurprisingly, the property that changes colour within a web page is color, although this itself is often attached to other properties such as background-color or border-top-color. If you bear in mind the comments above about using hexadecimal code, this is an extremely easy property to use. Typically, you may wish to provide a different colour scheme for headings

on a page and body copy, using rules such as the following:

```
h2 {color: magenta;}
p {color: darkgray;}
```

Each of these colours could also be represented by hexadecimal code, for example #ff00ff for magenta and #a9a9a9 for darkgray. If you want to generate the hexadecimal numbers for a wide range of colours, a useful tool can be found at www.colorpicker.com.

Creating a rule for the body element is also a good way to define a number of colours. For example, using the color property here will establish a base colour for text across the page, and entering background-colour changes the shade of the page, such as:

```
body {
color: red;
background-color: #a9a9a9
}
```

When defining colours for any element on a web page, such as borders, hyperlinks, columns or table cells, it is always advisable to use CSS. You can set up classes if you wish, so that one type of column could employ one colour scheme, and another a different set of values.

TABLES, FORMS AND LAYOUT

Tables

Tables are useful for laying out data in rows and columns. Until the late 1990s, they were also the main way by which web designers could have some means to provide more complex layouts on pages, but with the development of CSS there are much better ways to control presentation of a page. This said, there are plenty of times when creating a page as a simple table can be much quicker and simpler for laying out certain elements – a grid of images, for example – than setting up specific code for the page.

A table consists of three elements: <table>, which defines the whole table, <tr> which defines a table row, and <td> which defines an individual table cell. A simple table with two rows and three columns is formatted in HTML as follows:

```
<table>
  <tr>
    <td>Row 1 Cell 1</td>
    <td>Row 1 Cell 2</td>
    <td>Row 1 Cell 3</td>
  </tr>
  <tr>
    <td>Row 2 Cell 1</td>
    <td>Row 2 Cell 2</td>
    <td>Row 2 Cell 3</td>
  </tr>
</table>
```

It is important to nest these three elements correctly within each other. A table definition (td) must have its opening and closing tags within a table row (tr) which, in turn, must have opening and closing tags within the table element. Some of the various attributes for each of these elements are as shown in Table 3.3 (note, all of these are optional values).

The following code shows how some of these attributes work in practice:

```
<table border=1
  cellpadding=3  table">
  <tr align="left" valign="top">
    <td rowspan=2>Rows 1 and 2 Cell
1</td>
    <td>Row 1 Cell 2</td>
    <td>Row 1 Cell 3</td>
```

```
  </tr>
  <tr align="left" valign="top">
    <td colspan=2>Row 2 Cells 2 and
3</td>
  </tr>
</table>
```

A number of deprecated attributes such as width and height were formerly used to handle the formatting of cells, but this is now done within CSS. There are also several other valid elements, all of which appear within the <table> element, that can be used to provide additional information on a table. The <thead>, <tbody> and <tfoot> tags allow you to group rows of data within a table – for example to provide a header describing the table, along with a series of rows of numbers in columns, and a final row that tallies results in those columns. Although valid HTML, these are rarely used because of poor browser support.

Table design with CSS

While the slightly more complex, but still rather basic, table above has a simple element of presentation in terms of a border, HTML really cannot match the formatting capabilities of CSS when it comes to presenting tables. Likewise, other presentation elements, such as height, width and colour (which used to be handled within HTML) and alignment (which can still be specified as an attribute of rows or cells), are also set within CSS. HTML formatting is very basic and using the border attribute can make a grid look very dated, whereas CSS provides complete control over how it will appear in the browser.

As with other elements considered so far, any type of text and colour formatting can be applied to content within cells, and by setting up different classes you can present individual

> Although it is possible to handle page layout using tables, these should be reserved for presenting tabular data and other elements of layout (such as columns) handled via CSS.

Table 3.3

Attribute	Description	Values
table		
border	The table border in pixels.	*number*
cellpadding	Specifies the amount of space between the cell walls and content in pixels or percentage.	*number*
cellspacing	Specifies the amount of space between one cell and the next as pixels or percentage.	*number*
frame	How the outer border of a table should be displayed.	above below border box hsides lhs rhs void vsides
rules	Specifies horizontal and vertical divider lines.	all cols groups none rows
summary	Provides a summary of a table; this should not be used in tables employed for design.	*text*

Attribute	Description	Values
tr		
align	Sets the horizontal alignment of content within a row.	center justify left right
valign	Sets the vertical alignment of content in a row.	baseline bottom middle top
td		
align	Sets the horizontal alignment of content within a cell.	center justify left right
colspan	Specifies the number of columns a cell should occupy.	*number*
rowspan	Specifies the number of rows a cell should occupy.	*number*
valign	Sets the vertical alignment of content in a row.	baseline bottom middle top

rows, columns or cells in different ways. Here is an example of how a table could be formatted using CSS:

```
table {border:1px solid black;}
tr.oddRow td {background-color: lightgray}
tr.evenRow td {background-color: black}
td.numberCell {text-align: right; color: blue;
    padding: 5px}
td.textCell {text-align: left; color: red;
    padding 10px}
```

This set of rules creates a solid black border around the table (although it could, of course, be a different colour, width and style such as a dashed or grooved line). Within the table, odd rows have a background colour of light grey while even rows are black, and cells containing

Adding a table in Dreamweaver

1 To insert a table, select the grid-like Table button on the Common toolbar. This displays a dialog box with several options for customising your table before it is added to your page. Rows, Columns and Table width (in pixels or per cent) determine the dimensions of the table, while Border thickness, Cell padding and Cell spacing determine its appearance.

Table   ✕

Table size

Rows: 3   Columns: 3

Table width: 75   percent ▼

Border thickness: 0   pixels

Cell padding: 3   ⊞

Cell spacing: 5   ⊞

Header

None   Left   Top   Both

Accessibility

Caption:

Align caption: default ▼

Summary:

Help   OK   Cancel

---

2 Once a table is created, its properties can be edited in the palette at the bottom of the main workspace. As well as the default options listed in the dialog box, it is also possible here to change background or border colour, as well as set a background image. It is also possible to modify settings for individual cells, columns or rows when these are selected.

3 Different parts of your table may be combined or merged together across columns or rows. To do this, select either a number of cells or an entire column or row and press 'm' on the keyboard. Similarly, a cell may be divided into two or more rows or columns by right-clicking inside it and selecting Table, Split Cell.

numbers are formatted differently from those with text. Modifying our original simple table, the HTML would look something like this:

```
<table>
    <tr class="oddRow">
        <td class="textCell">Q1 Sales</td>
        <td class="textCell">Q2 Sales</td>
        <td class="textCell">Q3 Sales</td>
    </tr class="evenRow">
    <tr>
        <td class="numberCell">3500</td>
        <td class="numberCell">2000</td>
        <td class="numberCell">4600</td>
    </tr>
    <tr class="oddRow">
        <td class="textCell">Apr-Jun</td>
        <td class="textCell">Jul-Sep</td>
        <td class="textCell">Oct-Dec</td>
    </tr>
</table>
```

Using forms

Forms are an important way of adding interactivity to a site by allowing visitors to provide information that is then sent back through the browser.

Forms are one of the main means of gaining feedback from visitors, and can operate from the simplest design such as the text box and search button in Google, to much more complex multiple choice and comment boxes that can perform a multitude of tasks. A form contains various controls, such as input fields and push buttons so that when the 'submit' button is clicked a data string is sent back to the server. Forms are one of the primary means of interacting with site visitors that we shall consider in chapters 5 and 7. For now, we will discuss the HTML elements of a form in conjunction with a simple email instruction that will pass information back to the site designer.

The form is the area of a web page that lies between the <form> </form> tags, and contains various input controls and fields as well as other images and text. The information passed on by interactive controls is referred to as values,

and once these values are entered by a visitor to the site they are passed to the server as what is known as a form data set which can then be processed by the form handler, the script or program that analyses this data.

The form element has to include an action attribute, which is the URL of the form handler, and may also include a method, set to get or post, that appends the information to the handler's URL. The handler then extracts values from the URL to process. Between the form tags are various components for collecting data, such as input boxes and buttons, so that the HTML for a very simple form, simply consisting of a text box and submit button, would look something like this:

```
<form method="post" action="../cgi-bin/
    formscript.php">
<p label for="username">Enter your
    name</label>
<input type="text" name="username"
    id="username" />
<input type="submit" name="submit"
    value="submit" /></p>
</form>
```

This very simple form has two components, both indicated by the element <input> and distinguished by their type, as well as a label that provides instructions to a visitor. Once the form is submitted, the value from the form (a username) will be appended to the URL and posted to be processed by the file formscript.php.

These are the main input types for forms, created in HTML by changing the value for the type attribute:

- **Text**   Creates a single line field into which a visitor can type.
- **Password**   Another single line field, but this obscures entered text with asterisks.
- **Checkbox**   A toggle for users to select among multiple options, this places a tick or small cross in as many boxes as the visitor wishes.
- **Radio**   Another toggle, but only one radio button can be selected.

- **File** Allows visitors to upload a file from their computer.
- **Submit** This submits the form data set.
- **Reset** This clears any data that has been entered into the form.
- **Hidden** A control that is not displayed but is used to pass along additional information with a form, such as an ID number.
- **Image** This functions in the same way as a submit button, but allows you to set an image instead of a standard button.

Table 3.4 shows the most important attributes for these input elements.

As well as these standard input types, three other useful elements are <button>, <textarea> and <select>. The button element can function just like a submit or reset button (or, indeed, have other functions assigned to it), with the added advantage that it may use an image as well as text; textarea is similar to the type="text" input but creates a multi-line field for entering larger amounts of text; select creates a

Table 3.4

Attribute required	Description	Values
name	This identifies the control so it can be matched with its value once the form is submitted.	text
type	Specifies the type of input.	see above
Optional		
alt	Provides an alternative text description (only used with type="image").	text
accept	Includes a comma-separated list of file types (only used with type="file").	comma-separated text, e.g. jpg, gif, bmp
checked	Sets an initial checked status for checkboxes and radio buttons (only used with type="checkbox" and type="radio").	checked="checked"
disabled	This disables a control so it cannot be used, and will be displayed as greyed-out.	disabled="disabled"
maxlength	Specifies the maximum number of characters that can be entered (only used with type="text" and type="password").	number
readonly	Specifies that a control will only display a value and cannot be modified, but is not displayed greyed out (only used with type="text" and type="password").	readonly="readonly"
size	Specifies the width of certain input controls (only used with type="text", type="password" and type="file").	number
src	Specifies the source file for an image (only used with type="image").	URL
tabindex	Specifies the order for moving between controls using the Tab key	number
value	Provides an initial value for a control before it is modified by a user.	text

drop-down menu. Finally, the <fieldset> element groups together related controls, for example a series of radio buttons or checkboxes: it must also contain a <legend> element which provides a title for the set of fields. Using the fieldset tags with our earlier, very simple form, we would have something like:

```
<form method="post" action="../cgi-bin/
   formscript.php">
   <fieldset>
      <legend>User name form</legend>
      <p label for="username">Enter your
name</label>
      <input type="text"
name="username" id="username" />
      <input type="submit"
name="submit" value="submit" /></p>
   </fieldset>
</form>
```

Form design with CSS

A visitor's experience of using a form will be affected by various design issues, and it is easy to use forms inappropriately. Design issues will come into play in terms of aesthetics (an ugly form will not be appealing to complete) and usability (in terms of such things as legibility and the logic of information being requested).

In general, forms are one area I would not recommend trying to construct by hand in raw code, although it is important to understand the HTML in order to troubleshoot and be clear what you are trying to achieve. Generally, however, it is much easier to line up various components in a WYSIWYG editor. In addition, CSS rules can help greatly with the presentation of any forms on your site.

You can use CSS, for example, to remove the default border and padding that appears in a fieldset with following instruction:

```
fieldset {
border: none;
padding: 0;
}
```

Alternatively, it is possible to create a border in different colours or styles, as well as increase the level of padding around content.

Another task that is extremely difficult to do in HTML, even with a WYSIWYG editor, but extremely easy with CSS, is to align labels. To do this, you should create a rule for an ID (indicated with a # sign) and then assign that ID (here #info) to all the labels you wish to align:

```
#info label {
float: left;
width: 150px;
text-align: right;
margin-right: 10px;
}
```

When applied to a series of labels with the same ID in HTML with code such as <label for="control_name" id="info">, then all labels will align to the right and have a space of 10 pixels between them and their controls.

Finally, HTML forms default to a monospace typeface, but you can also modify this in CSS with a very simple instruction that will apply to all controls you specify (remembering, of course, that most of these controls are of the <input> type):

```
input, select, textarea, button {
font-family: inherit;
}
```

Now all controls in a form with the attached style sheet will use the same typeface applied to the parent object in the HTML document.

> While it is important to understand the underlying code behind creating a form, this is one area of web design that is generally better handled in a WYSIWYG editor rather than coding by hand.

CSS design

So far in this chapter, we have concentrated on CSS as it affects particular groups of elements such as images and forms, but these can also be placed inside containers that are themselves formatted using CSS. This type of positioning can be much more accurate than XHTML and is also useful when designing a page for different types of device. Containers are usually attached to paragraphs, but can also be linked to other HTML elements such as the body tag.

One common part of such a container that is formatted is the margin, defining the space around it, for example:

    p.boxout {margin: 12px 8px}

If you set two values, as in the example above, then the first value applies to top and bottom, the second to left and right. One value is set to all four sides, and four values set margins for top, right, bottom and left in that order. As well as margins around a container, padding will set the space within and works in very much the same way depending on whether you set one, two or four values:

    p.boxout {padding: 10px 15px 10px 5px}

Containers can also have a border, as with tables and form elements, which may also be styled:

    p.boxout {
    border-width: medium;
    border-style: solid;
    border-color: gray;
    }

Other features for a container are its size (width and height) and how content flows within it. By default, a container will be big enough to contain all its content, but if you specify a height it may not be large enough, causing that content to overlay other elements on the page. The overflow command deals with this additional content, telling the container whether it should display a scroll bar or not (scroll sets a scroll bar whether content overflows or not, while auto only does so if there is any overflow):

    p.boxout {
    width: 200px;
    height: 250px;
    overflow: auto;}

These styles can be combined more concisely as follows:

    p.boxout {width: 200px; height: 250px;
        overflow: auto; border: medium solid
        gray; margin: 2cm 3cm; padding 10px
        15px;}

The properties and values considered so far are the default for positioning within HTML and are what is known as static positioning. However, CSS also allows you to create relative, absolute, fixed and floating containers. Relatively positioned containers can move as the browser window changes size, and are determined via the property position and co-ordinates for top and left depending on where another element is located, for example:

    p.boxout {position: relative; top: 10px; left:
        50px;}

Changing the value for position to absolute will give a precise specified distance from the left-hand side and top of the screen, regardless of whether the browser window changes size or another element moves. Otherwise it functions in the same way, as does the fixed value, although in this case a container will remain locked in that position even if the user scrolls down the browser window.

The float property is slightly different in use, creating a box that is shifted to the left or right, with rules presented as follows:

    p.boxout {float: right;}

When floating a container that contains content other than images, it is best to set a width for the container, otherwise it can have unwanted effects.

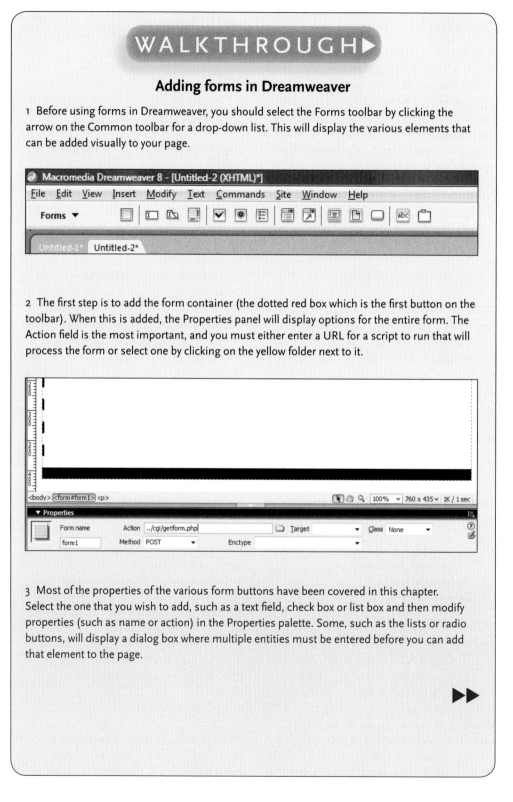

WALKTHROUGH▶

Adding forms in Dreamweaver

1 Before using forms in Dreamweaver, you should select the Forms toolbar by clicking the arrow on the Common toolbar for a drop-down list. This will display the various elements that can be added visually to your page.

2 The first step is to add the form container (the dotted red box which is the first button on the toolbar). When this is added, the Properties panel will display options for the entire form. The Action field is the most important, and you must either enter a URL for a script to run that will process the form or select one by clicking on the yellow folder next to it.

3 Most of the properties of the various form buttons have been covered in this chapter. Select the one that you wish to add, such as a text field, check box or list box and then modify properties (such as name or action) in the Properties palette. Some, such as the lists or radio buttons, will display a dialog box where multiple entities must be entered before you can add that element to the page.

▶▶

Core skills considered

This chapter has moved at considerable pace through the techniques and procedures required to create a website from scratch. While certain sections have demonstrated how to use an application such as Dreamweaver to create your site, on the whole the focus has been on mastering XHTML and CSS. These are the key skills that allow producers not simply to create a static site, but also to customise the various publishing platforms (such as blogs and wikis) that will be covered later on in this book.

For more information and updates on web design, visit www.producingforweb2.com/design.

CHAPTER 4

Creating dynamic sites

The previous chapter has looked at the requirements for creating relatively static sites. However, the vast majority of contemporary web design is dynamic, making use of databases and scripting languages to create a much more interactive experience for visitors. Any web producer wishing to explore more than the basics must engage with these technologies.

CLIENT-SIDE SCRIPTING WITH JAVASCRIPT

We have already discussed JavaScript in chapter 2, but now we shall look at some of the ways you can use client-side scripting to make pages more dynamic and responsive to users' actions.

While there are plenty of server-side scripting languages and technologies, such as PHP, Java and ASP.NET, that will work with most web browsers, there is only one client-side language that works across all the major platforms that users are likely to use on your site. JavaScript allows you to create mini applications that run in the browser: whereas the code for server-side scripts is executed on the server and the results

are passed to the browser as HTML, JavaScript code is downloaded and then executed on the client PC. The result of this is that it can respond faster. As JavaScript can do such things as change CSS values, it is a useful tool to learn for creating more exciting pages.

In this section, we shall cover the basics of using JavaScript, but you will also be able to find more examples on the *Producing for Web 2.0* site.

JavaScript basics

JavaScript, as has previously been pointed out, is not Java: whereas Java is a compiled (self-sufficient) language that can be installed and used in a variety of ways, JavaScript has to be run as a scripting language within the browser. Nonetheless, over the past decade it has developed into a pretty powerful tool providing many built-in functions to perform specific tasks. Here we will concentrate on the basics of the syntax for using JavaScript.

Unlike older versions of HTML, JavaScript is case-sensitive, so myJavaScript is not the same as myjavascript or MYJAVASCRIPT. Likewise, a built-in function

> A client-side scripting language is one that is run in the browser on the visitor's PC, rather than on the server that hosts web pages. JavaScript is the dominant scripting language supported by just about every browser available today.

such as alert("Hello World!") will not work if you type in alert("Hello World!"). At the core of the language is the statement, an instruction which will perform a task, and which is typically marked by a semicolon with values to be displayed presented between curly brackets, as in the following example:

```
if(userAge<18) {
    alert("You are too young to vote");
}
else {
    alert("You may vote now!");
}
```

When creating a script for a web page, the general script is either written in a separate file that is then linked to the HTML document via the element src="javascriptfile.js", or the script is written between the <head> tags in the document itself and then called when needed in the body. Thus, for example, if you had a JavaScript file called mycommand.js, it would be linked to your web page as follows somewhere in the head of the page:

```
< script src="../js/mycommand.js">
</script>
```

In XHTML, the script command must always be closed with a final tag, and this would call up mycommand.js when the web page was loaded in the browser. Alternatively, if you were including the entire script (such as our brief example for the alert userAge) in the web page, it would look like this:

```
<head>
    <title>A brief JavaScript</title>
    <script type="text/javascript">
    <!--
        if(userAge<18){
            alert("You are too young to vote");
        }
```

```
    else {
        alert("You may vote now!");
    }
    //-->
    </script>
</head>
```

For this script to do something, there would have to be an input box in the main page called userAge: when a number was entered that was lower than 18, the first message would be displayed in an alert box, while 18 or higher would cause the second alert to be displayed. The lines <!-- and //--> indicate that this section of the HTML document should be skipped by older browsers that cannot work with JavaScript.

In the rest of this section, we shall consider the other essential ingredients of JavaScript, such as variables, expressions, statements and functions, but it is also worth remarking that JavaScript code can become quite complex, and it is a good idea to place comments in any work that you do. The purpose of a comment should be to guide you when you return to a script to edit it – no matter how clear it appeared to you when first written, things can get confusing after a while. Comments are added with double forward slashes (//) or, if a comment is to be extended across multiple lines, with a slash and asterisk:

> /* This comment will contain detailed instructions on a script. As such, it is expected to run across several lines with text that will not be executed by the browser. */

Get into the habit of commenting your scripts frequently: when you return to them later, it will help you orient yourself to different commands or sections much more quickly.

> **Adding comments to your scripts will help you understand what you were trying to do when you come back to edit your code.**

Using variables and operators

Variables were introduced briefly in chapter 2 when discussing PHP language, and are as important to JavaScript as they are to any other programming language. A variable is a container for data that, as its name suggests, can vary the content that it stores. For example, as in the example of userAge above, you may need to collect a visitor's age and this will have to change as different visitors enter different values.

There are several rules when naming variables in JavaScript:

- As with the rest of the language, all variable names are case sensitive so userAge is not the same as UserAge.
- Variables can only use letters, underscores and numbers, but numbers must not appear in the first position.
- Certain words, such as 'abstract' or 'volatile', are reserved, that is they are used for other purposes within JavaScript and should not be used as variable names. You can find a complete list at http://www.javascripter.net/faq/reserved.htm.

JavaScript makes use of certain data types but, as with PHP (but unlike many other programming languages), these do not necessarily need to be declared, the only exception being that any variable value that appears in quotations marks will be treated as a text string. The data types are:

- **Boolean**   This can only contain the values true or false.
- **Null**   Contains no value, or more accurately, it shows that the value is unknown (the value null is not the same as 0 or an empty string).
- **Number**   A numeric value.
- **Object**   One of the built-in JavaScript objects, such as Date, or an object you build yourself.

- **String**   Characters within quotes that are treated as strings of text (so 10 is a number that can be added to other numbers, but "o" is a string).

When setting a variable, the variable name is placed on the left of an equals sign, along with the keyword var that declares it is a variable, and the value to the right, as in the following examples of Boolean, number and string values:

```
var _aComplete = false;
var userAge = 39;
var fullName = "Joe Bloggs";
```

After variables have been defined – either specified in your code or collected from the user, for example via a form, then you will often wish these variables to interact with other variables. For example, to add a first name to a last name:

```
firstName = "Jane";
lastName = "Bloggs";
fullName = firstName + " " + lastName;
```

Because the first two variables are strings, the last variable will similarly output a string – 'Jane Bloggs' (the empty space between the two names, indicated by a space between two quotation marks, is important. In this case, the plus operator (+) works by 'concatenation', literally placing the two strings together. However, with numerical data types it works as a mathematical operator:

```
vAge = 18;
wAge = 47;
rAge = vAge + wAge;
```

This returns the value 65. If both vAge and wAge are strings ('18' and '47'), it will return 1847.

Operators, then, perform actions on variables, with the most common operators indicated in Table 4.1.

> **Variables store data in a format that can change as information is updated, for example when a visitor selects one option on a page.**

Table 4.1

Operator	Example	Description
Arithmetic operators		
+	a + b	Adds a and b together.
-	a - b	Subtracts b from a.
*	a * b	Multiplies a and b together.
/	a / b	Divides a by b.
a++	a++	Increments a by 1.
a—	a—	Decrements a by 1.
Comparison operators		
=	a = b	Sets a equal to b.
==	a == b	True if a and b are the same value.
===	a === b	True if a and be are the same value and same data type.
!=	a != b	True if a and b are *not* the same value.
!==	a !== b	True if a and b are not the same value nor the same data type.
>	a > b	True if a is greater than b.
<	a < b	True if a is less than b.
>=	a >= b	True if a is equal to or greater than b.
<=	a <= b	True if a is equal to or less than b.
||	a || b	True if either a or b is true.
&&	a && b	True if both a and b are true.

Arrays

Arrays are a special type of variable that hold more than one value, which are then called from an index in brackets. Strictly speaking, in JavaScript an array is an object, that is a collection of functions and attributes grouped together in a common theme, and these are defined via an index in square brackets. Arrays are declared using the keyword Array(), as in the following example:

```
var myMeals = new Array();
var allMeals;
```

```
myMeals[0] = "Breakfast";
myMeals[1] = "Lunch";
myMeals[2] = "Dinner";
allMeals = "";
for (i=0;i<myMeals.length;i++)
{
    allMeals = allMeals + myMeals[i] + ", ";
}
alert("Here are the meals I eat each day " +
    allMeals);
```

In this example, the index number after the array name in square brackets distinguishes each value in the array – and this must start at

0 not 1. The variable allMeals is initially set with an empty value, and the conditional statement beginning for (dealt with in the next section) assigns a simple counter, i, to count each of the values contained in the variable myMeals. The statement myMeals.length uses a built-in function for arrays, length, which returns the number of elements in the array – as long as the counter i is less than the number of elements, it will continue to add 1 to the index for myMeals using the operator ++. Finally, each of the values contained in myMeals is ascribed to the variable allMeals and displayed in a message box.

Statements, loops and functions

Variables and operators are used in statements, which perform various actions. A general statement is an expression, which returns a value, such as wAge = 65 – 18, in this case returning a value of 47 for the variable wAge, or fullName = firstName + " " + lastName, which returns 'Jane Bloggs' when firstName is Jane and lastName is Bloggs. Expressions are usually the easiest type of statement to use and understand.

But what do you do if you want to check values against a number of variables, for example to return one message if a visitor to your site enters an age in one particular range, but a different message for different ages, say over 18. We have already seen an example of this at the start of this chapter, and it is known as a conditional statement. Conditional statements do a comparison between two values and returns a Boolean value of true or false. The simplest type of conditional statement uses the command if to check whether a value is true:

```
if(userAge<18){
    alert("You are too young to vote");
}
```

This statement compares the variable userAge to the condition under 18 and, if true, returns a message, but does nothing else if the condition is false. To extend it slightly, we can add an else statement:

```
if(userAge<18){
    alert("You are too young to vote");
}
else {
    alert("You may vote now!");
}
```

Now, if the condition is 18 or over, the message 'You may vote now!' is displayed. By adding an extra line of code (and slightly modifying our original script), we can check for multiple conditions.

```
if(userAge<5) {
    alert("Ooh! You liar");
}
else if(userAge>=18) {
    alert("You may vote now!");
}
else {
    alert("You are too young to vote");
}
```

In addition to conditional statements, which check whether values are true, and expressions, which return a value, another useful type of statement is the loop. This is used when you need the same action (that is the same piece of code) to be performed again and again. The syntax for a loop is as follows:

```
for (loop init;test condition; loop counter)
{
    code to be looped
}
```

For example, if you wanted simply to count from one to ten and display it in the browser, you would add the following code:

> **Loops are useful types of statements to include in your code when you need to repeat the same action more than once.**

```
<head>
    <title>Looping from 1 to 10</title>
    <script type="text/javascript">
    <!--
        var newline = "<br />"
        var iCount
        for
(iCount=0;iCount<=10;iCount++);
        {
            document.write("iCount = " +
iCount);
            document.write(newline);
        }
        document.write("Loop completed");
    //-->
    </script>
</head>
```

This code will count from zero to ten (using the incremental operator ++) and write out each number using the function document.write. Once the condition is met, that is the number 10 is reached, the code finishes looping and a final message is displayed in the browser. There are other types of loops that can be executed in JavaScript which we do not have space to cover here, using the commands do and while, but you can see examples of them on the *Producing for Web 2.0* website.

> **An event is an action that the user or the browser performs and is important for JavaScript in providing interactivity to a page.**

Functions

The final important concept to using JavaScript – and one which, like variables, operators and functions, is also important to PHP – is the function. A function groups together a series of statements that are to be performed in a particular order: a function, then, can be considered as a mini script or block of code that can be called and re-used again either in the same web document or across different web pages. These are particularly useful for another reason: if you do not want code to execute automatically when a page loads, for example you only want certain elements of a page to be displayed when the user clicks a button, then you can put that code into a function – then it only runs when it is called (that is, when the user clicks the button).

JavaScript, like other programming languages, has several built-in functions such as alert() and write(), which display a message box and write something to the web page respectively, but the main use of the function keyword is to write your own blocks of re-usable code.

For example, assuming that your JavaScript regularly adds two numbers together: rather than retyping the code, you may define a function addNumbers that can take two values and output the result to be used elsewhere in your script as follows:

```
function addNumbers(value1,value2) {
    return value1 + value2;
}
```

With this code, whenever the function is called the two values will be added together and returned to your code. To call a function, you simply use the name that you assigned it, as with:

```
var totalNumber =
addNumbers(54,82);
```

Now the variable totalNumber is assigned the value of 136. Functions are extremely important for creating efficient JavaScript, and assigning large blocks of code to a function will help simplify your scripts.

Handling events

Event handling is one of the most important uses for JavaScript, an event being an action that either the browser or the user performs in or with the document, for example loading the page or clicking a button. Table 4.2 shows some of the events that can be attached to JavaScript code.

There are several ways to use these events

Table 4.2

Event	Occurrence
abort	When a user cancels the page load.
click	When a user single-clicks an element in a page.
dblclick	When a user double-clicks an element.
keydown	When a user holds down a key on the keyboard.
keypress	When a user presses a key and releases it.
mousedown	When a user presses a mouse button.
mousemove	When the user moves the mouse around the page.
mouseout	When the user moves the mouse out of an element.
mouseover	When the user moves the mouse over an element.
mouseup	When the user releases the mouse button.
onload	When the page loads.
reset	When the user clicks a button to reset a page.
resize	When the user changes the size of the browser window.
select	When the user clicks a radio button or checkbox.
submit	When the user clicks the submit button on a form.

with JavaScript. The simplest, which we shall deal with here, is called the inline model: you simply state a function in the head of your document and then call it from within the body, for example:

```
<head>
    <title>onload event</title>
    <script type="text/javascript">
    <!--
        function fn_load()
        {
            alert("page has loaded");
        }
    //-->
    </script>
</head>
<body onload="fn_load()">
</body>
```

This will display a message box (and nothing else) telling you that the page has loaded. As can be seen from the example above, events are usually associated with a function and the function is not executed before the event occurs.

SERVER-SIDE SCRIPTING WITH PHP

PHP, or PHP: Hypertext Preprocessor, was introduced in chapter 2 as one of the most commonly used server-side scripting languages on the net. Unlike JavaScript it runs from the server, processing commands before converting them to HTML that is sent to the browser. Because the document will be saved with the .php extension, the server will process the command before it is displayed and output an HTML file. This can make it a little slower to execute than JavaScript (although rarely noticeable other than for the longest scripts), but it provides one of the most adaptable languages for creating rich web pages, particularly when employed with the database MySQL.

> It is very easy to integrate PHP code with HTML, which is one reason why the language has become so popular.

PHP has a shallow learning curve, which means that it is possible to begin employing it quickly to get results, building up to much more complex applications as you go. As with JavaScript, the language (its basics at least) is relatively easy to understand, and most of the concepts that apply to JavaScript also apply to PHP – meaning that learning one will give you a good grounding when getting to grips with the other.

PHP and HTML

In chapter 2 we saw a very simple example of HTML code – possibly the simplest that can be written and still be referred to as code in any meaningful sense:

```
<?
echo "Hello World!" ;
?>
```

This introduced the basic format for using PHP, with code contained between two angled brackets and question marks, with the command 'echo'. This has been described as the most fundamental command within PHP because it outputs whatever follows it into the HTML document that will be displayed in the visitor's browser.

When simply working with text in a PHP document, this should be contained within quotation marks – whether they are single or double does not matter as long as you are consistent, for example:

```
echo 'using single quotes to display
     "double" quotes' ;
```

```
echo "using double quotes to display
     'single' quotes" ;
```

One thing to be aware of: when PHP encounters an apostrophe, it will expect to find a matching end quotation mark and so return an error. To use quotation marks within lines of PHP code, you must use the escape character \, which tells PHP not to parse the following character, as with:

```
echo 'using the backslash means that PHP
     won\'t interpret the apostrophe as an
     ending quote' ;
```

While it is possible to output every line of HTML, both plain text and HTML markup, as PHP code this is not the most efficient way to create PHP documents. Thus while the following is perfectly acceptable, it would also be very time-consuming:

```
echo "<table>";
echo "<tr>";
echo "<td>";
echo "A one cell table";
echo "</td>";
echo "</tr>";
echo "</table>";
```

Rather than this laborious approach, you can mix PHP code and HTML markup in the same document, switching from one to the other by simply using an opening or closing bracket and question mark:

```
<? PHP code to go here ?>
<table>
<tr>
<td>
A one cell table
</td>
</tr>
</table>
<? more PHP code here ?>
```

One extremely efficient use of PHP is to use the include command to insert what are known as included files. If you have a common set of menu links, for example, or another snippet of code that you wish to include on every page of your website, it is extremely useful to be able to write that code in an external file that can then be linked to all your other documents. As with using CSS, you then need only to change one file to modify all the pages on your site.

To use included files, first you must create your external document, which might be HTML, PHP or simply plain text, and save it on your server, for example as mymenu.php. Then, in the document which will call that content, insert the following code at the point at which it is to appear on the page:

```
<?
include "mymenu.php";
?>
```

Using variables and operators

The general principles that apply to variables and operators in JavaScript also apply to PHP, so we shall concentrate on the minor differences that apply, as well as how to use variables in your PHP code, rather than repeating general statements. If you need reminding what variables are and how they work, consult page 76.

The main difference between JavaScript and PHP variables is that while variables are declared in the former using the keyword var, in PHP they are declared with the initial prefix $. This must come before all variables, whether they are Boolean, strings or integers, and the good news is that PHP decides which type of variable you are using automatically. Thus declaring a variable $myNum = 10 will be treated the same as $myNum = "10", and PHP is also flexible enough to work out that in the statement 'my

age is $myNum' it is to be treated as a string, while in '5 + $myNum' it is to be treated as an integer, or numerical variable.

As well as beginning with the dollar sign, variables in PHP must not contain blank spaces (although an underscore character is acceptable, so $first name is not acceptable, but $first_name is). As with JavaScript, they are case sensitive and also should not begin with a number, although numbers can appear elsewhere in the variable name.

When outputting a variable, it must be defined first in your code and have a value assigned, otherwise the PHP code will return an error. To do this, simply use the = sign:

```
<?
$myDrink = "tea"
echo "my favourite drink is $myDrink."
?>
```

An important point that is worth repeating, although we have already covered it when discussing JavaScript, is the reason for using variables. You could simply type out the above example as: echo 'my favourite drink is tea'. Indeed, you do not need to use PHP code at all. However, as the values for variables can change throughout a document (being pulled out of a form, for example, as we shall see later), so defining key elements of data as variables allows your code to be much more flexible and dynamic.

An easy way to see this in practice is to use the mathematical operators, which are the same as for JavaScript on page 76. The following example first defines a variable, $result, and then performs a series of mathematical operations on it, each of which changes the value of the variable (note: as with JavaScript, the use of double forward slashes comments the code):

> While it may appear easier to type in values directly into HTML, the virtue of using variables is that they can be modified to hold different information as a page changes in response to user actions.

```
<?
$result = 5
$result = $result + 7 // returns 12
$result = $result / 4 // returns 3
$result = $result * 2 // returns 6
echo "The final result is $result"
?>
```

Again, as with JavaScript, PHP makes use of a special type of variable known as an array, which is implemented in a similar way. The array is declared using the array() function (lower case, unlike in JavaScript) and collects together a series of variables, for example the elements height, weight and hair_colour in the following example, which are known as keys:

> The while loop is a particularly useful form of control statement that first establishes a condition and then executes it for as long as the condition remains true.

```
$vital_stats = array("height" => 190;
     "weight" => 90; "hair_colour" => black)
```

There are two ways to call an element from an array, either to use a number beginning from 0, or to use one of the named keys. Thus both the following will return the value 'black':

```
$vital_stats[2]
$vital_stats["hair_colour"]
```

Statements and loops

Also similar to JavaScript is PHP's use of conditional statements and loops (or iterative statements), both of which are referred to as control structures.

The use of a conditional, or if, statement, is very similar to JavaScript and so here we will present a slightly modified version of the one presented on page 78:

```
if(userAge<5) {
     echo "Ooh! You liar." ;
}
elseif(userAge>=18) {
     echo "You may vote now!" ;
```

```
}
else {
     echo "You are too young to vote" ;
}
```

The only differences to note are that this code uses the command echo rather than alert to output text to the main window of the browser rather than to a message box; also, the second part of the control statement uses the function elseif rather than else if as in JavaScript.

The syntax for loops is similar to JavaScript, employing either the command for, or while/do. As with JavaScript, a for loop must give a starting value, a condition, and the action to be looped, followed by the statement, as in:

```
for($i=1; $i<=0; $i++;) {
     echo "This line will repeat 10 times" ;
}
```

There is another, more specific loop, foreach, which is used with arrays. This works by listing each of the variables that is contained in an array by assigning them to a variable, for example:

```
$meals = array("breakfast", "lunch",
     "dinner");
echo "My daily meals are:<p>";
foreach($meals as $myFood) {
     echo "$myFood<br />";
}
```

In this example, each element of the array $meals is ascribed to the variable $myFood and then these are listed in the browser using the echo command.

The while or do/while loops, which we did not cover in the section on JavaScript, are useful control structures in programming, establishing a condition first and then executing an action for as long as that condition remains true. The variable is defined first, then the condition declared using either the command while or do, followed by the statement to be executed as in:

```
$i = 1 ;
while($i <= 10;) {
    echo "This line will repeat 10 times" ;
}
```

or

```
$i = 1 :
do {
    echo "This line will repeat 10 times" ;
} while($i <=10;)
```

While each of these looks very similar, there is one important difference between them. If the variable $i was set to 10 in each case, in the first case the loop would finish before executing the echo statement, while the second do/while loop would execute it at least once before breaking out of the loop.

Functions

As with JavaScript, PHP makes use of functions, blocks of pre-written code that are either defined by the user or built into the programming language. The latter are much richer than in JavaScript so that many features you may require are already available without the need to program additional code. A list of the many different types of functions can be found at www. php.net/manual/en/funcref. php.

These predefined functions can be called anywhere in a page simply by naming them and inserting relevant arguments in the brackets. Thus, for example, if you had defined several variables for sending email as $recipient, $subject, $message_body and $message_header, you could call the mail function to send emails from a web page as follows:

```
mail($recipient, $subject, $message_body,
    $message_header);
```

Functions that are defined by the user, by contrast, must be declared in your code before they can be called as part of a web page. Functions are declared using the function command, with a very simple function using the following syntax:

```
function welcome_function() {
    echo "Welcome to my web page!"
}
```

Once this function has been defined, it can be called simply by entering the command welcome_function() in your code. A more complex function would also specify arguments within the brackets, such as:

```
function add_VAT($total, $rate) {
    $total = $total + ($rate/100);
    return $total;
}
```

This function would then be called from within the page with values provided for the variables $total and $rate. If you wished to add standard UK VAT at 15 per cent to a figure of £100, this would be as follows:

> **PHP makes use of two types of functions: those which are predefined and can be called anywhere in a page, and those which are defined by the user and must be explicitly declared before they can be called.**

```
add_VAT(100, 15);
```

Which would return a figure of £115. If, however, you wanted a discounted VAT of 5.5, you would call the function add_VAT as follows:

```
add_VAT(100, 5.5);
```

Which would return the figure of £105.5.

A final point to bear in mind about functions is this: in most cases it does not matter where your functions are defined on a page, as long as they are listed somewhere in your code. It is good practice to declare a function before you call it in PHP, but if you have not done so the parser will simply search through the page until it locates it.

Talking to the browser and handling sessions

Thus far we have concentrated on PHP code that works within a single web page, being processed by the server and then passed onto the browser as one document. But what happens when you want to pass information between web pages, collecting information from a form, for example, and then displaying the results in a new page? Before going onto forms themselves, it is important to understand a couple of key concepts around how PHP can talk to the browser and temporarily store information via the use of such things as **cookies**.

One way by which information can be passed is through the URL using what is known as a query string, for example http://www.mybook.com/index.php?chapter=3&page=34, which tells the browser to view page 34 of chapter 3 at www.mybook.com. To use this information, PHP has to make use of the $_GET variable which is what is known as a 'superglobal'; that is, it can be called anywhere in any PHP script (for a list of these go to www.php.net/manual/en/language.variables.superglobals.php). $_GET is actually an array which stores a number of variables that can then be used in your web page, as in the following:

```
<?
$chap = $_GET['chapter'];
$pageNo = $_GET['page'];
echo "You are reading page $pageNo in
    chapter $chap";
?>
```

The $_GET variable is tied to the get action which was introduced in chapter 3 when discussing forms in HTML, and there is also a $_POST variable that is linked to the action post. Both of these will be discussed in more detail in the next section when dealing with how PHP handles forms.

Before this, however, it is necessary to discuss two ways in which PHP can make use of information temporarily stored between sessions. When data is transferred between sessions. When data is transferred between a server and a browser, it is usually 'stateless', that is there is no connection made by the server between a request for a page and any other subsequent requests. However, when browsing a site – for example when purchasing goods online and then moving to the checkout – it is necessary to store some information from the pages visited previously.

> **Cookies are text files that are used to store information temporarily that can then be passed back to the browser, such as a password or site preferences.**

This can be done either via a session variable, information that is stored for however long the 'session' lasts and is finished with when the browser closes (or the user moves to another site), or via cookies, which are text documents that are stored on the user's computer and remain valid until an expiry date is reached. There is some controversy over the use of cookies: they can be used to track a user's browsing habits, and so privacy settings will often turn them off. However, they are a preferable way of storing session information because if a visitor goes to a different website during a session, any data stored in the session variable will be lost.

To set a cookie to store information, PHP uses the setcookie() function with up to six arguments, of which three – name, value and expire – are the most commonly used. If the third is left out, expire will automatically default to 0 which means that the data is cleared once the browser is closed. If you wish to use a long-term cookie, you need to use what is known as a timestamp, measured in seconds and – for clarity – usually recorded in multiples of 60 (for seconds) times 60 (for minutes) times 24 (for hours) and so on. If you wished PHP to record when a user voted, for example, and store that information for two weeks, you would enter the following code:

```
setcookie('user_vote', '1', time() +
    (60*60*24*7*2))
```

To retrieve this data, the contents are stored in the superglobal variable $_COOKIE, and the argument required would need to be linked to a variable. For example, if you created a simple cookie that stored a user ID, as in setcookie('user_id'), the code to retrieve that would be:

```
<?
$user_id = $_COOKIE['user_id'];
echo "The user is $user_id";
?>
```

The final thing to note in this section about using cookies is that data is not entered into the $_COOKIE variable until the next time a visitor requests a page. This means you cannot set a value for the cookie arguments and then call them from the same page during the same session.

Handling forms

Designing forms in HTML is one area where PHP really begins to display its value as a programming language. To be useful, a form must come in two parts: there is the actual form itself which collects data from a user, and then there is some means by which that data is processed to be displayed in another format. The simplest type of form will email data to an address that is defined in the <form> element, but with PHP you can use that information in much more interesting ways.

The actual form itself does not need to make use of any PHP at all, so let's revisit the very simple form in HTML from chapter 3:

```
<form method="post" action="../cgi-bin/
    formscript.php">
    <p label for="username">Enter your
    name</label>
```

```
    input type="text" name="username"
    id="username" />
    <input type="submit" name="submit"
    value="submit" /></p>
</form>
```

When a visitor enters their name into this form and clicks the submit button, it is passed on via the post method to the file formscript.php. The data that is passed is stored in the superglobal variable $_POST. The form above has two possible values – username and submit – only one of which is really of interest to us. To display a user name on a page, the code for formscript.php could be as simple as the following:

```
<?
echo "Your name is $_POST['username']";
?>
```

To extend this form slightly, and combine it with a conditional statement, let's modify it with an additional input. Thus the code for the original form would be:

```
<form method="post" action="../cgi-bin/
    formscript.php">
    <p label for="username">Enter your
    name</label>
    <input type="text" name="username"
    id="username" />
    <p label for="userage">Enter your age</
    label>
    <input type="text" name="userage"
    id="userage" />
    <input type="submit" name="submit"
    value="submit" /></p>
</form>
```

Then, by extending the PHP code we could display a message depending on whether the visitor was over or under 18:

```
<?
$username = $_POST['username'];
$userage = $_POST['userage'];
echo "Your name is $username. <br />";
if(userAge<18) {
```

```
        echo "You are too young to vote." ;
    }
    else {
        echo "You may vote now." ;
    }
?>
```

PHP also includes rules for validating and cleaning data which go beyond the scope of this chapter, but the basics here should allow you to understand how this programming language works to process information that is passed from the browser to the server, which is an important principle when working with a database – as we shall see throughout the rest of this chapter.

> One of the most common uses of PHP is to process information passed to the server from a form in order to modify content held on a server or execute other commands.

DATABASE-DRIVEN SITES WITH MySQL

Perhaps the most commonly employed database software used to drive websites is MySQL, at the time of writing available in a stable version (5.1) with a new release (6.0) currently in development. As well as being very scalable and suitable for the vast majority of sites that users may wish to create, it is also free, open-source software which, when used with PHP, accounts for its popularity. In addition to being used from scratch, it is also the technology that lies behind a number of open-source content management systems such as Joomla! and Drupal.

Introduction to databases

A database must, obviously, store information, but more importantly it must make that information easy to retrieve. Databases full of megabytes, gigabytes or even terabytes of data are useless if there is no simple way to access information, and while a complete understanding of the principles of database design is beyond the scope of this book, some knowledge of the essentials will be useful when you start creating your own database-driven sites.

The earliest computerised databases simulated the record systems used in paper-based archives and libraries, and are known as flat-file databases. The easiest type of database to create and retrieve information from, discrete files could be stored in a virtual library and called up by the computer when required. Consider the example shown in Table 4.3.

Because of its layout, such a file is referred to as a table, with each row being a record for Joe Bloggs, Jane Doe and Jill Smith. Each column is a field that stores a particular piece of information for that record, such as Jane Doe's email address or Jill Smith's last name. After several decades during which computer spreadsheets have become commonplace the ideas behind such database records are not at all difficult to understand. The important point when designing your own database is to

Table 4.3

First Name	Last Name	Email	Telephone
Joe	Bloggs	joe.bloggs@mydomain.com	012-345-6789
Jane	Doe	janed@mysite.org	098-765-4321
Jill	Smith	smith.j@mycompany.co.uk	012-987-3456

decide which fields you want to include and, a related point, what format they will be in. Although it is slightly beyond the scope of this chapter, databases such as MySQL allow you to determine whether a field will be such things as a text or string, or an integer (number) or date.

There is, however, a problem with this very simple type of storing information: to find data, such as Jane Doe's email address, the computer would have to search every record from the beginning. As files build up into hundreds of thousands of records, this becomes a very laborious and slow process. To speed things up, databases use what is known as a 'primary key'. Usually called something such as 'ID', this is a number that is automatically generated by the database and assigned to records as shown in Table 4.4.

> Databases such as MySQL make use of what is known as a 'primary key', an ID number assigned to records that allows information to be found much more quickly during searches.

The advantage of a primary key is that once a record is assigned to a key, the database can search this rather than the entire database. Not only is this faster than searching strings of text in itself, primary keys are also typically indexed by a database, that is the database maintains a separate list of where exactly to find a record. In addition, assigning keys to individual records means that specific records can be defined – there may be two, three or more people by the name of Joe Bloggs or Jill Smith in your database, but there will only ever by one ID 1 or ID 3.

However, while this has many benefits for speeding up access, the flat-file system still poses a number of problems, the most important of which is data redundancy, where information is repeated in multiple fields or records. Consider the example shown in Table 4.5.

Table 4.4 Personal details

ID	First Name	Last Name	Email	Telephone
1	Joe	Bloggs	joe.bloggs@mydomain.com	012-345-6789
2	Jane	Doe	janed@mysite.org	098-765-4321
3	Jill	Smith	smith.j@mycompany.co.uk	012-987-3456

Table 4.5 Results

ID	First Name	Last Name	Subject	Grade
1	Joe	Bloggs	Mathematics	B
2	Joe	Bloggs	English	C
3	Jill	Smith	Chemistry	B
4	Jill	Smith	French	A

As records for the grades of Joe Bloggs and Jill Smith proliferate (not to mention those for the hundreds of other students on a course), so the database expands and bloats. Not only does it become larger (and thus slower to search, even with a primary key index), so the information from individual records is not as easy to manipulate as it could be. It is more likely, for example, that you will want to know all the grades for Jill Smith rather than just what she gained for chemistry.

There have been various attempts to overcome this problem (such as the hierarchical or network model), but the one that really concerns us here (because it lies behind MySQL) is the relational model. A relational database stores data in tables as demonstrated above but, more importantly, it provides a link between those tables. Using the example in Table 4.5 , the personal details in the second entry for each person's name would not be entered separately into each record for results but would be linked instead to the personal details table. Thus by searching Joe Bloggs in the first table, we could quickly find the results for all the exams he had taken. Alternatively, we could search the results table for anyone who had received an A grade and then look up their personal details to email or phone them.

MySQL is just such a relational database, storing different types of records in different tables. Before you begin creating your database using MySQL it is worth spending some time considering which types of records cluster together into different tables: thus for a bibliography, you might want a separate authors' table and another containing lists of titles with associated details, while an accounts database will want separate tables for clients and orders.

Using MySQL commands

MySQL comes with a command line interface, that is instructions are typed in from a rather bare interface. Although we would not generally recommend creating a database this way, it is worth learning the essential SQL commands because they are useful to understand when working with PHP to create a dynamic site. A much more user-friendly way to administer your database is provided by phpMyAdmin, which can be downloaded from www.phpmyadmin.net.

The necessary commands for MySQL are easy to understand and generally make clear sense even to novices. By convention, the commands themselves are written in capital letters to distinguish them from database and table names, and – as with the scripting languages we have considered in this chapter – SQL statements end with a semicolon, as with:

> SELECT name, address FROM contacts
> WHERE category='registered user';

In this example, the SELECT command finds a name and address of registered users in the table contacts.

To create a database, all that is needed is the CREATE DATABASE command with the name of the new file followed by a semi-colon, as in:

> CREATE DATABASE site_users;

Before working with a database to retrieve or add records, the USE command is employed with the name of the database you wish to work with:

> USE site_users;

Once a database is created, it is an empty shell to store information, and so a table with columns needs to be added. Each column will create a field in the database and, as they are added, records will be stored as rows within the table. Before creating a table, you should determine

> A relational database makes use of links between tables to prevent the duplication of data between different types of record and so makes searches much faster while keeping down file sizes.

what columns/fields will be required, and also what data types. There is a large number of data types available to MySQL, and you can see a full list of these at dev.mysql.com/doc/refman/5.1/en/data-types.html. We shall only deal with a few in the sample below, but an important point to remember is that numeric and string columns come in 'tiny', 'medium' and 'long' or 'big' formats that store between 256 and over 4 billion (for text) and 18 million trillion (for numbers) characters.

Keeping things simple, for our database site_users we will add a table for registered users that includes a primary key, ID, a first name, last name and a date of birth. Thus, having changed to the database with the USE command, the code to create a table would be:

```
CREATE TABLE registered_users (
id TINYINT UNSIGNED PRIMARY KEY
    AUTO_INCREMENT,
first_name TINYTEXT,
last_name TINYTEXT NOT NULL,
birth_date DATE);
```

A couple of elements from this code require some explanation: the column ID for the primary key is relatively clear (when you understand that MEDIUMINT refers to a tiny integer allowing for 65,535 records), but the command AUTO_INCREMENT is important: this instructs the table to automatically increase the ID for each added record by 1. TINYTEXT allows up to 255 characters to be entered for first and last names, but the command NOT NULL means that this field has to be completed by a user when they enter information into the database. Finally, the DATE command inserts a date field in the format YYYY-MM-DD, so that 19 August 1975 would be formatted 1975-08-19.

We have already seen that the command to retrieve information is SELECT, and to add a record into a database using the command line you use INSERT INTO, as in:

```
INSERT INTO registered_users VALUES
(DEFAULT, 'John', ;Doe', NULL);
```

In our simple table, the entries in brackets correspond to each column that we added with the CREATE TABLE command. DEFAULT is very useful when you wish MySQL to handle the value entered (in this case the primary key in the ID column) and NULL leaves a particular value empty (in this case the date of birth). We have thus added the name John Doe to our database – note that values have to be in single quotes – and allowed MySQL to generate a primary key for that record.

The MySQL command line is actually very flexible, but it is not the recommended approach for users who have little experience of database programming. However, even a limited knowledge of SQL commands will allow you to create sophisticated database driven sites with PHP.

Connecting to MySQL with PHP

PHP provides a convenient way to work with MySQL databases from a web page, and the module mysqli is a set of functions that allows you to open and close connections to a database to search, retrieve and insert records.

The first step to working with a database is to open a connection, which is done via the mysqli_connect command. For this to work, you need four pieces of information: the host name of the database server, a username, a password and the name of the database to connect with. You will need to get the name of your database server from your ISP for a live database, but when testing on a local PC you will use the name localhost. For convenience, we shall assume in the following example that the user name is 'root' (the default for database/server installations, although for security reasons this should always be changed), with a password 'mypassword' to connect to the database site_users. The connection command, assigning mysqli_connect to the variable $data_link, is as follows:

```
<?
$data_link = mysqli_connect('localhost',
    'root', 'mypassword', 'site_users');
?>
```

Depending on the setup of a server, a database can only have a certain number of open connections, so once information is processed from a database it is a good idea to close the connection. This is done using the mysqli_close command, as in:

```
<?
mysqli_close($data_link);
?>
```

Making a connection to a SQL database is the slowest part of the operation, so it is not a good idea to open and close connections too often. In general, recommended practice is to open a connection once per page just before the first query is made – for example when you need to get a user's name from the database site_users – and then close it when you are sure that the last result has been processed and another call to the database won't be required on that page.

A final point to be made is that hard-coding connection strings into every page on a website that will make a call to the database is not a good idea. If you need to move your database to a different server, the connection string will not work. Rather, the mysqli_connect code should be included in a separate file, for example db_connect.php, and then added to your web pages via an include command, such as include 'db_connect.php'. This way, you only need to change one file for your database to continue working with your web pages.

Extracting and displaying records

So far we have a database, site_users, with a single table, registered_users, and we can connect to this via the PHP variable $data_link. The next stage is to search and display results from a database, and to do this requires three steps: first to build a query, an instruction using the command SELECT that will search through the database; next to execute this query; and finally to build the table that will output the results of the query – you cannot simply use the echo command for this, as a search may return a number of results. All the following code must

follow the line that opens a connection and come before the line that closes the connection.

For the first step, building the query, you use SELECT with the fields you wish to search and assign it to a variable that can be executed by PHP:

```
$select = "SELECT first_name, last_name
    FROM registered_users WHERE id=1";
```

$select is the PHP variable attached to this query which will extract the first and last names from the first record in the table registered_users. Now this query needs to be added to a variable that will also contain the connection string using the command mysqli_query():

```
$result = mysqli_query($data_link, $select);
```

The results of the query are now stored in the variable $select, and to display this as a single record, you need to make use of the mysqli_fetch_array() command which places fields into an array so that they can be referred to individually: once this is done, each array element is given a variable of its own and these can be listed on the page. The code for displaying a single record is as follows:

```
$display_row = mysqli_fetch_array($result);
$fName = $display_row['first_name'];
$lName = $display_row['last_name'];
echo "First name: $fName <br />";
echo "Last name: $lName";
```

When you wish to display more than one record, then the best way to do this is by using a while loop. If our query consisted of $select = "SELECT first_name, last_name FROM registered_users";, this would extract all first and last names from the database, and these would need to be displayed on multiple lines. Adapting the previous block of code would give:

```
while($display_row = mysqli_fetch_
    array($result)){
$fName = $display_row['first_name'];
$lName = $display_row['last_name'];
```

```
        echo "First name: $fName <br />";
        echo "Last name: $lName";
    }
```

The important difference here is that the mysqli_fetch_array() command is placed as part of an argument in a while loop, and the other parts of the statement – assigning variables to the first and last names then printing them out using the echo command – are placed within curly brackets and executed as long as there is a record to display.

Adding data

Adding data to our database requires a form that can receive information as well as a script to handle inputs and add them using the INSERT command. To keep things simple at this stage, we shall concentrate on adding a first and last name to the registered_users table, but you can see a full listing of this code, as well as validation messages (to check that the process went smoothly, or to return an error message if it did not) on the *Producing for Web 2.0* site.

To create the variable that PHP will be able to work with in a form, add the following code after establishing a connection with the database:

```
    $insert = "INSERT INTO registered_
        users (first_name, last_name) VALUES
        ('fName', 'lName')";
```

This will take the values assigned to the variables fName and lName from our form and add them to the fields first_name and last_name. The full code, including the code to insert values, will be as follows:

```
    <?
    include 'db_connect.php';
    mysqli_select_db($site_users);
    $insert = "INSERT INTO registered_
        users (first_name, last_name) VALUES
        ('fName', 'lName')";
    mysqli_query($query) or die('Error, add
        record failed');
    $query = "FLUSH PRIVILEGES";
    mysqli_query($query) or die('Error, add
        record failed');
    mysqli_close($data_link);
    ?>
```

While this section only covers a basic introduction to client- and server-side scripting, as well as database programming with MySQL, it is important to have at least this essential familiarity with them as they drive so many Web 2.0 technologies.

For more information and updates on scripting and database-driven sites, visit www.producingforweb2.com/dynamic.

CHAPTER 5

Using multimedia

Multimedia in any viable form first began to be used on PCs in the mid-1990s with the growth of CD-ROM and the emergence of video cards that could handle compressed MPEG video as well as 16-bit sound (which moved towards more realistic audio sampling), with rapid developments in DVD technology in particular.

Online multimedia, however, took another five years to begin to catch up, especially as bandwidth lagged far behind processing power. The first major step came with the rise of MP3, which enabled much better sounding audio to be transferred across the internet in smaller file sizes. In addition, the popularity of web radio meant that by the end of the decade online audio was a well-established medium for many websites.

Video took longer to catch on, and has only really become a popular format in the past three or four years. Prior to this, while it was possible to find video online, it was usually restricted either to clips that were poor-quality and postage-stamp sized, or of very short duration. As more and more users were able to connect with broadband, accompanied by improvements in compression rates, so the web experienced a video boom – most notably observed in the recent popularity of YouTube for sharing movies.

In this chapter, we shall consider the requirements for preparing multimedia for the web, starting with the basics in terms of images (the oldest accompaniment to text) and then concentrating on audio, video and Flash as the most widespread means of creating media rich, interactive sites.

DIGITAL STORYTELLING

An important way of thinking about the use of multimedia, which has started to become very popular in recent years, particularly as promoted by organisations such as Apple and the BBC, is digital storytelling. The origins of digital storytelling lie outside the web, using images, sound and video to tell personal stories without professional mediation, concentrating on telling a narrative in a short format.

The phrase is often used to refer to movies made mainly from still images with an accompanying soundtrack. The rise of consumer software such as Windows Movie Maker and iMovie has enabled plenty of non-professionals to quickly create short narratives that would have been impossible only a few years ago. Because the technical skills required are relatively easy to master, this allows much greater focus to be given to telling the story, building a script that will capture the essence of the narrative. Once this has been determined, a series of still images can be captured that will convey the story: the use of 'Ken Burns' effects (after the photographer and documentary film-maker who devised a zooming and panning technique to bring life to still photographs)

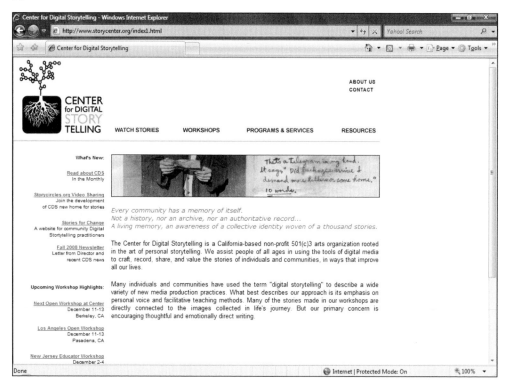

Digital storytelling is one of the many ways for sharing experiences, as with the Berkeley Center for Digital Storytelling.

means that it is easy to animate such photographs in an interesting fashion.

While this is the more restricted meaning of digital storytelling, the term is also used more broadly to refer to a range of narrative techniques employed in journalism, video games and interactive texts. The Center for Digital Storytelling at Berkeley, California (www. storycenter.org) places an emphasis on the personal voice that can be shared communally at the centre of all these different approaches.

Much of this chapter is concerned with the technical aspects of producing multimedia and preparing it for the web, but the notion of digital storytelling is extremely useful for two reasons: first of all, it emphasises ways in which the use of digital media has become simpler than ever; second, by not having to learn complex skills to tell a narrative, users can concentrate on the story that they wish to convey – shorter narratives being a perfect medium for the web.

ASSETS AND RIGHTS MANAGEMENT

While storytelling emphasises the accessibility of using the web with multimedia, and is usually grasped by students and inexperienced producers very quickly, issues around digital asset management and digital rights management are generally counter-intuitive to the same groups of users.

Most of the issues that affect asset management will be considered in the chapter on content management systems (CMSs), but it is an important concept to introduce here because it affects the way that producers look on the various elements that constitute multimedia, such as images, video, audio and animation. Such elements are, obviously, stored digitally – otherwise they are of no concern to anyone involved in web design. But to be considered as assets they must also include information that provides extra support for storing, finding and retrieving such components.

The key to this lies in *metadata*, or data about data, that is data that tells the system additional information about a particular piece of digital media in this case. A common type of metadata that many users encounter is Exif data, or the Exchangable image file format commonly employed with many types of digital cameras. Exif data records such things as the time and date when an image was taken, camera settings including aperture, focal length and shutter speed, descriptions and copyright information, and a thumbnail of the image.

More generally, the metadata employed in asset management will describe what a particular asset consists of (such as video or an image), how it is encoded (for example via MPEG compression for video or JPEG for photos), when it was created, who has access rights, whether there is a proxy copy (that is one at a lower resolution or quality for online use), and categories for storing and cataloguing an item. For example, when preparing images for a website, it is useful to maintain the original, high-quality file from a camera alongside a lower resolution proxy that is displayed on a page. Applications such as Adobe Bridge (part of the Adobe Creative Suite) provide tools to manage files in this way.

The issue of access leads onto digital rights. Although this will also be returned to in chapter 8 when dealing with copyright, it is worth looking at here because digital rights management (**DRM**) is more often applied to the multimedia elements that comprise a website than to individual pages or an entire site (which is covered by more general rules of copyright). DRM software, such as the Content Scrambling System (CSS) employed on DVDs or the Advanced Access Control System (AACS) for HD DVD and Blu-Ray discs, is designed to prevent or limit how items may be copied or shared. In addition to this type of copy protection, professionally produced digital media will often include some form of digital watermark to record the copyright owner: these do not themselves restrict access, but as part of a DRM system are useful for determining legal ownership of a file or document.

IMAGES

Ever since Marc Andreessen introduced the <img> tag into early versions of the Mosaic browser, adding images to a web page has been fundamental to developing online multimedia. Although graphics by no means push the limits of contemporary websites, though you will frequently encounter pages without video, audio or Flash animation, you will hardly ever find one that does not make use of images in some form.

Graphics enliven the visual appearance of a page and frequently work as logos, background interest and navigation cues, as well as important objects conveying significant information in their own right to the visitor, for example, portraits or depictions of scenes. While the web has benefited greatly from this expansion of visual material, there is a downside in that too many graphics can make pages slow to load, cumbersome to navigate and even impossible to use for visitors with visual impairment.

Nonetheless, the importance of illustration in making a point cannot be underestimated. Not only does it contribute to the aesthetic appeal of a page, if visitors can see a scene or item it will help them understand the significance of a page in a way that verbal description alone simply cannot achieve.

This section will consider the underlying principles of how digital images work, as well as offering advice on how to employ your graphics most effectively. There are certain elements – such as what constitutes a good photograph per

> Thinking of your multimedia files as digital assets focuses attention on the ways in which they can be stored, catalogued and accessed by different applications and websites.

se – that are beyond the scope of this book, but this chapter will show you how to get the most from your graphics, whether captured with a digital camera or scanner, or created from scratch in an image editor such as Photoshop.

Image formats and colour depth

The types of image file suitable for display on a web page were briefly introduced in chapter 2, and here we will consider the pros and cons of each type, as well as other file formats that you may encounter.

Most images you will see online are JPEGs and GIFs, with a few PNG files, but there are a few other formats of which you should be aware. The BMP (bitmap) file format, sometimes known as DIB (Device Independent Bitmap) is very common in graphical user interfaces such as Windows, but its uncompressed nature makes it unsuitable for the web. Another common format for print is the Tagged Image File Format (TIFF, or TIF), the copyright to which is now owned by Adobe. TIF is actually a very flexible format in that it can be adapted to handle a number of other types of file, the important element being the header which is 'tagged' with further information about the file, such as its size, compression, and a great deal of other data. While extremely important for print publishing, the fact that most browsers do not display it by default means that it is – again – not commonly used on the web. Some digital cameras also give access to all the information they capture in what is known as the RAW file format: such images have not been processed and so are not ready to be used in an image editor or to be printed, but when capturing initial images from a scanner or camera this is the preferable option because it will give the highest-quality image.

Before turning to the commonly used formats, it is worth understanding a little about the principles behind digital images. Of the two

main types of digital image – raster and vector – we shall concentrate most on the former here. A raster image has a finite set of pixels that represent the brightness of a colour at any given point. Vector images, by contrast, do not define an image pixel by pixel but rather describe lines and colours using mathematical equations: this means that they can produce much smaller files that are also scalable with greater accuracy, but they are less useful for photographs.

Computer images are generated via combinations of the primary red, green and blue colours – or the RGB colour model – in contrast to printed images which use the secondary colours, cyan, magenta and yellow, along with black (or CMYK). How many colours may be displayed in an image depends on what is known as the colour depth of an image. The most basic form of digital image is a binary image that has only two values for each pixel – usually black (off) or white (on). By increasing the number of bits that can store values for colours to three, this gives 8-bit colour (2^3), with a possible range of 256 different hues (there are 256 colours because the blue is actually only 4-bit, thus $8 \times 8 \times 4$ gives the maximum combination of values). Although not commonly used, this provides the palette for GIF image files. Much more common is HiColor, or 16-bit colour, which uses five bits each for red and blue (but six for green), to allow a palette of 65,536 colours ($32 \times 32 \times 64$ possible shades of red, blue and green), and Truecolor, or 24-bit colour: this, which comes closest to mimicking human perception of colour, allows for more than 16.7 million shades by combining variations of 256 colour values for each red, green and blue pixel. You may also come across references to 32-bit colour: actually, this does not affect the perceived colour, but uses an extra eight bits to determine other factors such as transparency (alpha) or texture (bump) data.

In practice, JPEG and PNG images are 24-bit images, with JPEGs being most

> **Computer generated images employ pixels of varying combinations of red, green and blue colours to generate up to 16.7 million potential shades.**

commonly used for photographs because, despite the fact that they are a lossy compression format (information is discarded when the file is compressed), they are very commonly supported by all graphical browsers.

For black and white photography, greyscale is a type of digital image that only preserves information about the intensity of light being displayed by the pixel, rather than any RGB colour information. Indexed colour, important to GIFs, is a way of handling a limited colour palette: information about colour values is not handled directly by the pixel, but points to a separate palette or index. Whereas Truecolor requires 24 bits, or three bytes, for each pixel, so that an uncompressed image at a resolution of 640×480 pixels would be 900 kilobytes in size ($24 \times 640 \times 480$), storing the most commonly used 256 colours in a palette would require only eight bits per pixel and reduce the file size to 300 kilobytes. Because of the restrictions of this palette, however, other compression methods tend to be used more to reduce file sizes.

A final point to note with regard to the principles of digital imaging is how images may be measured in terms of hue, saturation and lightness (HSL, sometimes referred to as brightness, or HSB), or hue, saturation and value (HSV). Hue is what is perceived as colour, with lesser or greater degrees of saturation, and lightness or value affect how those colours and saturations are applied in different models. In HSL models, maximum saturation takes place when the value for lightness is at 50 per cent (0 per cent = black, 100 per cent = pure white); in HSV models, the maximum intensity for a colour is when V = 100 per cent. HSV is better when more perfect saturation is required, but HSL models represent brightness better.

Camera versus scanner

There are three main ways to create graphics through the web. One of these, using an image editor or drawing program such as Photoshop or Illustrator, we shall leave to one side for the moment, concentrating instead on the other two ways: via a digital camera or using a scanner.

The recent advances in digital cameras mean that it is possible to buy 20 megapixel SLR cameras for between £5,000 and £6,000 – although anyone who would wish to attach 20Mb plus image files to their web pages would need seriously to reconsider how much they want to get involved in web design. Such high-quality devices are really aimed at print, but while images for the web can be captured in sufficient quality using much lower-powered cameras (and even then will need to be resized and reformatted for a site), ensuring that you have a high-quality lens is just as important if you are going to portray images that are a few hundred pixels – rather than several centimetres – wide.

The virtue of digital cameras, of course, is that transferring pictures to a computer hard drive is simplicity itself. For images caught on film, you will need to use a scanner: here, as with cameras, high pixel counts are irrelevant. Much more important is the quality of the CCD (charge couple device), the collection of light-sensitive diodes that convert photos (light) into electrons (an electrical charge that can be measured and interpreted as graphic data by a computer). The cheapest scanners may offer 9,600 dpi (dots per inch) resolutions, but as graphics are displayed on a screen at 72 or (more rarely) 96 dpi, this is utterly unimportant if the image is blurred or fuzzy because of poor optics.

For creating original images, a good-quality camera with a decent lens is much simpler and more convenient. However, for artwork a scanner is still a necessary item, although a film scanner that works with negatives may be preferable to a conventional print scanner.

Preparing images for the web

It is highly unlikely that images from a scanner or camera will be immediately suitable for use on a web page. If the image has been saved in a format such as TIFF or BMP, then it must be converted to the correct file format. Although most cameras can save images as JPEGs, you will probably want to preserve the original as a RAW file as this will be the best quality. What's

Resizing low resolution images in an editor will simply show up jagged anti-aliasing in a final, poor-quality image.

more, the image should be saved to a screen resolution of 72 dpi, rather than 150 or 300 as is common with images used for print.

The next step will be to create an image at the correct size. If your web page needs a photo with dimensions of 300 × 200 pixels, then uploading a 1600 × 1200 pixel image will take up unnecessary space and slow down your page when it loads. In addition, resizing an image in a web editor can cause jagged anti-aliasing to occur around lines, so that your photo will appear poor quality.

Beyond these two stages – converting to the correct file format and to the appropriate size – which are essential tasks, most other steps will depend on what you require from an image. It is, however, highly unlikely that the image will be perfect for your requirements. In particular, the focus of the composition may not be quite right and you should crop an image so that it zooms in on the most appropriate part of the graphic.

Further steps usually involve such things as colour-correction and sharpening the image in your favourite image editor (resizing often results in unwelcome blurring).

One important point to bear in mind: each time you save an image to the JPEG format, it will use compression to discard information. This means that if you perform a series of edits and continually save your work (which seems perfectly reasonable), then the graphic will degrade more and more with each save. Therefore, as many edits as possible should be performed in one session, to keep saves to a minimum or – a better alternative – save the file in a lossless format (such as TIFF or Photoshop's PSD format, which is useful if you wish to work with such things as layers), and only save to JPEG when you need a final version for the web. Plenty of image editors now offer a save to web option, which allows you to preview how a photo or graphic will look before it is converted to a JPEG or TIFF.

Shape and position

No matter how stunning your images, if they always appear in the same position on the page and show similar elements, your whole website will start to appear a little dull. Using a little variety, such as images in a landscape or even banner format across the top of a page, can add drama to your page and make the whole much more visually appealing to the visitor. Alternatively, long, vertical pictures can have an unusual effect because when images are not square or portrait-sized, we are used to seeing them in landscape format, which fits the way peripheral vision works to 180 degrees across the horizontal plane.

Square images tend to be the dullest, while rectangles, being asymmetrical, offer the most scope for variety. The technique employed by tabloid-style magazines, for irregular polygon shapes such as stars, tends to be much less commonly encountered on the web. One reason for this is the difficulty of flowing text in HTML around any image that does not have straight edges, so that attempts to do this end up looking rather amateurish.

In addition to deciding where an image goes on the page (so that it does not always appear in the top left-hand corner, for example), and what shape it can take, it is important to reiterate the value of cropping. Important details must be framed within the picture rather than lost amidst irrelevant background or space. Ideally, this should be decided when taking a photograph in the first place, but the perfect photo cannot always be captured first and this is where image editors are a godsend. Zooming in on a subject is one way to create drama, and taking a shot at an unusual angle can add suspense and tension.

While most of these comments are directed towards photography, which still constitutes the most obvious visual element on web pages, do not forget graphic components such as buttons, text created in an image editor if you need to use an unusual font (although this is not recommended as a matter of course, in that without the ALT tag such elements become unworkable for people with visual disabilities), and logos. Finally, as we shall see in the section on Flash, there are also tools available that allow you to present your images in a stimulating way as animated slideshows online.

Effects and filters

Sometimes images require something different to make them stand out, and image editors provide a great many filters and special effects to modify photos and graphics. Indeed, the problem with filters is often that there are too many available and they are too easy to apply, making them tempting but ultimately ruining the image. Professional sites, rather like other media such as magazines, will use special effects sparingly to enhance rather than completely distort a photograph.

That said, some ranges of filters can be very useful, particularly those which apply an artistic effect to an image (to make it appear like a drawing or watercolour, for example). In addition, if you need to create a graphic from scratch, such as a logo, then the ability to apply different layers of texture or to do such things as emboss text, can provide for such things as a pseudo-3D appearance without the need to invest in 3D software.

In general, however, most image manipulation once it moves beyond cropping and resizing a photograph or graphic, tends to concentrate on tweaking, adjusting such things as the colour balance or contrast to bring out details. However, it should also be realised that no amount of tweaking can save a bad image. Before you even think of applying effects and filters to a photograph, the important point is to prepare your shoot beforehand.

> While some filters can be very useful when preparing images, over-enthusiastic application of special effects to photos can make them look amateurish.

WALKTHROUGH ▶

Preparing images in Photoshop

1 Images from a digital camera or a scanner are highly likely to be far too large to be used directly on a web page and so will need to be optimised in an image editor such as Photoshop. After saving your image to your hard drive, open it in Photoshop and (using the magnifying glass) zoom into 100 per cent so you have a clear idea as to its dimensions.

2 The first step is to resize the image. To do this, go to Image, Image Size from the menu, which will display the relevant dialog box. Of the two sets of dimensions it is the top one, Pixel Dimensions, that is important (the other, Document Size, is for print). However, do ensure that the image resolution is set to 72 dpi (dots per inch), then change the pixels to the settings you require. Clicking the Constrain Proportions box will ensure that the image is set to a suitable scale if you change just the height or width of your image.

▶▶

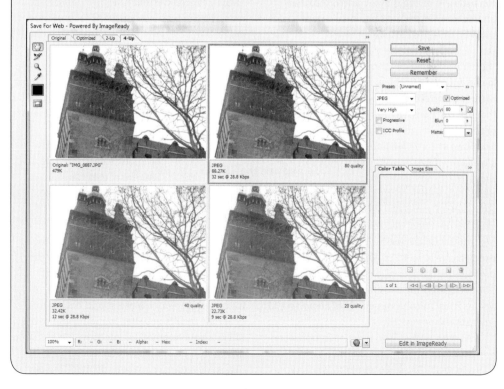

3 Depending on the source for your image, it may be in one of any number of formats, but for a photo it ideally needs to be saved as a JPEG. The best way to do this is to select File, Save for Web. This displays a dialog box with multiple variants of your image using different compression rates, allowing you to compare the final version. Make sure that the JPEG format is selected, then experiment with different compression rates before clicking Save.

AUDIO

Working with audio comes in two stages: first you have to record your sound and then you have to edit it and prepare it for a suitable format online. Uncompressed audio, while producing sound files of the highest quality, will also result in large file sizes that are unsuitable for downloads. In addition, simply converting a sound file into another format may not be quite enough in itself to prepare your audio for general consumption, so in this section we shall also look at how to use a free sound editor, Audacity.

Sampling and formats

The popularity of CDs from the late 1990s onwards made digital audio a commonplace, while the growth of MP3s as a means of sharing music in recent years has familiarised the concept of compression for reducing file sizes for easy online distribution.

Audio signals are continuous, or analogue, consisting of changes in air pressure as they hit our ears. Digitising this signal means that it must be converted to a series of bits, steps that sample each part of the wave. Inevitably, this means some loss of information. However, while aficionados often claim that there is a degradation of sound quality, in general sampling at 44.1 KHz (a Hertz is a measure of frequency), which provides CD-quality audio, is more than sufficient: 44.1 KHz allows a maximum of 22 KHz in either direction, and the highest frequency that humans can perceive is 20 KHz. This does still leave a problem for the size of sampled sound files, however: sampling two channels at 44.1 KHz results in an uncompressed file of about 10.5 Mb (megabytes) per minute.

As with images, two types of compression are used with audio – lossless, such as MPEG-4 SLS and Dolby TrueHD, and lossy, such as MP3 and WMA. In lossless compression, the compressed file will be an exact replica of the original, but it still results in rather large file sizes and so is uncommon online, being a preferred format for DVD and HD audio. We shall therefore concentrate on MP3 as an example of lossy compression which is only an approximation of the original file: obviously compression and decompression affect the quality of a sound file, but a typical MP3 file can store a minute's worth of data in about 1 Mb of space.

MP3 files (or MPEG-1 Audio Layer 3 to give the format its full title) was approved as a standard in 1991. The format became popular after 1995 and was quickly associated with illegal file sharing – one result of which was that online music providers typically preferred different standards that could be encrypted in an attempt to prevent piracy. Drawing on work done in psychoacoustics, the developers of MP3 take advantage of the fact that the brain actively interprets sound so that the differences between certain waveforms may be imperceptible. The human ear can normally hear frequencies in the range between 20 Hz and 20 KHz, but some ranges can be aggressively compressed without significant loss in terms of perceived quality (for example someone clapping their hands will sound very loud in a library, but not be heard next to someone else drilling).

Audio quality can also be affected by the bit rate, the amount of data transferred for each segment of a file. The shorthand for how this is calculated is referred to as ABR, CBR and VBR for average, constant and variable bit rates. VBR as its name suggests, varies the amount of data output per second with more storage for complex segments of a sound file. As this generally results in better sounding audio, it is the preferred method for encoding but has some downsides, most notably that it takes longer to encode and may not be supported by older

> Since the late 1990s, audio has become an increasingly important part of preparing online multimedia and one that is – in the right settings – expected by web users.

hardware. Too low a bit rate will result in 'sound artefacts', noise and/or distortion that was not present in the original recording, but too high a bit rate will result in larger file sizes. An average bit rate of 128 Kb per second results in file sizes about a tenth the size of CD-quality files with only a relatively small loss of perceived sound quality.

While MP3 is the most popular audio format online, there are other commonly used file formats some of which offer superior compression techniques (although most are not as widely supported by browsers or other software). These include the open-source Ogg Vorbis format, which was intended as an entirely free replacement to MP3, AAC (Advanced Audio Coding), another replacement for MP3 and best known as the standard for Apple and Sony PlayStation applications, and two proprietary formats, Microsoft's WMA (Windows Media Audio) and RealNetworks' RealAudio. All these formats sample the original sound; by contrast MIDI (Musical Instrument Digital Interface) synthesises music from scratch. Strictly speaking, MIDI does not generate or transmit sound, but rather is the interface between computers, synthesisers and sound cards for sending information about such things as pitch and tempo.

Recording, editing and adding sound files

The ideal conditions for recording audio, of course, would be a sound studio where every aspect of the environment can be carefully controlled. In practice, such a setup is rarely available (although media students may be able to take advantage of college or university facilities). In addition, the compression required to make audio usable on the web means that production standards do not need to be as high, but it still makes sense to make your recording as good as possible. Indeed, for some of the simplest audio-visual presentations on the web, good-quality audio is in many ways more important than video: a crisp, clear sound file will add pizzazz to what could in effect be little more than a slide show.

Preproduction is therefore important – preparing your equipment and setup before you begin recording. For a podcast, prepare and rehearse a script, and consider the format of what should be an appealing show for listeners. If you do not have access to a sound studio, then a room that is as clear of ambient noise as possible (ideally with carpets and soft furnishings to absorb echoes and dampen sounds) will do. If you are recording on the move, try to find a quiet alcove to perform your recording. While buying an expensive microphone is not absolutely necessary, a good directional mic will make a big difference to how sound is recorded and where you place it can have a huge impact on the quality of your final sound file. Before you begin recording, sample different sound levels and positions to find which one works best.

As with image editing, there is only so much that an audio editing package can do to save a poor-quality sound file. Nonetheless, an important skill that is worth learning is the ability to 'read' a wave file: the vertical axis of a file shows the level (volume, or amplitude) of a sound file, and the horizontal axis represents it over time. One thing that often generates distortion in speech is 'plosives', the burst of air that accompanies sounds such as 'p' and 'b': when you learn to identify these, it is possible to select the section of the wave that corresponds to a plosive and apply compression just to that part of the file. In addition, editors such as Audacity allow you to remove ambient noise: by selecting part of the file where such noise is clearly audible, the editor analyses the background noise and then applies a filter to the rest of the file. This should be used sparingly, however, as it can have the side effect of deadening the rest of your audio.

Other important skills include mastering volume fades, creating a transition between clips or ending a clip gracefully so that it does not jar the listener. Audio editors usually represent these as a line across a section of the clip, and the default will be a linear fade, but adding transition points so that the line curves (what is known as either a fast or a slow fade depending

WALKTHROUGH ▶

Editing audio with Audacity

1 With a microphone attached to your PC, you can begin recording with Audacity by opening the program and clicking the red record button. Press the yellow stop button when you are finished. To save your recording, go to File, Save Project As, and to export it as MP3 go to File, Export Selection as MP3. Files are imported by going to Project, Import Audio.

2 When sound files are loaded, the main use of Audacity is to clean up and edit your work. The selection tool allows you to highlight just that part of your file that you wish to work with (useful when sound quality is not uniform across the wave file), while zoom is extremely helpful when you need to focus on a particular section in detail.

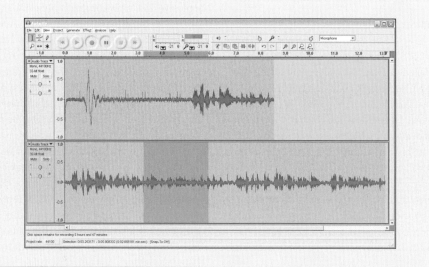

3 Time shifting is employed when working with multiple tracks, one or more of which needs to be moved in relation to time so that they can be synchronised. More commonly employed is the envelope tool: you should click on the purple lines that appear when you select this tool, then drag your mouse towards or away from the centre of the file to decrease or increase the volume.

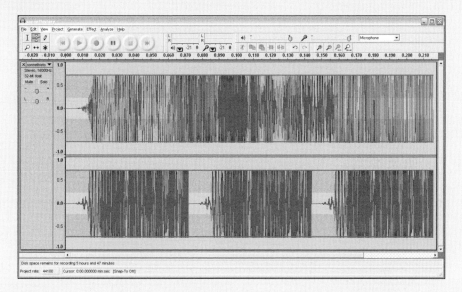

4 Basic editing techniques include trimming and cutting. If your file has unwanted silence at the beginning or end, use the selection tool to highlight the part you wish to keep and click the Trim outside selection button in the toolbar. Cut works in the opposite manner, removing the selected parts.

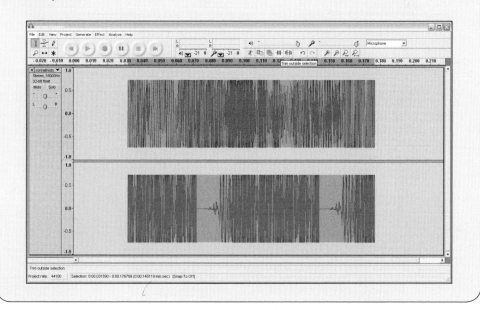

5 You can use the program to mix tracks, for example to add voice over music. From the Project menu, import a new audio file or, if necessary, go to Add new track (for example to record a voiceover). When you have edited the tracks to your satisfaction, go to Project, Quick mix to combine the selected tracks into one.

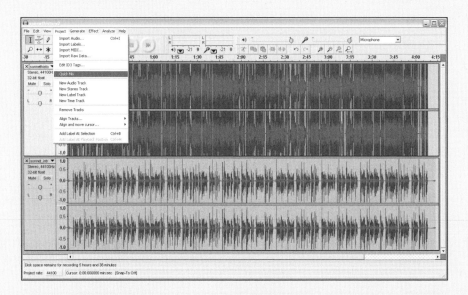

6 Audacity has a number of effects that can be applied, either to the whole file or to a selection. These include, but are not limited to: Bassboost (increase the volume of a specific frequency), Fade in/Fade out, Noise Removal (to remove background noise), Wahwah (emulates the effect of a wahwah pedal), and Echo.

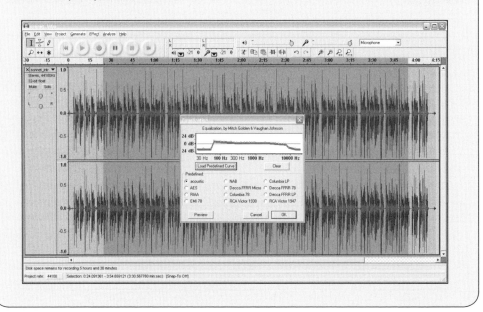

on the direction of the curve) is often a much more aesthetically pleasing effect. It is also worth experimenting with equaliser effects in an editor, which corrects (makes equal) extremes in audio frequencies to balance and harmonise a sound.

The most interesting way to add audio to a site is as a podcast, which we shall consider next, but if you want quick and easy ways to include sound on a web page, the first step is to simply upload the file to your server and include a link to it. When visitors click this, the sound file will play in an external player. It is possible to embed sounds using the <object> tag: while the older <embed> tag was simpler to use, it has been deprecated under XHTML and so should be avoided. The following code adds the default media player to a web page with a link to a sound file, test.mp3:

> A podcast is more than simply a sound file uploaded to a website. It should also include a syndication feed (usually RSS) so that subscribers can see when files are updated.

```
<object type="audio/mpeg" data="sound/
   test.mp3" width="150" height="20">
   <param name="src" value="sound/test.
   mp3">
   <param name="autoplay"
   value="false">
   <param name="autoStart" value="0">
   alt : <a href="data/test.mp3">test.mp3</
   a>
</object>
```

This code specifies the **MIME** type for the file (audio/mpeg), as well as its source and sets dimensions for the player. The other parameters determine whether the sound file starts automatically when the page is loaded, or waits until the user clicks on the player.

Podcasting

The success of digital audio on the web has given rise to the phenomenon of podcasting. Today, the term is just as likely to be used for video as well as audio, but the principles remain largely the same for both media types.

What distinguishes a podcast from simply embedding a media file in a web page is the fact that it is attached to an RSS or similar syndication feed, the functions of which will be looked at in much more detail in the next chapter. The use of RSS means that with appropriate podcasting client software, such as iTunes or Zune, the audience can easily catch up with new downloads that are automatically listed depending on which feeds they subscribe to. Furthermore, software can then be set up to download files automatically, as well as synchronise them with other devices such as MP3 players. Work on integrating audio media with RSS feeds began in 2000, with podcasting catching on some three or four years later.

One of the real virtues of podcasting has been the fact that it emphasises the use of audio for much more than music – although this obviously remains an important part of such downloads. Spoken word podcasts can be found on a huge variety of websites, from the obvious places such as news and radio sites, through education and entertainment to very special interest sites such as farmpodcasting.com and cosmology podcasts at www.universetoday.com.

To create a podcast requires an XML file that contains the RSS information used by a podcasting client to look for updates that can be downloaded. Without this RSS/XML feed, placing MP3s on a site cannot really be considered a podcast as there is no mechanism for automatic distribution. A sample RSS/XML file is as follows:

```
<?xml version="1.0" encoding="UTF-8"?>
<rss version="2.0">
<channel>
<title>My Channel</title>
<link>http://www.mysite.com</link>
```

```
<description>A sample podcast channel</
   description>
<language>en</language>
<copyright>(C) 2008</copyright>
<pubDate>Mon, 17 Sep 2008 13:00:00
   GMT</pubDate>
<image>
<url>http://www.mysite.com/images/
   podcast.jpg</url>
<title>Podcast image title</title>
<link>http://www.mysite.com</link>
</image>
<item>
<title>My First Podcast</title>
<description>A sample podcast from a
   site</description>
<pubDate>Mon, 17 Sep 2008 13:00:00
   GMT</pubDate>
<enclosure url="http://www.mysite.
   com/podcasts/myfile.mp3"
   length="1048576" type = "audio/mpeg"
   />
<guid></guid>
</item>
</channel>
</rss>
```

When this is saved as an XML file and uploaded to your website, clicking a link to the file will automatically load it into your default podcasting reader (additional details not included in the above example are required to make it compatible with iTunes). Of the details provided above, the <channel> tag indicates the channel for a variety of individual podcasts (each one indicated by its own <item> tag), with links to the actual MP3 file and associated images. As more items are added to the channel, so they will be automatically listed in a visitor's podcast reader. One extremely useful tool for creating an RSS/XML file (which was used to generate the above) can be found at podcast.redevelopments.co.uk/podcasting/podcasting.asp?podcasts.

> **Despite some difficulties with licensing, the boom in internet radio has proved to be one of the massive (and even unexpected) hits of online multimedia.**

While the source code for an RSS feed looks complicated (but is actually fairly simple to generate with the podcast code generator listed above), the process of creating podcasts for your websites is actually very straightforward: create and upload an MP3 file, generate the RSS/XML source code, upload the XML file to your site and then create a link to it from a web page. However, if you wish to make this process even easier, a number of sites such as podbean.com and podhoster.com have started to appear that integrate hosting and RSS generation so that there is no code to learn at all.

Internet radio

Internet or web radio is an older phenomenon than podcasting, having first been pioneered in the early 1990s and achieving some widespread recognition when a Rolling Stones concert was multicast in 1994. Audio from radio sites is typically streamed using a lossy format such as RealAudio or MP3, reducing the file size as much as possible, and often using a transfer protocol, UDP (user datagram protocol) which, unlike the standard **TCP** (transfer control protocol), does not guarantee the reliability or order of bits sent across the internet. Although this can result in omissions in the final broadcast when it is reassembled, it is faster and so more efficient for services such as radio that are time sensitive.

Internet radio is one example of streaming media, where the audio file is constantly delivered by a server and received on a client PC. Media streams may be on-demand or live: the latter are closer to traditional broadcast media such as analog television and radio, being transmitted only for a particular event, while on-demand streaming – made popular by developments such as the BBC iPlayer – store streams for a longer period of time and make them available to the user to download when he or she requests them. Popular radio

SHOUTcast is one way to stream internet radio from your site.

sites include Rhapsody (www.rhapsody.com), Live365.com and Pandora (www.pandora.com).

Although setting up an internet radio station is a little beyond the scope of this book, there is a relatively easy way to do so (with regard to the technology at least) using the SHOUTcast radio server (available from www.shoutcast.com/download). Available for Windows, Unix/Linux and Mac OS computers, installation of the DNAS (Distributed Network Audio Software) is fairly straightforward, with most of the complex configuration options working in default mode or being optional. To listen to streaming audio broadcast using SHOUTcast, visitors to your site should use the Winamp media player.

While the technology is generally simple to set up, copyright issues are another matter. It is illegal to transmit recordings without the permission of the copyright owner: webcasting can now be applied for under a statutory licence (in the US) and licences for performer's rights and composer's/songwriter's rights (for the UK and many other countries), which means that a producer does not need to approach each individual copyright owner. Strict limitations apply when using such licences and more information on each of these can be found at www.copyright.gov/licensing (for US radio stations) and www.ppluk.com (for the UK).

VIDEO

While video lagged considerably behind online audio because of the obvious restrictions of bandwidth and computer processing power required to transmit and play movies, since 2004 there has been a considerable explosion of its use on the internet, of which YouTube is the best example. Formed in 2005 by Chad Hurley, Steve Chen and Jawed Karim, YouTube offered a revolutionary means to upload and share videos and within a year more than 100 million videos were being watched on the site every day, with 50,000 being uploaded daily. The *New York Times* reported that in 2007 the site was estimated to use the same bandwidth as the entire internet did in 2000 and its success led to it being acquired by Google for $1.65 billion.

As with the earlier generation of music sharing typified by Napster, the rise and rise of YouTube brought with it a host of legal complications around internet sharing and copyright. After the Google buyout, companies such as Time Warner threatened legal action, while others such as Sony BMG signed revenue-sharing arrangements, in which back catalogues were made available in return for advertising shares.

Concentrating on copyright issues, however, draws attention away from one of the most remarkable aspects that YouTube represents, which is the growth of user-generated video. Throughout the 1990s, digital video cameras dropped in price and became increasingly easy to use: coupled with more powerful computers, this meant that it was simpler than ever for amateurs to create their own movies that could then be shared online. Added to this, the inclusion of video recording hardware in mobile phones meant that users could participate in new forms such as mblogging, or mobile blogging, publishing photos and videos in a simple format.

Video compression and formats

Although digital video cameras can produce high-quality and (depending on the model) uncompressed video, while extremely useful for editing this is unsuitable for display on the web due to file sizes. One second of uncompressed video at 30 frames per second (fps) at a frame size of 640 × 480 pixels, for example, would be 27 Mb in size.

Video compression has therefore been as important to movie distribution across the web

> Unlike audio, there is a wide range of competing video file formats, each of which has advantages and disadvantages in terms of compression, quality and compatibility.

as increased bandwidth. As with audio, video compression works by exploiting the fact that there is a limited amount of information that we can realistically perceive. While 24-bit colour can produce over 16 million different shades, in practice we rarely detect more than about 1,000 of these in any particular scene. Similarly, if the same object appears throughout a clip, there is no need to store information for it in every frame. Psychovisual compression, then, works in a similar fashion to psychoacoustic compression, discarding information that we cannot perceive while watching movies.

Compression can be intraframe or interframe. Interframe is commonly employed, for example in MPEG video, because it can offer the most efficient results, working by comparing earlier and later frames in a sequence, copying those elements that do not change from one frame to the next. While this can be very effective for playback, it makes such videos more difficult to work with when editing, and there is also the danger that, if a reference frame is cut, no information can be transmitted to subsequent parts of the sequence. Many interframe compression techniques insert regular frames that contain much more information than those on either side.

Intraframe, by contrast, compresses a video frame by frame, being much closer to image compression. Editing intraframe compressed video, for example that taken from a DV (Digital Video) format camera, is almost the same as editing uncompressed video.

When describing video file formats, there are two different parts: the container and the codec. The container describes the entire file structure and includes the codec, or compressor/decompressor, the software that enables video compression for storage and transmission and decompression for viewing. Common container types that are found online are:

- **AVI**   The audio visual interleave format was developed by Microsoft and, due to its wide support on Windows, became popular online despite the fact that commonly supported codecs, such as some of the older Sorensen ones, are not as efficient as for other file formats. One popular codec that is increasingly employed is DivX, which is an implementation of the MPEG-4 codec. While this can be extremely efficient, it is worth bearing in mind that it is not automatically supported in a number of media players, and so if you encode videos this way visitors may be forced to download additional software before they can view your movies.
- **FLV**   Because of the widespread use of Flash and its ability to stream video, the Flash Video format has been adopted by a wide range of sites in recent years, most notably YouTube. Recent releases use variants of the MPEG-4 codec, such as H.264, to produce highly efficient compression rates, and another advantage of the format is that it can be used within Flash applications.
- **MPEG**   A standardised format produced by the Motion Pictures Expert Group, this first came to general public attention via MPEG-2, the audio and video compression codec used in DVDs. MPEG-4 is the codec most commonly employed online which offers better quality at smaller file sizes.
- **QuickTime**   The format developed by Apple, and usually indicated by the file extension .mov. It is compatible with both Windows and Macs, and recent versions usually employ the MPEG-4 codec or variants. Despite its cross-platform compatibility and the fact that QuickTime movies offer good quality at high compression rates, the fact that the QuickTime player has to be installed first to view videos produced in this format makes it less popular than many of the others listed here.
- **WMV**   Microsoft's own video format, Windows Media Video, was designed for streaming media online (along with the associated WMA format for audio). Although popular because it is the built-in format for Windows Media Player, it is worth bearing in mind that PCs not using Windows will not necessarily be able to play WMV files.
- **RM**   The RealMedia format, developed by RealNetworks. This is available for video and audio but generally requires RealPlayer to view on both Mac and PC. It is most often employed for low-quality, low-bandwidth streaming video.

When creating videos for a website, these are the most common formats to be used online, with MPEG-4 and its variants probably offering the best compromise in terms of compression, quality and support on different platforms. There are also other, less commonly encountered formats such as ASF (Advanced Streaming Format, a variant of WMV) and 3GP, originally designed for 3G mobile phones.

Video encoding

Such things as the file format depend on how you are going to eventually deploy your video as well as the platform used for editing. Mac users, for example, will probably prefer to encode footage as a QuickTime movie, while Windows users will usually tend to save files as MPEG or WMV files (variants of the MPEG-4 file format, which includes QuickTime, are preferable).

When encoding video, as with audio, it is possible to select different bit rates: the more data that is transferred each second, the higher the quality of the video – and the higher the file size. There is always, therefore, a compromise to be achieved between quality and file size (this is true of all multimedia). Streaming codecs will typically use a constant bit rate (CBR), although there are technologies such as RealNetworks' SureStream that can encode multiple transfer rates so that the server will select the one that is most appropriate for the connection. DVD, by contrast, uses a variable bit rate (VBR), so that scenes with lots of motion increase the amount of data transferred to 8 Mbps (megabits per second) as opposed to the more usual 3 Mbps (HD DVD and Blu-ray have average bit rates of 36 and 54 Mbps respectively). For sending video across a network, typical bit rates are between 128 and 384 Kbps (kilobits per second).

Another feature to take into account in editing video is the aspect ratio of the image – the relation of width to height. The most commonly used aspect ratios are 4:3 for regular video and 16:9 for widescreen. If you encode video at a different aspect ratio, the chances are that it could be distorted when played in some applications. The 4:3 aspect ratio is typically employed by video editors when outputting footage to standard sizes measured in pixels, for example 320 × 240 and 640 × 480.

Because of its ubiquity, it is worth considering the specifications for encoding video for YouTube, as this will affect the settings for output when creating video with your favourite application. When preparing video for YouTube, the suggested format is as follows:

- MPEG-4 video, ideally with the DivX or XVid codec, although it is possible to upload other formats such as QuickTime movies that employ the MPEG-4 format,
- a frame size of 640 × 480 pixels,
- video captured at 30 fps (frames per second),
- a bit rate of 1 Mbps (megabits per second): although lower bit rates can be used, this will provide the best quality,
- MP3 stereo audio, ideally with a bit rate of 128 Kbps, and
- 100 Mb file size limit.

In addition, to preserve the quality of your upload, it is suggested that during editing you select the sharpest possible settings, and also increase brightness by about 10 per cent and contrast by 20 per cent, as these will suffer slight degradation and possible pixelation during the conversion (what is known as transcoding) to Flash. YouTube transcodes videos to 250 Kbps Flash 7 video in normal mode: this is not particularly high quality, but does have the advantage of playing in the vast majority of browsers. Encoding your video at the highest possible settings will give the transcoding process more to work with.

Finally, keep the aspect ratio at 4:3, otherwise the video will be degraded. In particular, if video with a frame size of 320 × 240 (a common setting for online video) is uploaded, it will be stretched out to 480 × 360 in high-resolution mode and so appear pixelated (normal mode displays videos at 320 × 240).

Recording tips

For new video users, recording footage can be rather overwhelming. Setting up and using a camera is beyond the scope of this book, so this section will concentrate on the basics for creating decent video with, obviously, an emphasis on preparing it for the web.

When first using a camera, it is important to experiment with all its settings and read the manual. Here are some very simple tips to improve shooting:

- **Use a tripod and microphone**   In the vast majority of cases, shaky, handheld footage will simply show up the amateurishness of your efforts, which is at best only partially offset by any stabiliser settings on the camera itself. Using a tripod will enable you to capture much better-quality video. Likewise, built-in microphones tend to be rather poor quality, so investing in an external mic is a good idea.
- **Avoid zooming**   Again, this is the mark of amateur video, with constant zooming in and out of a subject likely to result in the viewer being disorientated. Some times you will need to zoom in on a subject, but keep this to a minimum. In addition, it is better to set up a zoom so that you can cut from a distance shot to a close-up later on in your editing program.
- **Do not use built-in effects**   A number of cameras come with the ability to capture video with effects such as sepia tones or black and white. The problem with this is that if you change your mind at a later date,

you will not be able to go back to the footage in normal colour. Any digital effects should be added in an editing package, when you can try something out before committing yourself.

- **Use appropriate lighting** For professional video, this means using a lighting rig, but even if you do not have this at your disposal you should ensure that a scene is as well lit as possible. Camcorders cannot record well in low-light conditions, and footage may be virtually unusable afterwards. If it is impossible to increase the amount of lighting, a low-light mode will give some benefit; some models will also allow you to increase the aperture and slow down the shutter speed manually.
- **Set the white balance** Whenever you work in different lighting conditions, it is important to set the white balance on your camera. Locate the white balance button on your own model and then point the camera at something white (a piece of card is useful for this purpose). With the camera zoomed in so that only the white is visible, press the white balance button.
- **Record extra time** If you begin your shoot exactly at the moment when the scene begins, you will probably run into trouble at the editing stage when you need to splice clips together, particularly if there is some kind of transition between them. Recording a few extra seconds at the beginning and end of the scene will provide you with something to work with.

As with a digital stills camera, video should be recorded at the highest possible settings. Converting it to the appropriate format for the web takes place during the editing and encoding stage.

Editing and adding video

Editing video with a PC is referred to as non-linear editing (as opposed to linear editing with tape). We considered some of the common video editing applications in chapter 2.

During the editing process, footage is laid out along a timeline, with at least one track devoted to video and another to audio. More professional packages allow for multiple tracks so that complex overlay effects can be achieved, while simpler programs aimed at consumers will often provide a 'storyboard' approach where clips are dropped into slots. The latter is helpful for providing a snapshot view of the progress of a completed video, but not so useful when it comes to editing within those clips.

In addition, as with image and audio editors, a video editing package typically provides a range of filters and effects that can be applied to clips, from transitions to much more complex special effects. The process of overlaying multiple clips for more complex effects is known as compositing (and has similarities to compositing in image editing). It is very commonly employed as a blue- or green-screen technique, where an actor is filmed against a monochrome screen so that he or she can be placed over background footage.

An editing program that allows for compositing will employ what is known as keying to remove the key colour, with most providing a 'chroma key' to the particular shade of blue or green used in these effects. Once video is shot, the background is imported into the first track then overlaid on the second track with a foreground clip: the chroma key is selected from the menu (usually by clicking on an area of blue or green), and so a large section of screen colour is made transparent.

As with shooting video, editing is a complex skill that deserves a great deal of space, but

> When editing video, the choice that is often presented to a user (depending on the professional level of the software they are using) is between working with a timeline or using a storyboard to compose their movie.

WALKTHROUGH▶

Uploading and using YouTube videos

1 To upload videos onto YouTube, you must first create a free account (this also allows you to create playlists and comment on other videos). Once logged in, click the Upload, Video file button to start the two-step process for adding videos. The video will remain online until you remove it unless it is deemed to violate YouTube's terms and conditions (for example copyright or adult content).

2 The first step is to browse to the relevant video (up to 1Gb in size) and then provide some information about the video you are uploading, including a title, description, category (such as Music or Sports) and tags – keywords which are used by other visitors to locate your video.

3 On the next page, you are asked whether you wish the video to be public or private: if you select the latter, then you can restrict it to friends or family. When you have decided this, click the Upload Video button, then click Browse to select a file on your hard drive. Depending on the size of the file you are uploading, this process can take between a few minutes and several hours.

4 YouTube has made it extremely easy to embed a video on your website or blog. When you upload or locate a video you wish to use, on the right-hand side you will see two fields, one labelled URL (the address of the page itself), the other Embed. Selecting the latter provides you with the HTML code you can cut and paste into your own page so that the video will be streamed from YouTube directly to your site.

the most important point to bear in mind is the transition between scenes. Plenty of video editors provide a huge amount of transition effects such as curls, explosions and pseudo-3D effects (such as when the moving image is wrapped around a sphere or cube). However, these almost inevitably look amateurish and it is best to keep things simple, using straight cuts, dissolves and a fade to black.

Once a sequence of clips with audio has been arranged to your satisfaction, it can be exported into a final movie. While many editors have a set of built-in settings for a variety of outputs (such as DVD- or web-compatible), if you have the space on a hard drive it is always best to create a high-resolution version of your movie as a backup, and then go back to the timeline and create a web-ready version.

Once your video is complete and saved in a suitable format, it can be added to a web page in a variety of ways. Video blogging, or vlogging, is one of the easiest, along with uploading movies to YouTube. To include a video directly, as with audio files, you should use the <object> element.

Vlogging

Because producing, uploading and sharing video has become so simple, a new trend that is starting to take off is vlogging, where video becomes the medium for posting and communicating with others. As with podcasting, a user moves from simple video hosting to Web 2.0 vlogging when syndication takes place, enabling visitors to subscribe to updates automatically via an RSS feed.

Because sites such as Blogger and TypePad in conjunction with YouTube make it so easy to upload and syndicate video, these have become the preferred option for many vloggers. If video is hosted on your own site, however, it is also possible to create your own RSS/XML file that will create a subscription link as outlined in the section on podcasting.

For producers with an iTunes account, it is also possible to use the Apple site to distribute video as a podcast. To do this, log into your iTunes account and click on the Podcast link. From here, select the Publish a Podcast link and enter the syndication feed of your blog, either produced automatically in a site such as Blogger or manually via Feedburner or your own XML file. Once iTunes has verified the link, you can select a category for your podcast and enter other information such as a long description of your file. When this is done, click the Publish button and your video will appear as a podcast once it has been approved.

FLASH

The principles behind Flash were introduced in chapter 2, under Web technologies. Produced for many years by Macromedia and now owned by Adobe, it has become one of the most popular tools for creating media rich applications – with good reason due to its versatility. Although this includes a range of games and interactive online programs, we shall concentrate on its origins as an animating tool (to introduce the important notion of the timeline), using scripting for some basic interactivity and – because it is so important to multimedia today – a closer look at Flash video.

> One of the most important pieces of multimedia software, Flash started life as a simple animation tool but has since grown into a complex program for creating complete online applications.

Animating with the timeline

In many respects the core application of Flash – certainly its oldest – is animation. The program began life as a vector graphic animator, these consisting of primitive objects such as circles, polygons and Bézier curves that can be displayed and manipulated very quickly.

When Flash is opened, the central white rectangle at the centre of the screen is referred to as the stage and is surrounded by toolbars and a property panel. This forms the canvas for all objects that appear on the stage, and these in turn – when drawn directly onto the stage or imported – form what are known as symbols. A symbol is a reusable object, such as a graphic, button or movieclip. When used on the stage, this is referred to as an instance of the symbol, and the virtue of this approach is that the file size of an individual symbol is calculated only once in an animation, no matter how many times it is used (that is, how many instances appear) in a movie.

As with a video editor, Flash presents the user with a timeline – although it looks slightly different being broken down into a series of frames. The number of frames per second can be set from preferences, with a smaller number of frames creating a smaller file size at the expense of fluidity. In practice, setting a frame rate of more than 30 fps (frames per second) is irrelevant as persistence of vision means that we cannot perceive any additional smoothness to the animation.

Once the timeline has been set up, certain frames are specified as key frames – that is the point where something happens that changes the appearance of the animation. The transition between one key frame to another is referred to as 'tweening' (from in-between), and Flash automatically calculates differences in the appearance of an object on the stage frame by frame. When creating an animation, there are several basic types:

- **Motion tween**   As its name suggests, motion tweening works by moving elements around the stage, and is one of the easiest animations to create in Flash. Once a symbol is placed on the stage, you select another key frame and then move that element to another position. After Motion is selected from the Tween panel of the Properties inspector, Flash then calculates all the intervening positions between the first and final key frames. As well as regular, linear movement, motion tweening can be set up to 'ease in' and 'ease out', beginning and ending slowly.

- **Shape tween**   As with motion tweening, a shape tween is fairly self-explanatory and employed when you wish to transform one shape into another, a circle into a star, for example. Again, two key frames are set up at the beginning and the end of the animation, with one shape being inserted at the start and another at the end. This time the Shape option is selected in the Properties inspector and, again, Flash calculates the intervening appearance of the symbol.

- **Frame-by-frame animation**   This type of animation is slightly more time-consuming than the previous two, but useful when you need to create something like animated text. Once a string of letters is entered, its elements are separated using the Break Apart command, then a series of key frames must be created. For each frame, the symbol should be moved into place. No tweening is involved in this kind of animation.

- **Guided motion tween**   A more complex animation, this is where guides are used to move an object along a path (such as a curve). When a guide layer is added from the insert menu, a line is drawn with the pencil tool and an object snapped to the first and final key frames on a timeline.

These basic types can be combined with other effects to create different forms of animation. For example, the motion tween, when combined with changes to the alpha (transparency) channel of a symbol creates a fade-in or fade-out effect, while changing the size of a symbol will create a zooming motion, again using the motion tween. In addition, the program offers a number of masking tools that can be used for more advanced effects.

Rich internet applications

Key to developing interactive applications is ActionScript, which, like the scripting languages considered in chapter 4 could easily take up its own chapter or even book and so can only be dealt with very briefly here. This section will concentrate more on the broad principles of creating rich internet applications (RIA) with Flash.

An RIA can be developed with a large number of technologies other than Flash – or rather, a number of technologies such as XML and JavaScript, are often combined with Flash to create an online application that has many (if not all) the features of a traditional desktop program. The term was first used by Macromedia (although its principles were known before this) to refer to using Flash on the client rather than the server to handle most of the processing, providing a more responsive interface that could also handle more media and data types more quickly, hence these being 'rich' applications.

As has already been indicated, RIAs are not by any means restricted to Flash (in conjunction with its Flex platform), but also include the Curl programming language, Microsoft's Silverlight web browser plug-in, and Adobe AIR – this last allowing internet applications to be run on the desktop with access to local file systems in contrast to programs run in a browser, which are much more limited.

Rather than running through all the complexities of creating a full RIA with Flash, important as this is to the future direction of web production, it is worth concentrating instead on some of the basics of ActionScript as it is used to create more interactive movies. With the current release of Flash CS3, as well as a new player to display files in a browser, version 9, the language has been completely rewritten and so requires a new virtual machine (called the AVM2) to run movies developed with ActionScript 3.

As it is based on ECMAScript, the syntax of ActionScript has many similarities to JavaScript, with the same kind of commands, use of variables and flow control structures. A very simple example of an ActionScript can be seen in the following, used to control two buttons so that they start and stop a movie with an instance of an animated symbol called 'my_symbol':

```
on(press)
{
my_symbol.play();
}

on(press)
{
my_symbol.stop();
}
```

Because it can be integrated with server-side technologies such as PHP, ASP and Ruby on Rails, ActionScript can be used to build extremely complex interactions between the user and the website – hence its significance to the development of RIAs.

Flash video

The Flash video format (FLV) has already been considered briefly in the section on general video. Here we will simply add some comments on preparing video within Flash, either to export it as an individual file or as part of a media-rich application. When using video within a Flash movie, cue points can be added which allow it to synchronise with other elements of the swf file, such as animation or text, so that at certain points alongside a video images or text will be loaded.

> The widespread adoption of Flash means that the Flash video format has become immensely popular.

Video within a Flash movie is treated like any other media type, meaning that it can be scripted and layered like any other part of a file. Alternatively, video may be exported to be played on a web page as a standalone object, using the default Sorensen Spark and On2 VP6 codecs included in the main program. Sorensen Spark is supported by Flash Player 7 and later, On2 VP6 by version 8 onwards: the latter supports better-quality video at the same data rate. The Professional release

WALKTHROUGH▶

Flash powered image and video galleries

1 Once you have installed Exposé, either as a standalone package on your site or as part of a content management system such as Joomla!, click the Album Manager link and enter your password. This will launch the back end where you can load up images to be displayed on your site.

2 Exposé uses collections which in turn host individual albums. In the first instance, click the Create Collection link in the bottom left-hand side, provide a name, and then the Create Album button. A collection can contain multiple albums, which appear in the front end as animated lists.

3   With your album created, the next step is to upload images or videos from your hard drive. Click the Upload videos/photos buttons in the bottom centre of the screen, then the Add videos/photos button in the dialog box that appears. Once you have added a list of files, click the Upload button.

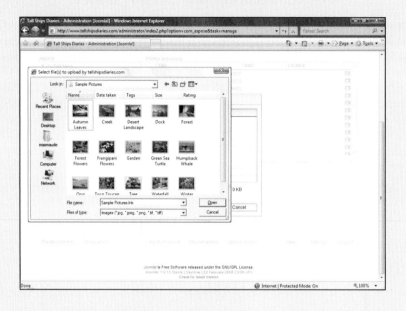

4   As images are uploaded, these will be resized automatically according to the settings in Exposé. To modify these and other settings, click the Main Configuration link. Here you can set such things as the width and height of your gallery, as well as a host of other settings.

5 Galleries display various elements for navigating between pictures and albums: when adjusting settings in the configuration panel, bear in mind that positions are measured from the top left-hand corner of your browser window, so you must change X and Y co-ordinates to move elements.

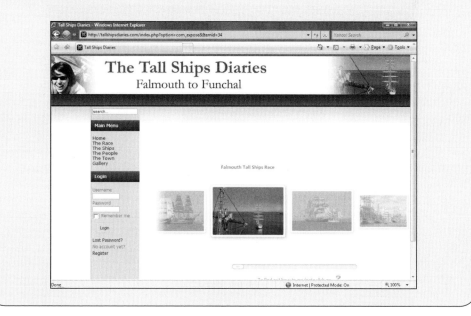

6 When your images are uploaded, they will be displayed on your website as a series of animated menus and slideshows (the number depending on how many collections/albums you have created). Simply select the album you wish to view then move your mouse over thumbnails to display them on screen.

7 For adding Flash video to a site, a useful free tool that allows you to embed slick videos into your pages is Flowplayer (flowplayer.org). It works with the .FLV videos, and you can convert MPEGs and other formats to Flash video with the free Riva FLV Encoder from rivavx. de/?encoder.

8 After installing Flowplayer on your site, click the examples folder on your server's hard drive. This displays a series of embedded videos from the most basic (a single file on a page) to much more advanced scrollable videos and playlists that you can modify with extra scripts.

9 Using the simple video as an example, go to View, Source to see the code you need to embed a Flash file using Flowplayer. The two important elements are the src argument, which links to the Flowplayer applet on your server, and the videoFile argument under config to link to your video.

```
simple-example[1] - Notepad
File  Edit  Format  View  Help

<!--
     A minimal setup to get you started. This configuration is the same
     as in our Quick Start documentation:

     http://flowplayer.org/player/quick-start.html
-->
<head>

     <title>Simple Flowplayer example</title>

     <!--
          include flashembed - which is a general purpose tool for
          inserting Flash on your page. Following line is required.
     -->
     <script type="text/javascript" src="js/flashembed.min.js"></script>

     <!-- some minimal styling, can be removed -->
     <link rel="stylesheet" type="text/css" href="css/common.css"/>

     <script>
     /*
      * window.onload event occurs after all HTML elements have been loaded
      * this is a good place to setup your Flash elements
      */
     window.onload = function() {

          /*
               use flashembed to place flowplayer into HTML element
               whose id is "example" (below this script tag)
          */
          flashembed("example",

               /*
                    first argument supplies standard Flash parameters. See full list:
                    http://kb.adobe.com/selfservice/viewContent.do?externalId=tn_12701
               */
               {
                    src:'../FlowPlayerDark.swf',
                    width: 400,
                    height: 290
               },
```

10 For more complex effects, such as tabbed videos that use a mouse scrollable wheel, you will need to download some JavaScripts such as flow.embed and jquery.scrollable from the Flowplayer website (links are on the examples page). Again, modify the source code to link to the videos you want to play.

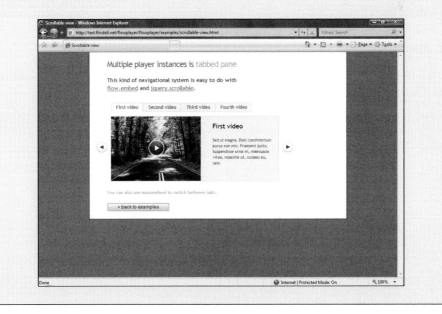

of Flash CS3 also includes a Video Exporter that can be used alongside a QuickTime plug-in to export FLV movies directly from within programs such as Final Cut Pro and Avid Xpress. Importing through the main Flash interface will encode one video at a time, while the Flash Video Encoder can batch process a number of files.

When importing video into Flash, you can use AVI, QuickTime, MPEG, WMV and DV (Digital Video) formats. Whenever possible, for the best quality, Flash video should be encoded from the uncompressed form; when creating a video, complex transitions such as cross-dissolves tend not to compress well. Sometimes, in order to get file sizes down, it is necessary to cut the number of frames per second, leaving the frame rate at its native fps will obviously look best, but if you must cut the best results come from dividing the frame rate by whole numbers (so reducing 30fps to 15, for example).

Video that is imported into a Flash file is placed onto the timeline; both the movie into which the video is embedded and the video itself must have the same frame rate. Embedded video such as this works best with smaller clips, typically with a playback of 10 seconds or less: longer clips only really work with the Flash Media Server, as otherwise file sizes become too large causing Flash Player to fail.

Flash alternatives

Flash has obviously become an important tool for creating multimedia for websites, but it is also a complex and expensive tool to use. For web developers who have specific requirements for a website, however, there are plenty of alternatives – most of which are much cheaper and many of which are free.

Here we will concentrate on adding two types of multimedia component to a site in order to provide animated galleries and a video player that can display plenty of different movie formats. While you will need to know a little bit of HTML to add these to your site, for the most part this simply consists of being able to enter the URL for your own media and follow the templates for creating such things as playlists.

The first of the two programs we will look at here, Exposé 4.4 (www.slooz.com/trinkets. php), is the most complex in that it can provide a standalone gallery to run on a desktop PC as well as work via a website. It works via a front and back end: the latter is where you set up and configure albums, which are then displayed in the front end as a series of animated, scrolling collections of images.

FlowPlayer (flowplayer.org) is an extensible video plug-in for a site. You will need to copy the relevant Flash and JavaScript files to your site, with samples provided to give you the code you need for your web page. The scripts offered on the FlowPlayer site allow you to do some fairly sophisticated things with your video, including animated scrolling between playlists.

For more information and updates on multimedia, visit www.producingforweb2.com/multimedia.

CHAPTER 6

Web 2.0 tools

Many of the technologies and techniques introduced so far are fundamental to so-called Web 2.0 tools. What is important, however, is that over the past five years or so, new ways of publishing information online have appeared that greatly simplify the process of getting content onto your site. This chapter will move from relatively quick and easy techniques, such as working with blogging software, through intermediate mashups such as Google's many and varied application programming interfaces (APIs) before concentrating in some detail on using MediaWiki, the content management software that runs Wikipedia among other things.

SYNDICATION AND RSS

While syndication and RSS has been discussed briefly in chapter 1 as one of the main principles behind Web 2.0 technologies, and encountered again as part of the discussion on podcasting in the previous chapter, this section will look in much more detail at how web producers can use web feeds to syndicate stories so that readers or other websites receive automatic updates.

The idea behind syndication dates back to the mid-1990s, although large-scale syndication only began just after the turn of the century. Because of its simplicity in sharing content, such as from blogs and news websites, or for snippets of data stored on servers in the form of financial or weather reports, it has become an essential ingredient in the development of Web 2.0 platforms. Previously, if a publisher wished to share information this would have required a considerable amount of effort in order to copy data between sites.

By contrast, web feeds provide a standard interface for transferring data between websites based on XML. Once a web feed is published, visitors to a site may subscribe to it and read it either in an aggregator or a feed reader. As should be evident from the previous chapter, as well as HTML pages various types of multimedia such as audio and video can also be syndicated. Furthermore, the protocols behind syndication have been developed to sort content automatically into different categories (once these are identified by the site producer) so that subscribers can select more easily only that type of content they wish to receive.

Because syndication tools are built into so many Web 2.0 sites, such as Blogger and YouTube, it has become extremely easy for millions of amateur web users to share their posts online. However, syndication has also unsurprisingly been taken up by professional organisations as a means of distributing information to partners on a commercial basis – commercial syndication having been around long before online technologies were even dreamed of. Thus Reuters and Associated Press, for example, will allow their news feeds to be taken up by third-party news sites. Such commercial feeds are either licensed (that is content is paid for) or supported by advertising.

In this section, we shall consider in greater detail how syndication works, concentrating in particular on RSS (although, it should be noted, this is only one of several types of web feed technology), as well as tips for using web feeds to promote your own site and as a basic building block of Web 2.0 sharing.

Web feed variants

There are several web feed formats, of which the most commonly employed are RSS and Atom. Atom is the newer of the two and was developed as an alternative to RSS which, because of its need to remain backwards compatible, was seen as sometimes being problematic. Thus, for example, there is no clear way to distinguish in RSS whether content being syndicated is plain text or HTML. In addition, Atom offers greater flexibility in terms of such things as internationalisation for sections of content, as well as a syntax that can be used in other feeds (such as RSS ones).

> RSS is the most popular web feed used today, but is quickly being caught up by alternatives such as Atom.

While Atom was an opportunity to overhaul web feeds, and became increasingly popular after its adoption by Google (it is, for example, the subscription method for Blogger), when most web producers think of syndication they tend to think of RSS. What RSS actually stands for is a matter of opinion, as it can be used to refer to a family of interrelated web feed formats: Really Simple Syndication (currently version 2.0.1), RDF Site Summary (1.0 and 0.9, RDF standing for the Resource Description Framework, or a specification for metadata about sites), or Rich Site Summary (0.91).

RDF Site Summary was the first variant of RSS syndication, developed by Netscape in 1999 and, following complicated claims to ownership of the original RSS format, this was followed by Really Simple Syndication. Throughout this section, we will concentrate on RSS 2.0 for

examples, this being the most popular format for many websites and podcasters, and easily identified by the orange and white symbol that appears on pages offering the service.

Both RSS and Atom allow visitors to a site to subscribe to a link that can then be displayed in either a dedicated news reader or an aggregator, such as NewsGator (online at www.newsgator.com or available as a download, FeedDemon) or RSSReader (www.rssreader. com), or as a subscription feed for portals such as iGoogle or My Yahoo! With a suitable dynamic site and appropriate plug-ins, it is also then possible for third-party web producers to take RSS feeds from multiple sources and display syndicated content. It is even possible to generate RSS feeds from sites that have not been formatted for RSS as described previously, a process known as scraping. However, as well as being much more difficult to do, this is dubious ethically as it effectively creates syndicated copy from sites that have not given their express permission. Google amongst others has taken steps to block this practice where possible.

Creating an RSS feed

In the previous chapter, we looked at a fairly complex RSS feed for a sample podcast, generated using podcast.redevelopments.co.uk/podcasting/podcasting.asp?podcasts. In this section, we will go through hand-coding a much simpler RSS 2.0 feed to explain the various steps involved.

RSS and Atom are both dialects of XML and, as such, must conform to the XML 1.0 specification. The top level element is the <rss> tag, beneath which is the <channel> element that provides metadata about the type of feed being offered, for example whether this is the entertainment, sport, politics or latest news feed for a site. These elements essentially surround the various items that constitute the web pages or podcasts that a feed will link to. Each item

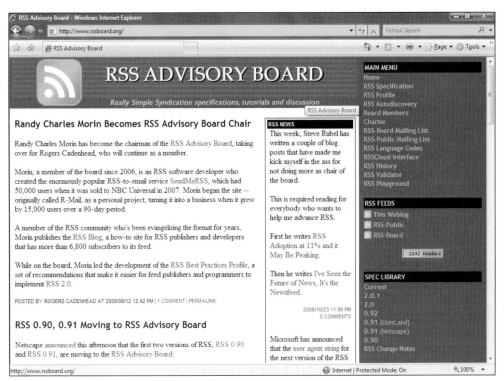

The RSS Advisory Board sets specifications for sharing content using Really Simple Syndication.

must then include a title, description and link which will then form part of the feed.

A single XML file for RSS can contain multiple items for the various pages that will be linked to a news feed. The simple version shown below is also backwards compatible with earlier versions of RSS, which means that it will display in just about any news reader or RSS-enabled site. For our example, we will consider a site that offers a subscription feed for reviews of new gadgets:

```
<?xml version="1.0"?>
<rss version="2.0">
<channel>
<title>New Gadgets</title>
<description>Cool new gadget reviews.</
    description>
<link>http://www.mysite.com/
    newgadgets/</link>
```

```
<item>
<title>Sonata HiFi</title>
<description>One for real audio buffs, this
    2.1 DAB receiver comes with its own
    iPod dock and choice of HD DVD or CD
    player.</description>
<link> http://www.mysite.com/
    newgadgets/sonata.html</link>
</item>
```

```
<item>
<title>AiGuru SV1 videophone</title>
<description>A VGA webcam and Skype
    means that you can use the videophone
    without a computer.</description>
<link> http://www.mysite.com/
    newgadgets/aiguru.html</link>
</item>

</channel>
</rss>
```

As can be seen from this sample, there are two items contained in our RSS channel, with title and description being displayed according to the preferences of a visitor's reader or browser. Once the file is saved (usually with the extension .xml or .rss, although neither of these is strictly necessary), it can be uploaded to the web server.

In addition to these required channel elements, there are also several optional ones outlined in Table 6.1.

Of the above optional elements, the <image> tag has three required sub-elements – <url>, <title> and <link> – and three that are optional – <width>, <height> and <description>. The element textInput has four required sub-elements – <title>, <description>, <name> and <link> (the latter to a script that processes text input from the user).

There are several applications available that will generate an RSS feed for you, such as Feed Editor (www.extralabs.net/feed-editor.htm) and RSS Editor (www.rsseditor.net), rather than having to create it by hand. One extremely useful address is Feedity.com, which can generate RSS feeds from just about any website.

Table 6.1

Element	Description	Example
language	The language of a site, which enables aggregators to select language-specific feeds.	en-us (US English) zh (Chinese) ja (Japanese)
copyright	Copyright notice for a channel.	Copyright 2008, Routledge
managingEditor	Email address for content manager.	joe@mysite.com (Joe Bloggs)
webmaster	Email address for site manager.	jane@mysite.com (Jane Doe)
pubDate	Date of publication for content in the channel.	Sun, 21 Sep 2008, 13:37 GMT
lastBuildDate	Last time the channel's content was changed.	Tue, 23 Sep 2008, 14:54 GMT
category	Used like the item element, this specifies categories that the channel belongs to.	<category>reviews </category>
generator	Indicates the program used to generate the RSS feed.	Extralabs Feed Editor
docs	A URL for any documentation that may be associated with the feed.	<http://www.mysite. com/rss-feeds.html>
ttl	Time to live: number of minutes that a channel can be cached before being refreshed from source.	<ttl>120</ttl>
image	Specifies an image to be used with the channel (see below).	(see below)
textInput	Provides a text input box with the channel.	(see below)
skipHours	Specifies hours in GMT that the channel is not to be read.	23 (not to be read at 11 p.m.)
skipDays	Specifies days in the week that the channel is not to be read.	Wednesday, Saturday

Validating and publishing a feed

Once a feed is created, it needs to be tested or validated to ensure that it works correctly. This is probably the easiest part of the process, in that once you have uploaded your XML file to a website all you need to do is enter the URL into the input box at www.feedvalidator.org. This works for both Atom and RSS 2.0 feeds, returning errors for such things as a missing <xml> element or too many days in <skipDays>. Use these error messages to correct your original RSS/XML file.

When you are sure your feed is valid, create a link to it on your site – either a straight text link or, even better, an image link with one of the standard RSS icons which you can find at www.feedicons.com in a variety of sizes and formats. Users who click the link to the XML file will then be able to view it in a compatible browser or reader.

The most complex part of creating a suitable RSS feed is, unsurprisingly, fashioning the file itself. Many guides suggest copying and pasting an existing RSS feed and then customising it to incorporate your own files. While this can often be useful for creating XML files in a hurry, it is always best to understand the basics of the file that you are modifying – otherwise, you could generate a number of confusing errors for visitors to your site.

A 'walkthrough' for creating a feed is on the next page.

BLOGGING

While syndication is the glue that often binds Web 2.0 sites together by providing easy sharing of content, or, to rephrase the metaphor slightly more accurately, the oil that smoothes the way for a flow of information, blogging is the tool that has completely revolutionised web publishing for the vast majority of users. At the beginning of 2008, Technorati claimed to be tracking more than 112 million blogs, although as an article in the *Blog Herald* pointed out, this did not include the 70 million plus Chinese blogs – and in any case, as Anne Helmond asked, was anyone really still counting? (Helmond 2008).

As Helmond observes, where once the internet used to be measured in web pages, for the past four or five years it has tended to be measured in the number of blogs available – which, as the *Wall Street Journal* pointed out in 2005, was a sign of the immaturity of the blogosphere as a medium. Nonetheless, throughout 2007 to 2008, particularly in spheres such as journalism, politics and technology reporting and commentary, blogging has very much become an accepted and mainstream activity. *The Guardian*'s Comment Is Free site (www.guardian.co.uk/commentisfree) has become as much an integral part of its activities as daily news, sports coverage and reviews, while the 2008 US presidential elections were fought out as much in blogs as in traditional media such as newspapers and terrestrial television.

As blogs are moving away from the previous perception as being little more than vanity publishing for cranks and specialist interests, so they have become the easiest way to get material online. At the end of the 1990s, commentators would often remark on the proliferation of personal home pages that were appearing as ISPs and third-party sites offered free web space – but although many of these sites increasingly offered design templates, the user still usually had to create web pages in an editor and then upload them manually by **FTP** (file transfer protocol). By contrast, contemporary blogs such as Blogger and LiveJournal require no real technical knowledge to get started, simply the ability to log on and start making posts.

Not that blogging has always been this way: indeed, the earliest blogs – or web logs – were really manually updated web diaries that

> **Blogging is one of the most important tools that has revolutionised the way in which millions of users publish to the web.**

WALKTHROUGH▶

Creating a feed with Feedity.com

1 After going to Feedity, the first step is to locate a suitable RSS feed from a site that you wish to use. Once you have the URL for this, it should be entered in the field in the centre of the page. Alternatively, Feedity provides some sample feeds such as those from YouTube or *Time* magazine.

2 Clicking the preview link will display what the feed looks like in terms of headlines. Links for Simple Refine and Advanced Refine allow you to customise what content is included in the feed. Once this is done, select a category for your feed (such as Arts & Literature or Games) and click the Get Feed button.

▶▶

3 Feedity generates a URL that can then be added to the HTML of your page. Signing up for an account will enable you to create multiple feeds or store them for later editing, while paying for a Pro account adds some extra features, such as the ability to add dates to feed headings.

differed from other sites not in the mechanics of publishing but in their content. It was with the launch of Blogger in 1999 (later purchased by Google), that the practice of blogging really started to catch on as a streamlined publishing system. As well as the automatic archiving of entries, the introduction of the permalink (a permanent link back to an entry once it had passed from the front page) began to make blogs a more useful resource. Introduced into Blogger in 2000, this meant that articles posted online were much easier to cite and return to, even if the content of a posting was modified at a later stage. Similarly, the introduction of support for such things as audio and video meant that blogs could become a media rich resource.

While personal blogs evolved out of diaries to become one of the most popular forms online today, these do not constitute the sum total of the blogosphere by any means. In recent years, microblogging, or the practice of posting short statements to communicate with friends and family, has begun to catch on. Twitter is a good example of this, and its immediacy is closer to SMS than email or more typical forms of web posting. Likewise, as we have already seen in the previous chapter, multimedia blogs such as vlogs are starting to catch on, as are moblogs or blogs maintained from mobile phones and similar devices. Likewise, the corporate blogs of businesses, traditional media companies, and institutions such as universities offer a relatively informal means of allowing readers and members of an organisation to keep up to date.

Adding and organising content

The simplicity of most blogging software allows web users to concentrate on their content rather than struggling with a complex package such as Dreamweaver. As the interface for applications such as Blogger or WordPress look very similar to a typical word processor, with few options to confuse potential users, bloggers can start adding text, images and video within

a matter of minutes. For more expert users, the ability to work directly with HTML allows for more complex effects to be added to a page. Although ultimately this will be less flexible than unfettered access to a web server with CGI access to run dynamic scripts, the variety of third-party services online means that it is possible to achieve sophisticated blogs with some expert knowledge.

Of course, simplicity does not guarantee quality, and if the software itself is virtually transparent this places a greater onus on getting the content right. The majority of content uploaded onto blogs is still text, and we shall consider writing for the web in greater detail in a later chapter, but a few pointers should be borne in mind if you wish your blog to appear professional.

> **Blogs today encompass a variety of formats, including microblogs, corporate blogs and vlogs.**

While blogging has, because of its relative immediacy in terms of publishing, tended to promote a rather informal approach to writing, quality always matters. Obviously errors in spelling and grammar and factual inaccuracies will earn your site a reputation for untrustworthiness. In addition, the values that make good copy for news are also relevant to a great deal of online writing: short, concise sentences that convey information and attract attention quickly. However, alongside this, writers who want a great deal of traffic will need to write with an eye on search engine ranking, part of the process of search engine optimisation (SEO) that will be considered in the final chapter.

With regard to maintaining interest, the hardest thing to advise on but also the most vital is the importance of generating ideas. Coming up with new posts to produce a lively blog is harder than it looks and is the simple reason why professional sites will hire writers. However, while this option is beyond the means of most readers of this book, there are a few tips that can help. First of all, the interactive nature of blogging should never be underestimated: the fact that it is so easy to comment on stories is a very useful way of getting feedback and suggestions. Similarly, while simply stripping junk onto a site is a good way to drive readers away, having fresh content is useful for attracting search engine traffic, and for this reason it is not a bad idea to subscribe to (relevant) RSS feeds to provide regular updates to your content.

A virtue of making your own virtual updates is that this is a useful way to get other bloggers to link to you, which in turn can generate traffic for your site. In recent years, this has led to the practice of so-called 'guest blogging', where writers are invited onto another site to make comments and write articles. As well as looking to the blogosphere to promote your work, it is also a good idea to be active on social networking sites, forums and so on, engaging in discussion and (where appropriate) adding links to your own blog. Actually, some discretion is required with this: blatant puff pieces are liable to attract adverse reactions, and if people simply see your posts as advertising for your writing you may end up with little more than hostile flaming on your own or other sites. Instead, being seen to be active online will raise your profile, and other users will be tempted to search for your other comments and posts online. Finally, more discreet tactics should never be ruled out: including your blog address in an email signature is not intrusive but can be very effective for promoting your work.

Blogging software tends to work by archiving content automatically according to the date on which it was created and in accordance with any preferences specified in the software. However, you may wish to archive your material in other ways, and a useful tool for this is to create categories or labels that establish sections for content. Finally, and this is something that will be looked at in the next section on social networking tools in more detail, it is also often possible to allow visitors to tag content so that it is added to sites such as digg.com or delicious.com.

> As well as using blogging software to create your content, a knowledge of core technologies such as HTML and CSS will allow you to customise a blog in innovative and interesting ways.

Customising your blog

Getting the content right for your blog should be your main concern in attracting visitors, but personalising its look and feel serves two main functions. First of all, it encourages a sense of ownership on the part of the blogger, enabling him or her to feel that this is more than a standard template. Second, as sites such as LiveJournal and Blogger offer only a few default designs, sticking to one of these can make your blog indistinguishable from the many thousands of others online.

The walkthrough on setting up Blogger indicated briefly how a user can begin to customise his or her blog. Elements such as fonts and colours are fairly self-explanatory, but it is worth paying a little more attention to the Page Elements and HTML sections.

These elements in a blog are powered by scripts that allow different kinds of content to be displayed on a page, for example a navigation bar, a heading for a logo and various sidebars. Each element includes an edit link, clicking which brings up different options for each section of the page. Some of the choices available are fairly limited (for example, the Navbar options), while others are more extensive (as with the options for the Blog Posts). It is also possible to drag and drop some elements, such as sidebar components, around the page.

Blogger also includes a range of what it calls gadgets. These are plug-ins such as quotes, photos of the day, chat options and games that can be added to a page. To install a gadget, simply click on the Add a Gadget link and select the plug-in you wish to install.

For more comprehensive control over the look and appearance of your site, however, the Edit HTML option is by far the best. It also draws attention to one of the features of contemporary web production which, in some ways, appears to have taken a step backwards.

W A L K T H R O U G H ▶

Using Blogger

1   Before you can create a blog at www.blogger.com, you will need to create a Google account (which you will already have if you use a service such as Gmail). If you don't have an account, when you click the Create your blog now link you will see a simple registration screen asking for an email address, password and display name. Once this is entered, click the Continue link.

2   The next step is to provide a name for your blog and a subdomain (http://mysubdomain. blogspot.com). Alternatively, if you wish to host your blog on an alternative address – for example you have web space elsewhere – click the Advanced Blog Setup link. For this, you will need information about your FTP server.

▶▶

3 The final stage of the easy setup routine is to select a template for your blog. To begin with, Blogger only provides a dozen or so templates, but these can be customised at a later date. Once you click the Continue button, the blog will be created and a Start blogging button appears.

4 When your blog is launched, the browser will display a screen with three tabs. The first is a tab to create a post, and is a simplified web editor. At the top is a field to add a title for your entry, and beneath this is the main workspace with buttons for basic text editing and adding images, videos and links. It is also possible to work with the HTML for your post directly by clicking the Edit HTML link. From this page you can also edit individual posts and moderate comments.

5 The Settings tab displays a wide variety of options for such things as controlling access to your blog and how it is published online. Under Permissions, for example, you can restrict access to named authors, Formatting sets such things as how dates and times are displayed, and Archiving determines the frequency of how often posts are moved into the archive as well as setting permalinks for pages.

▶▶

6 The final tab for modifying your blog, Layout, controls its appearance. The final link, Choose New Template, offers a few additional templates, but where you can really make a blog your own is via the other links at the top of the page. Page Elements determines where components are laid out on the template, while Fonts and Colours uses CSS to modify text, background and sidebar colours. Finally, for expert users, the Edit HTML link allows you to modify the code for your template, although it is advisable to back up a copy first.

By the end of the 1990s, the vogue was to create personal home pages with graphic, WYSIWYG editors, but the modern blogger who wants to update the look and feel of his or her site will need to get their hands dirty with code. In fact, because the structure of a page is clearly separated from its content and design, this represents an extremely effective way of modifying presentation. For a completely non-technical user, the graphical interface will provide plenty of opportunities to modify colours and position, but a grounding in XHTML and CSS will prove invaluable for the blogger who simply wishes to hack an existing template, or even create one from scratch and upload it to the site.

It should be stated very clearly, however, that before you edit a blog template directly you should always back up. An error with code could ruin your design or even stop the page loading altogether. A typical template will include a series of CSS entries that define such things as the colour of the background and margin for a page, links and formatting for entries. Expert users, by studying the various entries, will also be able to emulate and create their own templates from scratch.

Using WordPress

So far, most of the blogging examples in this chapter have drawn on Blogger which is the most popular third-party site and probably the easiest to use. But what options are open to the web producer who wishes to make a blog from scratch, either for him- or herself or for visitors to use?

There are several open-source applications that are available for free downloads, such as Movable Type, GreyMatter and WordPress. Here we shall concentrate on this last to explore some of the options that are available when producing a blog for your own site.

When installing WordPress, you will need to provide an administrator user name and password. By default, WordPress installs an administrative folder, wp-admin, where you will need to log on to manage the site. So, for example, if you installed the software into a subdomain blogs.mysite.com, the admin folder would be accessed at http://blogs.mysite.com/wp-admin. This is also the folder that authors will need to access to contribute to your site.

When logged in, the default page for an administrator shows the Dashboard with main links on the top left for writing, managing, designing and moderating comments, with smaller links on the top right for controlling settings, WordPress plug-ins and users. A summary of posts, plug-ins and comments then appears in the main Dashboard.

For a blog that will be employed by multiple users, the first thing that an administrator will probably want to do is set up log-ins. WordPress does not allow users to register themselves, so they must be set up by the main admin and provided with a user name and password. Users can be allocated different roles, from a subscriber who cannot post to an administrator with full rights. Those with author status and above can log in and make posts by clicking on the Write link in the Dashboard.

Under the Manage link, an admin will see options to set such things as categories and tags for posts, as well as to manage any media items uploaded to the system and to import or export posts and comments from other blogging software. The Design link, in turn, is very similar to that in Blogger, although it refers to widgets rather than gadgets, but also allows you to edit HTML directly as well as download other themes.

WordPress is, in effect, a very simple to use content management system (CMS). Rather than setting up multiple blogs for different users, it is best deployed as a single, multi-user blog that can be tweaked and

> **WordPress is one example of blogging software that you can install on your own site and fine tune to match templates and styles used with your other pages.**

WordPress is a popular alternative to Blogger that can be installed on your own site.

customised even more thoroughly than Blogger because it also allows you the ability to install more extensions on your own server.

SOCIAL NETWORKING AND TAGGING

Social networking as a concept far predates the web, with its origins lying in the work of social scientists such as Georg Simmel, W. Lloyd Warner and Elton Mayo in the first part of the twentieth century. Such theorists began to consider the ways in which interactions between individuals created complex effects that amounted to more than their roles as individuals. Social networking is not simply the creation of traditional organisations (workplace, church, government), but includes also the ties between actors within a network; this becomes particularly important for the distribution of information.

Various analysts have emphasised the relatively small number of so-called strong ties that we can make as individuals (usually estimated at around 150 or so connections). Beyond this, it simply becomes too much effort for us to maintain communication. However, in recent years the importance of 'weak' ties between individuals and groups has come to be seen as just – if not sometimes more – important. If a group of friends do everything together, then the opportunities for sharing information become relatively limited because they will tend to know the same things. Across a network of weak ties, however, social networking becomes invaluable for distributing and sharing new experiences and data, which is why the phenomenon has become so important on the web.

Although social networking sites are a relatively recent appearance in terms of their name, computer mediated communities have played a significant role online since the early days of ARPANET and **Usenet** in the 1970s. The move from these general online communities to ones that explicitly drew upon existing social networks and friendships began in the mid-1990s with sites such as Friends Reunited and SixDegrees.com allowing users to build up lists of friends – either already known or attracted on the basis of interests listed in profiles.

Between 2002 and 2004, sites which also allowed greater control over content started to attract a huge number of members, including MySpace, Bebo and Facebook (the last starting as a college community network for the US, only opening up to the wider world in 2006). Shortly afterwards, sites such as LinkedIn and Plaxo began to employ social networking techniques to link business and professional users.

The popularity of social networking sites increased in the early years of this century with the introduction of MySpace, Bebo and Facebook among others.

The numbers of users creating accounts on these sites can be staggering: MySpace passed 100 million by the middle of 2006, and although a significant number of these were also inactive by mid-2008 it was estimated to have more than 110 million active users. Facebook follows most closely, with more than 60 million active users (and twice that many registered accounts), and is the sixth most visited site in the USA according to comscore.com.

Production uses of social networking

Obviously, millions of people are using social networking sites for a variety of reasons – to communicate with friends, share music and video or locate professionals in related fields.

MySpace is one of the most popular social networking sites online.

Here, however, we shall concentrate on some of the ways in which these sites can be employed by web producers as an adjunct or alternative to a main website.

In the first instance, sites such as MySpace and Facebook offer another way of creating and distributing content. MySpace in particular has become an extremely important way for new bands to distribute music, for example, while if you wish to set up a discussion forum then creating a group in Facebook could be a better option than setting up one in your own web space. In both instances, the large number of potential users can be a useful way of generating traffic.

These are relatively simple means of using social network sites to generate content, but Facebook in particular has also begun to generate a thriving industry for web developers via the use of its API (application programming interface). The Facebook platform, launched in 2007, allowed third parties to create applets that could be added to members' pages, for example, for games, file sharing, learning languages, sharing photos, video and music, or creating interactive maps. The next section on mashups and APIs will look in more detail at some of the ways in which the Facebook API can be used to create a mini applet for sharing with other members.

As an adjunct to your main area of web production, social networking is also extremely useful in a number of ways, not least of which is that it provides a means of promoting your site to a wider sphere of users. This is probably the most mundane way to make use of these kinds of sites, however. More innovative uses for established social networking sites include providing customer support and connecting with experts, and also collaborative working and preparation: as a cross between instant messaging and email, the private messaging systems on these sites are often more immediate than email (as well as being less exposed to

> **As well as using social networking to connect with friends and colleagues, web producers can employ such sites to generate their own content.**

spam), but also keep a record of any important decisions.

So far, we have concentrated on making use of existing social networking sites, but for the more ambitious there is also the possibility of building a social network. The next chapter considers adding social networking features to a content management system in some detail, but there are various packages available that allow web producers to create such networks. Some, such as DynaPortal (www.dynaportal.com) are very much aimed at the corporate market, but one alternative for small-scale developers is to consider KickApps (www.kickapps.com). This is available in two versions: one is free to use, but is supported by advertising, while the other will display no third-party advertising if you pay a usage-based fee.

KickApps is an interesting example of Web 2.0 software created for deployment on different sites. It is run as a web application, on a software as a service (SaaS) platform that is hosted and managed from KickApps's own servers. As such, there is no software required for installation: instead, after signing up and choosing a pricing plan, customisable profile pages are created for subscribers from which they can connect with other friends, exchange private messages, form groups or display favourite media and feeds. A range of other widgets also exist for sharing such things as photos and videos, again hosted on the KickApps server but directed to your own URL.

Folksonomies and collaborative tagging

When web pages began to proliferate in the early 1990s, and before the rise of search engines, sites such as Yahoo! (whose name referred jokingly to 'yet another hierarchical officious oracle') sought to offer some order to the chaos of the web by providing a range of links to interesting material. In its earliest form, Yahoo! began as Jerry Yang and David

Filo's Guide to the World Wide Web, effectively a list of bookmarks to their favourite sites. As the lists became too long, they organised them into categories and then subcategories, creating a hierarchical directory of links through which visitors could browse.

The directory approach worked well for a while, but the increasing number of sites meant that it was impossible to keep track of all the information appearing online. Before the rise and rise of Google (launched in 1998), a number of commercial search engines began to appear such as Lycos, Infoseek and Webcrawler. And yet although search engines soon became ubiquitous, the lack of human intervention always meant that results could be slightly random and the need to discriminate between links meant there was always a place for more personal recommendations.

Yet the traditional approach to organising information via directories represents a significant bottleneck. When only a few experts determine what is relevant, the vast majority of websites simply cannot be scrutinised – and the real needs of visitors may be overlooked.

In 2003, the launch of the site delicious. com (formerly del.icio.us) introduced the concept of social bookmarking, followed quickly by others such as Furl, Simpy and Digg. Social bookmarking allowed for sites to be saved as public lists, and with the related concept of tagging meant that visitors could also enter their own searchable keywords for other users. The flat-file rather than hierarchical nature of tagging provided for much faster categorisation of online content than traditional subject organisation, with the advantage over search engines that the significance of a web page is determined by people who understand that content.

In 2007, Thomas Vander Wal coined the term 'folksonomy' to refer to this method

> In contrast to traditional ways of organising information via directories and web taxonomies, social tagging or folksonomies works from the bottom up, relying on multiple users to identify what type of content is being displayed.

of 'ad hoc labelling', defining it as 'the result of personal free tagging of information and objects (anything with a URL) for one's own retrieval' (http://www.vanderwal.net/folksonomy.html), done in a social context for sharing with others. While immensely popular, tagging and folksonomy are not without their critics: while visitors may understand the content of a page, their own personal interpretations may result in inconsistent and contradictory tags – not forgetting that spelling mistakes may make plenty of tags redundant. However, as with a considerable amount of other Web 2.0 practices, because tags are user-generated they are cheaper to implement than traditional taxonomies and do offer one valuable means of organising information on a site.

For web producers wishing to implement some form of tagging on their site, there are several options open. Two very popular options are to use the Add This or Share This buttons, available at www.addthis.com and sharethis.com. These create one button for several social tagging/networking links or feeds, and once you have registered for an account you can click the links on each site to generate the code needed to copy it onto your own web pages. Some content management systems such as Joomla! and Drupal also have plug-ins that can be integrated into sites: these CMSs also have some fairly sophisticated add-ons for creating such things as tag clouds, which provide a visual representation of tags or searches across a site.

Alternatively, it is possible to add manually the code for different tagging sites. Although this is more laborious, it does have the advantage of allowing greater control over what social bookmarking sites are linked to, as well as probably loading a little faster. An example of the code required to add a delicious link is as follows:

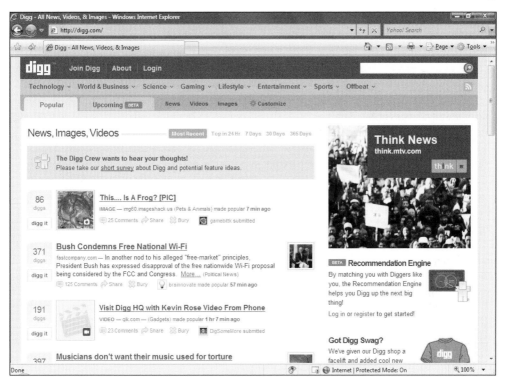

Digg, like delicious, is a **social tagging** site for sharing content and links easily with others.

```
<a href="http://delicious.com/save"
    onclick="window.open('http://delicious.
    com/save?v=5&amp;noui&amp;jump=
    close&amp;url='+encodeURIComponent
    (location.href)+'&amp;title='+encode
    URIComponent(document.title),
    'delicious','toolbar=no,width=550,
    height=550'); return false;"> Bookmark
    this on Delicious</a>
```

When users click the link, it will be added to their delicious.com bookmarks.

MASHUPS AND APIs

While there is no doubt that the technical end of programming web applications is a very complex task, getting these to work with your websites is becoming simpler with each passing month. Technologies such as Ajax, a combination of JavaScript and XML used by many of the Google APIs among others, means that it is now possible to take sample code and plug-ins from one site and create something extremely sophisticated without too much programming.

In this section, we will look at how to create an application for Facebook using mashups from online sites such as Popfly, as well as taking just one of the many APIs available from Google, in this case Maps, and adding it to your site. The key is being able to use information from more than one source (your photos on one site, your friend lists on another, a geographical location) and bundle them into one easy-to-use page that can be hosted elsewhere.

Because so many of the companies and sites that are driving the Web 2.0 revolution have made their programming interfaces freely available, including Google, YouTube, eBay and Flickr, a new breed of editor is emerging to take advantage of them. Mashup editors such as

Dapper, AlchemyPoint and Yahoo! Pipes feed through content from sources all around the world wide web to your site.

Web 2.0 widgets and mashups

One of the advantages of the Web 2.0 approach to design is that it allows visitors to a site to customise it according to their own requirements. A widget is a code that is portable – that is it can be transferred across to more or less any HTML web page. It also tends to be compact, making it fast when installed on a page or blog. A related concept is the mashup, a hybrid application that takes data from more than one source, such as weather reports from around the world, and creates them into one tool for display on a page.

Examples of widgets include: Google Gadgets such as clocks, maps, translators and an aquarium that can be added to your page (www.

google.com/ig/directory?synd=open); Yahoo! Widgets such as stock tickers and mini games (widgets.yahoo.com); and Microsoft Gadgets such as photos, messenger displays and weather reports – these being slightly different in that they sit on the Vista desktop but, in most cases, draw data from the web.

These particular examples tend to be designed for a particular site (iGoogle, My Yahoo! or Microsoft Live), but it is also possible to find a range of more general widgets at sites such as Widgetbox.com and SpringWidgets.com. Many of the widgets listed on these sites are Ajax-powered, making them compact and compatible with most web pages. These sites often allow you to customise your chosen widget (for example, changing the colour of the widget, its title and any other relevant parameters), and then a script is generated which you can copy and paste into your web page. Sometimes this runs simply as a JavaScript in the client browser,

Widgetbox is one of several sites for adding applets or widgets to your own pages.

at other times it is hosted on a third-party web server but, in general, appears seamlessly on your website.

When it comes to creating mashups, some popular sites include Yahoo! Pipes (pipes.yahoo.com), Dapper (www.dapper.net) and AlchemyPoint (www.orch8.net/ap/index.html). Such sites work by aggregating feeds from multiple sources to generate a single chunk of code that can be copied to your site. What is most useful about such sites for the general web developer is that they often employ an extremely easy to use visual interface: with Yahoo! Pipes, for example, you drag modules (such as search queries or Flickr photos) into a design area before linking them together.

For example, if you wish to find pictures of cats on Flickr, you enter this search query into a module and then link it to what is called a Pipe Output. Once a Pipe is created, it can be used to power an RSS feed or a widget on your website, with the source code hosted on Yahoo! servers.

Mashups in Popfly

One fun and fairly simple example of building some quite complex mashups and applications is Microsoft's Popfly (www.popfly.com). At the time of writing, this is in beta stage (and, if a truly Web 2.0 application, may always remain that way, although it is unlikely that Microsoft would remain happy with that state of affairs) and available for free. You will need a Microsoft Live account to make use of the site (available if you use Hotmail or Messenger, for example), but joining the site is extremely straightforward.

Popfly makes use of a wide range of open standards – such as XHTML and Ajax – as well as Microsoft's proprietary technologies – most notably the Silverlight graphics engine – to create its innovative interface. By dragging and dropping components within the browser, Popfly enables users to create 2D games, build mashups mixing content from other sites, design web pages, and create other web gadgets that can be hosted elsewhere such as in Facebook.

The principle behind creating mashups in Popfly is that of using blocks: blocks are visual representations of collections of code or resources. For example, one block could represent a set of photos and another block the code that creates a rotating carousel in a browser: dragging links between these two blocks will make a mashup that displays those photographs in the carousel. The visual design environment then allows developers to modify properties and change the appearance of elements as they are added to the applet.

The site is fairly flexible even without any knowledge of programming, but with some JavaScript it is possible to refine any mashups that you create within Popfly. Selecting the advanced view in the program displays the JavaScript editor which Popfly uses to call different blocks, and which can be edited directly to fine tune applets. One of the real virtues of Popfly's approach is that the huge number of blocks – essentially pre-configured code libraries for such things as playing videos, displaying stock graphs, or adding maps – provide an extensive collection of tools and utilities that can be incorporated into a mashup. To get the most out of the program, however, understanding JavaScript is a definite advantage.

Once a mashup has been created, it is hosted on the Popfly site and can be shared, generating customisable HTML that provides a link to the applet. You can then make this available on your website, blog or social networking site.

> Popfly is a good example of the new breed of web programming tools that is relatively simple and fun to use.

Working with the Facebook API

The Facebook API was launched in 2006 as a means for third-party developers to create applications for the site. While we have concentrated on a quick and easy route

WALKTHROUGH ▶

Creating a mashup in Popfly

1 While you can create a Facebook application from scratch, it's easier to use a site such as Popfly which allows you to create applications without coding that can then be integrated into your profile. Here, we will draw up sample images that can be mapped onto a rotating sphere, using third-party graphics or your own photos from Facebook.

2 Popfly applications are called mashups, and you begin making one of these by clicking the Create, Mashup link. This loads the Popfly developer, with a series of building blocks (code objects) that can be dragged onto the design surface. Each block can be modified to make it act as you want, and then linked to other blocks to build a complete application.

▶▶

3 In this instance we drag the Live Image Search block into the design surface and then click the wrench next to it to modify its properties. This zooms into the block and lists elements that can be changed (such as type and number of images). When you have finished this, click the wrench again to return to the main screen.

4 The next step is to set up a rotating sphere that will display the images: find the Photosphere block and drag this into the design surface so that it is displayed alongside your first block. Click once on the Live Image block and once on the Photosphere block to join them, and your basic application has been created.

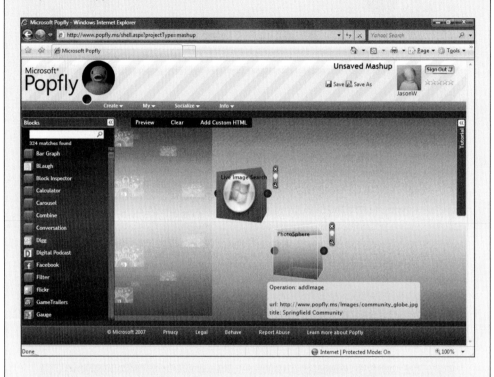

5 You can preview your application by clicking the link at the top of the design surface, and save it by clicking Save above this in the top panel. To view your project once it has been saved, click My then Projects which will display any work you have on Popfly. The last step is to share it so that Facebook users can access it.

▶▶

6 After clicking the Share link, you will see a screen where you can enter details about your project and also, under the heading Publish, an option to provide a link to it on Facebook. Select this and click Post. Once you have logged into Facebook, you will see a link to the new application under your Profile.

using Popfly, there is also a great deal of documentation for constructing an app from scratch in PHP at developers.facebook.com.

To begin working with applications in Facebook, first of all you need to set up your account to work with the right tools. To do this, click the link Developers at the bottom of the screen and then the link Get Started. Next, click Add Facebook Developer Application to include this in the list under your profile.

The last step is to get people using your application (in this case adding the mashup in the following walkthrough). To do this, on the Developer page select your application and click the Share button at the top of the screen. Select Send a Message to start communicating with friends – once five of them have added it to their profile, you can click the Submit Application to share more widely.

Google tools and Google APIs

For many web users, Google is most famous as a search engine, although for a great many users it also provides a range of invaluable services such as email (Gmail), document editing (Google Docs) and map finders (Google Maps). For web developers, Google is also increasingly important as one of the largest providers of APIs, programming interfaces that enable these and many more utilities to be incorporated into web pages and external sites.

The Google Open Source Programs Office (code.google.com/opensource/) is the hub for much of this development, and in recent years the company has released over a million lines of code and over a hundred projects, as well as providing a central location for other programmers to develop and host their own projects. The various products available from the code website include Ajax tools for creating websites and mashups for collating data from Google services, such as the general search engine, book search or maps; full APIs that are more difficult to use for the beginner, but provide access to many more Google offerings such as its calendar tools or the SketchUp 3D program; and gadgets, mini-applications created

in HTML and JavaScript that can be run in a web page.

Some of the web services offered by Google that offer greater or lesser degrees of integration into a website via tools or APIs include:

- **Google Data API**   A standard protocol for reading and writing data on the web, which uses Atom or RSS syndication formats to share data between different sites and lies behind many of the other Google services.
- **Blogger API**   Using this, you may use other web applications to view and update entries made to a blog.
- **Gadgets API**   Gadgets are HTML and JavaScript applets that can be embedded in other applications and web pages, and this API uses the Google Gadgets Editor to help you construct applets more quickly.
- **Ajax Language API**   This enables developers to detect and translate blocks of text using Google translation services.
- **Google Analytics**   With Analytics, you can gather, view and analyse information about your website: a code snippet is inserted into the page and then sent to Google servers, which in turn generate a number of reports on site activity.
- **Calendar APIs and Tools**   An API for adding web calendars that can be generated from events databases stored on a third-party website.
- **Document List Data API**   Allows users to view and search through documents created using Google Docs, which is itself a valuable web application for creating word documents, spreadsheets and presentations.
- **Google Earth API**   Using this, developers can plug 3D maps and globes into their web pages.
- **Google Maps API**   This provides customisable maps from the popular Google Maps website. The related Static Maps API allows you to embed a map without requiring any dynamic scripts.
- **Google Mashup Editor**   This is an Ajax development framework to quickly create

WALKTHROUGH ▶

Adding a mashup to Facebook

1 In your profile under posted items, you will see a link to any applications created with a third-party site, such as Popfly: click this link to get the URL. You will need to add it as an application within Facebook. Then click Post to add the item to your profile so that you can start to work with it.

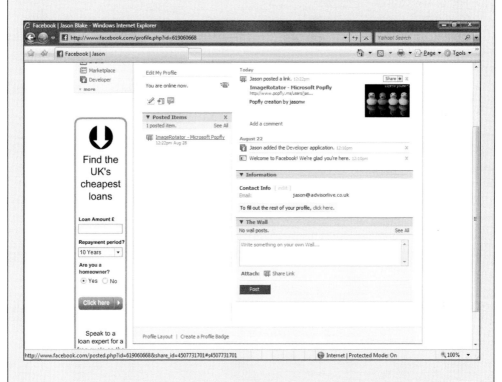

2 Next, select the Developer link under Applications on the left-hand side of the screen. From here, you will see a list of applications that you are working on – which is currently empty. To get started, click the Set Up New Application button at the top of the screen, which will load the page to start adding necessary details.

▶▶

3 On the New Application page, you will see the various details that you can begin entering to set up your application for others to share. You have to enter a name for your application, as well as a support email and check that you have read the terms of using the Facebook Platform. Once you have done this as a minimum, click Submit.

4 To continue work at any time, from the Developer page click See My Apps and then select the edit link above your application. This will reload a very similar page to the New Application one, and in here you will need to enter the URL of your third-party mashup under the entry Installation Options, Post-Add URL.

5. Your application is now nearly ready to use on the Facebook platform. The final step comes when you click the link for your new applet: here you will see a button Add Application. Also, on this page are links to start discussions of the application (for example, if you want to add news of development) and reviews from other users.

6. When you click the Add Application button, this will display the add screen for that particular applet. To include this in your profile, you have to allow the application to know who you are, but other options such as adding a link to the left of the screen can be deselected. If you add information about your application, this will be available from the about page link.

web applications from other services, such as Google Maps.

- **Open Social** This API creates access to a social network's list of friends and feeds to make them accessible across other websites.
- **Google Talk for Developers** A tool to provide chat on your website.
- **YouTube Player Tools and API** A series of applets for incorporating YouTube videos onto a third-party site.

This is only a very small selection of the Google tools and APIs that are available to web producers, and we shall concentrate in more detail on using just one of them, the Google Maps API, to integrate with your site.

Using Google Maps

While plenty of people use this site (maps. google.co.uk) to find locations or look at satellite images of their own homes, it is also possible make use of these maps on your own website.

This is one of the many projects that make use of a Google API to provide services to different websites. With it web designers can add a map to any site so that visitors can view one or more locations. In addition, it is possible to display different types of information and it is even possible to create a mashup that is loaded onto the main Google Maps site.

As with the other APIs – such as Google Calendar or Blogger – this is free to use for end users, with certain restrictions. If you want to use a map commercially, or on a private website, you can sign up for a 30-day trial of Google Maps Enterprise. This allows users to view maps behind a firewall or with a paid subscription login, as well as providing extra features for such things as customer relations management and marketing support.

There is a lot to do even with the free version. As well as localising a map, it can be modified to respond to zooms and pans to find other places. Information windows can be added to provide visitors with updates, or markers and route lines shown to indicate positions or directions.

It is also possible to perform advanced functions such as geocoding (converting an address into latitude and longitude co-ordinates), or add a Google-powered local search engine to a site. If you really want to try out your coding, it is even possible to create custom controls and add driving instructions to reach a location. However, these are beyond the scope of this section.

WORKING WITH WIKIS

Wikis first began to be developed in the mid-1990s as an easy way for multiple users to add and edit content, using a simple markup language that removed a great deal of complexity so that contributors could concentrate on adding material to a site. The name was given by Ward Cunningham to the software he invented after the fast bus service at Honolulu International Airport, emphasising the speed with which material can be added to a wiki site.

Wikis are designed from the ground up as collaborative software, but omit many of the features around user management that is familiar from other types of content management systems that will be discussed in the next chapter. This means that the vices and virtues of wikis are very closely intertwined, with any registered user able to edit the pages of any other contributor. The emphasis is always on simplicity of use, and this raises its own problems because moderation of content has to operate in a very different fashion

> **Wikis have become one of the simplest means to provide content management for multiple users.**

from traditional CMSs: it is not possible with a true wiki to restrict some users to certain types of page or content, and instead new strategies have to be developed to moderate content, as we shall see at the end of this chapter.

The most famous wiki is Wikipedia, which, at the time of writing, has some 2.5 million articles written and edited by more than 75,000 contributors. The software it is based on, MediaWiki, is completely open source and can be installed on any server running PHP and MySQL. This is the software we shall concentrate on in this section and it is available for download from www.mediawiki.org.

If you want to try out a wiki but cannot or do not want to install MediaWiki on your own server, one very useful alternative is to try out Wikispaces (www.wikispaces.com). This is a free service to the end user, funded by Google ads that appear in your wiki, and it is an excellent way to try out many of the features in this section. Wikispaces itself runs using proprietary rather than open-source software, but its format is very similar to the wikitext employed by MediaWiki.

MediaWiki markup

MediaWiki uses a simplified markup language based on XML and with various similarities to XHTML. An important point to remember is that wiki markup languages are not necessarily compatible, so if you decide to use software other than MediaWiki the examples shown here may not work. However, because Media Wiki drives Wikipedia, the version we cover here (sometimes referred to as MediaWiki Markup Language or wikitext) is generally the most extensive and most useful to learn.

If you have worked through the chapters on web design, then you will have no problem with this markup once you have grasped a few basic points. Most important with regard to the syntax is that a number of characters, or tokens, are reserved to create tags within MediaWiki. For example,

WALKTHROUGH▶

Adding a Google map to your site

1 To get started using Google Maps, you will need to sign up for an API key at code.google.com/apis/maps/ (you will need a Google account for this). Log in and click the Sign up . . . link, then enter your domain name (http://www.mysite.com) and click the Generate API Key button. This will create the key along with some sample code that can be pasted into an HTML file to create a basic map.

2 If you are familiar with hand-coding, study the 'Hello World' example at code.google.com/apis/maps/documentation/introduction.html. This will give you the essentials for fine-tuning your file in any number of ways. If, however, you simply want to make a few essential changes in order to customise your map, continue with the steps outlined here.

▶▶

3 The first thing you will want to do is to change the start location for your map (the sample code brings up a map of Stanford University). In the code in the head section, locate the entry map.setCenter and change the two co-ordinates after GLatLng to your new latitude and longitude entries. Now you have a new central location for your page.

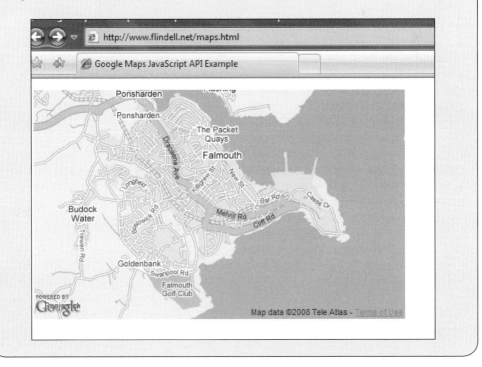

4 So far we have covered the basics of adding a map to your home page, but there is much more that you can do. For example, locations can provide additional information to visitors and, to include one of these windows, add the following line of code:

    map.openInfoWindow(map.getCenter(), document.createTextNode("Hello, world"));

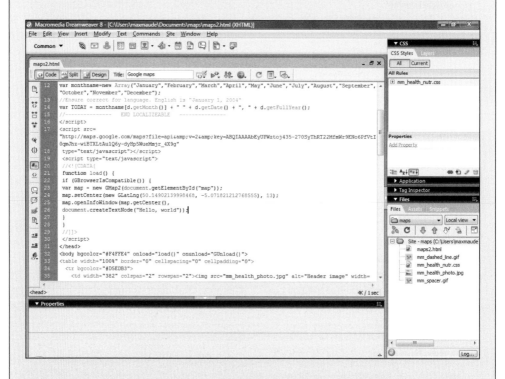

5 When you view Google Maps, you can see them via normal or satellite views. To change the view of your map from standard to satellite view, add the following line of code underneath the latitude/longitude co-ordinates:

    map.setMapType(G_SATELLITE_MAP);

Changing the instruction to G_HYBRID_MAP creates a combination of both views.

▶▶

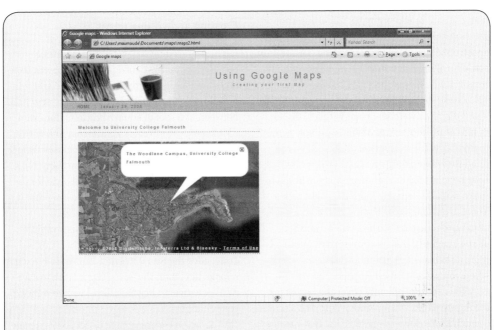

6. To create an overlay that allows you to zoom in and out of your map, or pan from side to side horizontally and vertically, add the line of code:

```
map.addControl(new GLargeMapControl());
```

If you use the instruction GsmallZoomControl instead, this inserts more discreet plus or minus buttons to control zoom levels.

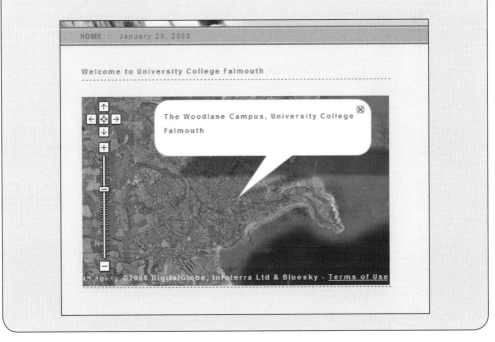

using square brackets creates either internal or external links, such as [my page], while sets of apostrophes are used for formatting. In addition, some html style tags such as <nowiki> (which removes wiki formatting) can be employed.

Once MediaWiki is installed on your server, it will display a welcome page with a number of tabs at the top: article obviously displays the main text, while discussion allows users and/or editors (depending on whether permissions have been set to allow anonymous postings) to make remarks separate from the main article. There are also tabs for the history of an article, or to watch the page (so you will be notified of any changes), but most important to our requirements is the edit tab, which you select when you wish to modify a page.

This section will only cover the basics for setting up pages within Media Wiki, but there is a much more extensive help manual at http://meta.wikimedia.org/wiki/Help:Contents.

Creating and editing pages

Getting started on a new page is extremely easy. Once you have navigated to a current page anywhere within MediaWiki, click the edit link or tab and simply type the title of your new page between two sets of square brackets, for example [[MyPage]]. This creates an internal link within MediaWiki that is set out with the tabs as listed above but without any content. Until anything is entered on this page, the default style for the program will show a red link indicating that it is empty of content.

For text, adding content consists of little more than typing in your copy. When this is done, click the Show Preview button to see what it looks like, then the Save Page button to save it. Alternatively, click the cancel link to remove your changes.

To begin editing a page or section of a page, click the edit tab in the top menu (this will load

An easy way to try out your own wiki is via Wikispaces.

==Definition==
{| align="right"
| __TOC__
|}
;Prosody
:The study or science of metre; the rules or laws of versification.

==Extended Definition==
An Internet keyword search for <i>prosody</i> will return a variety of results; many of the links generated by the search engine are likely to take web surfers to material linguistic or perhaps musical in nature, scattered among which would be some results relevant to the study of poetry. The linguistic usage of <i>prosody</i> denotes the rhythms and movements of speech, covering things such as intonation, tone and other phonological properties. It deals with small sound units such as phonemes and also with syllables. Musical prosody (the word in fact derives from the Greek <i>prosodia</i>, meaning "tune") runs along similar lines: it designates sound characteristics: for example, pitch, timbre and other acoustic factors that can be measured.

As a body of knowledge associated with poetry, <i>prosody</i> signifies "the study of verseform" (Preminger and Brogan 982)

Clicking edit anywhere in a wiki brings up the editing page where any user may change content.

the entire page), or the edit link next to a section. This will load the editor for that page, comprising a basic text editor and several icons at the top of the screen. For essentials such as inserting subheadings, basic text formatting or creating links, these icons will be sufficient. However, more sophisticated formatting requires tags to be inserted into the body of the text.

The starting point for formatting is to begin adding section headings, which is an extremely simple task. While some entries in a wiki will be very short and not require subheadings, section headings (also known as level 2 headlines) are useful in longer documents. As well as being helpful in terms of formatting the page, these headings are also used by MediaWiki to generate an automatic table of contents (TOC).

To insert a section heading, click the large A icon above the text editor. Alternatively, type two sets of double equals (=) marks around the heading text, for example == My Section Heading ==. It is also possible to generate level 3 and level 4 headlines simply by adding more equals marks, such as ===My level 3 heading===.

A table of contents (TOC) is useful for navigating within longer pages, and is created using the tag __TOC__, for example using the following code:

```
{| align="right"
| __TOC__
|}
```

Adding this code will automatically generate a linked table of contents in a blue box and, in the above example, will align it on the right-hand side of the page. Although you can simply use the tag __TOC__ by itself, this example also demonstrates some other features of wikitext, notably the use of pipes (|) to separate different elements of a section of code, and the use of curly brackets to identify more extended instructions that must be grouped together.

Working with text and links

The presentation of elements such as text, links and tables is governed by the MediaWiki cascading style sheets, which are then applied when certain symbols or tags are used on a page, with the following providing the essential markup for formatting text in the MediaWiki:

- **Bold**　click the B icon in the toolbar or type two sets of three apostrophes, e.g. '''bold'''.
- **Italics**　click on the I icon in the toolbar or type two sets of two apostrophes, e.g. ''italics''.
- **Bold and italics**　Type two sets of five apostrophes, e.g. '''''bold and italics'''''.
- **Unordered lists**　Type an asterisk (*) to create a bullet point in an unordered list. Use two asterisks to nest one list inside another.
- **Ordered lists**　Type the hash (#) key to create an ordered list. As with unordered lists, these can be nested within other lists.
- **Definition list**　On a new line, type a semi-colon before the word that is to be defined, with a colon before the line that defines the word. For example:

;XHTML
:eXtensible Hypertext Markup Language

Note: The colon indents a line; using two or three colons at the beginning of a line will indent it two or three times. In addition to these basic tags, the use of the tilde (˜) symbol will insert some pre-defined styles:

- Three tildes gives any signature that has been specified in preferences: ˜˜˜
- Four tildes provides the signature plus the date and time: ˜˜˜˜
- Five tildes gives the date and time alone: ˜˜˜˜˜

The wiki markup for linking to other pages within the MediaWiki is very simple, being the same as for creating a page: insert two pairs of square brackets around the title of the page you want to link to, for example [[MyPage]].

To link to an external site, click the External Link icon in the toolbar (the world image). Alternatively, type in a single set of square brackets with a title for your link containing the URL and a name for the link for example [http://www.producingforweb2.com Producing for Web 2.0]. This will insert the text in the second part of the brackets as a hyperlink. If you simply wish to include a URL as a hyperlink, enter it without any square brackets.

Creating tables

As with HTML, you can use tables in MediaWiki to present in, with the code for a basic table looking like the following:

```
{|
|-
! header 1
! header 2
|-
| row 1, cell 1
| row 1, cell 2
|-
| row 2, cell 1
| row 2, cell 2
|}
```

This would create a table that looks like this:

Header 1	Header 2
row 1, cell 1	row 1, cell 2
row 2, cell 1	row 2, cell 2

Unlike HTML encoding, which uses <tr> and <td> elements, tables in wikitext simply use pipes to compose a table, with rows indicated by a dash and the beginning and end of a table marked out with curly brackets. In the example above, header data, which is separate from the main data contained within the cell, is indicated using an exclamation mark rather than a pipe.

Using HTML style attributes and properties

(some of which have been deprecated in HTML 4.01 and XHTML, but are still valid in wikitext), it is also possible to create quite sophisticated effects, as with the following example:

```
{| width="75%" cellpadding="0"
    cellspacing="0" align="center"
|- style="background:black; color:white;"
! header 1
! header 2
! header 3
|- align="center"
| row 1, cell 1
| row 1, cell 2
| row 1, cell 3
|- align="center" style="background:gray;
    color:white;"
| row 2, cell 1
| row 2, cell 2
| row 2, cell 3
|- align="center"
| row 3, cell 1
| row 3, cell 2
| row 3, cell 3
|- align="center" style="background:gray;
    color:white;"
| row 4, cell 1
| row 4, cell 2
| row 4, cell 3
|}
```

A table created with this code would look like the following:

Header 1	Header 2	Header 3
row 1, cell 1	row 1, cell 2	row 1, cell 3
row 2, cell 1	row 2, cell 2	row 2, cell 3
row 3, cell 1	row 3, cell 2	row 3, cell 3
row 4, cell 1	row 4, cell 2	row 4, cell 3

Looking in more detail at the code for this table, we see that the formatting for the table as a whole, after the first pipe, sets it to 75 per cent of the width of the browser window, and removes spacing and padding between and within each cell. The row elements, indicated by a hyphen, set alternate text and background colours for each row, with black for the header background.

Images and media

MediaWiki can handle a range of multimedia files, although the default list of gif, jpeg, ogg and png files has to be changed by modifying the includes/DefaultSettings.php file that you will find in the MediaWiki installation directory. In addition, before images and other media files can be added to pages they must be uploaded to the site. To do this, click the Upload button in the top menu. From here you can browse to a file on your hard drive, enter a description of the file (as well as an alternative name) and then click the Upload File button. This is also the same place where you can search to see whether a file has already been uploaded into MediaWiki.

To insert an image into a page after it has been uploaded, click the Embedded image icon on the toolbar and enter the name of the file stored on MediaWiki. Alternatively, you can add an image using the same syntax as for internal links, that is double square brackets, [[ ]], for example: [[Image:MyPic.jpg]].

To align an image on the left or right, use the same code as above for a table of contents, but the image link in place of TOC, for example:

```
{| align="right"
| [[Image:MyPic.jpg]]
|}
```

The default image link will insert an image at full size, but there are several arguments that you can pass to this embedded image, including resizing it and adding a caption, as in the following:

```
[[Image:MyPic.jpg|thumb|200px|This is my
    image as added to MediaWiki]]
```

The first part of the tag is obviously the file type (image) and file name. The next part tells MediaWiki to display this as a thumbnail image which will go to the full size file when selected. Finally, the last part of the tag is a caption that is displayed at the bottom of the blue box that surrounds this thumbnail when it is displayed on a page.

Tracking updates

As a wiki is open to all registered users to edit, quite a lot of activity can take place on a site and MediaWiki provides fairly simple means to keep track of updates. The History tab at the top of each page shows all edits and updates to a page (while the default recent updates list shows them for an entire wiki). It is possible to reduce or expand the number of edits displayed by clicking a number from 20 to 500 at the top of the page, which will change the list of entries that appear in the main screen. When creating or changing a page, it is possible to identify any changes as a minor edit. The advantage of doing this (when just tidying up a page, for example) is that minor changes can be ignored when viewing Recent Updates.

To view an older version of a page, simply select it from the list of entries under History. To compare different versions, select a radio button on the left- and right-hand side of the central column and then click the Compare Selected Versions buttons. This will display each version side by side.

Moving a page is sometimes necessary – for example, when a page has been misnamed. To do this, click the Move tab and in the field in the middle of the page provide a new title for that page. Moving a page should move all discussions and history to the new title, with the old page creating a redirect link. However, it can sometimes cause problems in that searches or old links will not correctly redirect; this feature should therefore be used with caution.

If you have done a considerable amount of work on a page, or engaged in discussion about its contents, you may want to keep track of any future changes. Clicking on the Watch tab will add this to a list of pages that will appear in bold when you select the Recent Updates menu option. In addition, you can set up MediaWiki to email you when changes are made. To remove the page from your watch list, click on the Unwatch tab.

To change your preferences for the site, select the Preferences option in the default wiki menu. In the page that appears you can select a number of options:

- **User data**   This is the most useful: if you enter an email address (and confirm this), you can set up MediaWiki to inform you via email when any changes are made to pages that you are watching. Entering a real name will also change your signature to your actual name when this is added to any pages.
- **Skin**   This changes the appearance of MediaWiki with a range of pre-installed skins.
- **Files**   This controls how images are displayed on preview pages.
- **Date format**   Select how dates are presented on pages.
- **Time zone**   Enter a plus or minus number to offset the time displayed from GMT.
- **Editing**   This includes a number of options for being able to edit pages on the site, the most useful of which are to mark all edits as minor unless indicated otherwise (useful if you engage in a considerable amount of tidying up of pages), and to show the Preview Page button.
- **Recent changes and stubs**   Allows you to determine how much text has to be on a stub (incomplete article) for it to be displayed, as well as how many updated pages are shown by default.
- **Search**   Sets the defaults for searches.
- **Misc**   Extra settings for displaying broken links, tables of contents and paragraph/heading settings.

For more information and updates on Web 2.0 tools, visit www.producingforweb2.com/web-20-tools.

CHAPTER 7

Content management systems

MediaWiki is an open and (relatively simple) content management system that allows multiple users to contribute to an online site in a relatively straightforward manner. In this chapter, we will look in much more detail at how to use such a system, considering what it entails and using a piece of open-source software, Joomla!, to create a much more complex site.

CMS PRINCIPLES

A content management system (CMS), as the name indicates, handles different types of content, although the core simplicity of this concept can mask a wide variety of nuances. In particular, an effective CMS should also be able to deal with multiple users in different roles.

The site Enterprise Content Management distinguishes the following three principal factors in defining a CMS: (a) content, the unit of information that is to be handled electronically, whether text, image, video, etc.; (b) content management, the rules, processes and workflows whereby this content is handled; and (c) the system, the tool or combination of tools that will provide the desired output, such as a website, brochure, printed magazine and so on.

> A CMS is a tool that enables a variety of (centralised) technical and (de-centralised) non technical staff to create, edit, manage

and finally publish (in a number of formats) a variety of content (such as text, graphics, video, documents, etc.), whilst being constrained by a centralised set of rules, processes and workflows that ensure coherent, validated electronic content. (www.contentmanager.eu.com/history.htm)

Convergence – in technology the movement of different systems and media towards one product or format that combines the advantage of all of them (such as with multimedia publishing across multiple platforms – television, computer, mobile phone, etc.) – holds out the promise of a single CMS that could cope with the demands of different users and media. In practice, the requirements of different electronic formats and different users have led to a multitude of content management systems, many concentrating on particular niche applications. The perfect CMS (the one that satisfies all requirements in all circumstances) does not exist and probably cannot exist, at least in the foreseeable future.

Background and applications

The term CMS is commonly used to refer to any electronic system, but it is worth pointing out that the final output for a CMS may not simply be for the web, such systems commonly being employed where multiple users have to produce output for different media such as print or broadcast. Here, understandably, we will concentrate on online systems.

The *CMS Review* currently lists about 200 commercial offerings and approximately 80 open-source systems available. In addition, many ISPs have transformed themselves in recent years into Application Service Providers (ASPs), using one of the many CMS applications available to offer services to end users for everything from creating simple web pages to online shopping portals. The value of using a CMS is that the technical end of constructing a website is separated from the task of providing content, allowing non-technical users to concentrate on getting media online.

It is a little facetious to claim that content management systems are as old as content itself (as the CMS wiki states), but the principles of library management and classification do give some insight into the workflows and organisations of a CMS. An electronic CMS will typically organise different assets into categories or sections (a system which has its roots in bibliographic cataloguing and classification systems), and also distinguish the rights and abilities of different users, both for content creation and for end users. Content management deals with content creation for the producer, content delivery for the consumer or end user, and general information retrieval (such as organising and searching) whether in print or electronic form.

An important principle behind the modern online CMS is that of the application framework. This is a series of standard rules and programming procedures implemented in software that promote standard structures for programs. The virtue of this approach is that because developers know the underlying structure of a system, they do not have to create a whole application from scratch but can work instead to build modifications or plug-ins that extend the features and functions of an existing

> **A CMS makes use of an application framework, a set of rules and programming procedures that enable developers to extend the capabilities of the CMS via plug-ins.**

CMS. This has been particularly important in the development and extension of open-source systems, whereby the source code is freely available and a wide range of plug-ins can be rapidly developed to provide functions that were not originally conceived by the CMS developers.

One specialised form of a CMS is a *course* (as opposed to *content*) management system, sometimes referred to as an LMS (Learning Management System), which emphasises such things as online assessment, the provision of e-learning resources and training resource management (facilities, instructors, equipment, etc.). Such packages include OLAT (Online Learning and Training), WebCT and eFront e-learning system. Strictly speaking, they are beyond the remit of this chapter, but common content management systems such as Drupal, Moodle and Mambo/Joomla! have been used to provide e-learning systems.

Types of CMS

There are hundreds of content management systems available today. It is important to remember that while some systems are designed to handle hundreds, even thousands of users (as consumers if not producers of content), others are essentially sole-author systems that enable a single user to get material online as quickly as possible. Some of the key distinctions in the current market are as follows:

- **Proprietary versus open-source** One primary distinction is between proprietary systems (usually paid for in one way or another with licences per processor and with source code not available for modification) and open-source systems (where the source code is always open for modification, and software is typically free to the end user although sometimes it will

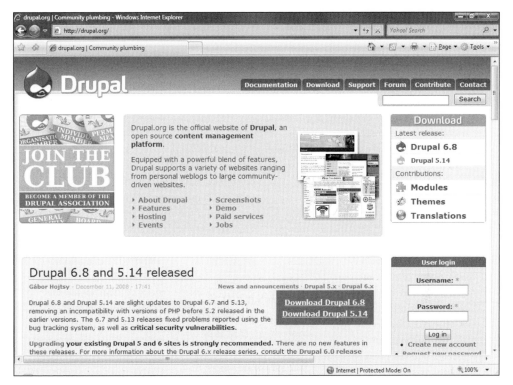

Drupal is one of many popular open-source CMSs.

be sold as part of a package). Proprietary systems are designed to serve thousands of web pages and millions of hits per day where reliability of service is key and the provider will act as a guarantor of that service. Free open-source systems may hide additional costs of training, consultancy and hardware infrastructure, but the best now compete with proprietary systems in terms of serving large numbers of users.

■ **Enterprise versus micro**   An enterprise CMS is designed to service large numbers of content producers and often a wide variety of digital assets; such systems can be complex and difficult to administer. A micro system, by contrast, simplifies the management of assets and is designed to be administered by a small group of users, or even an individual.

■ **Web publishing**   Although many systems may be used for different media formats, the majority of CMSs available on the market are employed to produce web pages, pulling information from a database that is then formatted for delivery on a website.

■ **CMS 'Lite'**   A term used to refer to multi-user content delivery systems that tend to focus on one element of online publishing, such as blogging software (WordPress, for example) or a wiki (MediaWiki). The virtue of such systems is that they are often extremely simple to use, although they are often limited in terms of their customisability or user management.

A CMS requires a set of standard technologies in order to function: a database, a software framework employing a scripting or programming language, and a server to deliver pages to the end user. Proprietary systems may run on Microsoft's .NET framework and server, but the majority of open-source systems use the SQL database MySQL, and the scripting language PHP.

User management and roles

Although the core function of a CMS is to handle content, as the name suggests, managing users is at least as important: without users any CMS is redundant regardless of the quality of content, and so this raises questions about the assignment of roles and usability.

The precise nature of user roles will differ from CMS to CMS, but the following may be taken as generic:

- **Guest/anonymous** If a site is open to the public, this group may include casual browsers or dedicated users who have a very restricted role in terms of content management. A key issue here is that information available to anonymous users should be clearly indicated and seamless at the point of delivery, and so a CMS will hide categories and sections of a site that are only available to registered users to prevent the frustration of clicking links only to find content is unavailable or to meet an error message.
- **Registered** The core group for content consumers; on some systems registered users will have only a limited role to play in content production, while on other, less hierarchical, systems they may have access to all features of a site.
- **Authors** These users will typically be able to produce content, but will be restricted to their own material and unable to edit the work of others. They may also have to submit this material for moderation by another user group.
- **Editors/publishers** Some systems distinguish various levels of content production, and this group will be able to modify content produced by others as well as to publish material onto a site.
- **Admins** Administrators will be responsible for running a CMS, in some

cases having very little involvement in content production other than moderation and concentrating instead on technical issues. Many systems, but not all, have a back and front end, the latter available to a wider group of users while access to the former is restricted to admins.

While this list describes some generic user group categories, classification of user roles can also take two extremely different directions. On the one hand, some CMSs (mainly proprietary ones) offer the ability to create micro groups, useful when members involved in a particular project may need to share restricted information, for example. On the other, those systems which may be considered as Web 2.0 applications, such as wikis, will tend to make no or few distinctions between users: simplicity of use and the ability to produce/edit content easily is more important than user management.

It is also worth considering another category of user: unwanted groups. These include spammers, hackers and disruptive users. For the first two of these, many CMSs will have some form of protection in place, although this requires constant monitoring; for the last group, this requires different types of protocol and interaction (for example banning users who consistently break the rules of a site).

Setting user groups raises questions of access and moderation, which will be discussed more thoroughly in the next chapter. Obviously if groups are employed access to some areas of a CMS will be restricted to different groups, while certain tasks may be moderated, requiring approval before material is posted to a site, for example. This does raise a difficulty for user experience, however, in that users expect information to be available immediately and so a CMS must provide feedback (usually a message informing them that moderation is taking place). In addition, this places an extra

> Managing users in a CMS is just as important as handling content, so that they can add, edit and publish material as appropriate.

burden on administrative groups who must be active. These issues, along with communication between users, are considered in greater detail in the section on workflows.

Finally, the definition of a CMS on page 165 emphasises the difference between technical and non-technical users. The majority of users on any site will fall into the latter group, and so a system must be as easy to use and as intuitive as possible for them.

Digital asset management

If a CMS must effectively handle users, ultimately this is so that they can exchange different types of content as efficiently as possible. Content will consist of all communication on a system, including messaging, but for issues surrounding digital asset management (**DAM**) we shall concentrate here on those materials which are published for public consumption.

DAM covers two related areas: the uploading, storing and cataloguing of an asset, by which we mean text, images, video and audio, as well as other forms of files and documents; and the protocols for downloading and maintaining those assets.

With regard to uploading, it is important to establish formats that can be used, and even the simplest asset on a site, text, can present its own problems. For example, the tendency of users to prepare documents in Word and then copy them to a site – while perfectly reasonable – can create difficulties in terms of formatting as Word inserts its own code. Many CMSs have developed tools to deal with this particular problem in recent years, but it must be said that none of them is immediately obvious to the non-technical user and this requires training and education. For other types of media such as images and video, formats have to be established and clear rules in place to ensure these are

complied with: the importance of such protocols is that they enable the presentation of content on the site to take place as smoothly as possible – obscure file formats (for example, videos that require additional codecs to be downloaded) can simply make consumers of a site believe that it is not working.

An important feature of DAM, and one that is handled more or less automatically by many CMSs, is indexing and searching. Site structure and planning will direct users to certain categories of information (such as galleries or news stories), but users of a site should also be able to access the specific information they are looking for and, in effect, bypass this structure. Nothing is more irritating for an end user than not being able to find information in the manner they require, and the fact that a CMS employs a database makes it easy to query records.

Automatic indexing, however, has its limitations, particularly when moving beyond text, and this is where metadata becomes important. Metadata, or 'data about data', describes an asset, for example information about an image type, its date, and keywords describing its content. Recent developments such as XML also mean that information about one piece of content can be passed between different pages and applications – for example data stored about an asset's creator can be linked to records about the creator more easily than before.

> Considering content such as images, video and audio as digital assets focuses attention on how these elements are managed on a website so they can be stored, catalogued and handled most effectively.

Workflow and messaging

The management of assets draws attention to the processes by which a CMS handles such content as well as users, that is the workflow. This is the sequence of operations required to achieve certain tasks which in turn may be modelled to provide assessments of future tasks.

On an abstract level, a workflow will often

be used to define the various functions, teams and projects involved in a task: for example, this may be the group of authors and editors/publishers (team) involved in creating specific content such as forums and articles (functions) for an issue of a projected journal (project). Another way of modelling such workflows is to consider input (material submitted), transformation rules and protocols in place (editing), and output (appearance of material on site). A workflow should also take into account some measure of effectiveness, which may be peer-review or the successful promotion of a feature. Finally, for an online CMS there will be other features of the workflow such as feedback for submissions and accessibility/Quality of Service (QoS).

One potential area of conflict between an effective workflow and user expectations arises between the requirements of a system to ensure levels of quality in published material and the fact that online users increasingly expect to see submissions appear immediately. If users make submissions and do not receive a more or less instant response, they can believe that the system is not working and so do not contribute in future. A CMS must therefore provide automatic responses that submissions have been received and, where moderation takes place, site admins/editors have an obligation to respond as quickly as possible. Furthermore, for ease of use you will probably benefit from certain areas on a site (such as forums, comments, blogs, etc.) which are more decentralised, not requiring moderation on the part of the admins.

A common workflow employed by many systems is that of authoring, editing and publishing. Authoring (creating content) should be as simple and efficient as possible, with editing and (possible) publication following on as quickly as possible, or at least feedback being returned to the content author rapidly. A

CMS must have an efficient communication system – usually email or some form of internal messaging – which informs admins when changes requiring authorisation take place.

This in turn draws attention to another feature of many CMSs which is the ability to send messages. Most users will not be on a site most of the time, and so emails will be the most efficient means of conveying information. However, to encourage a sense of community and participation in a site, an internal messaging system is vital, as a useful means to connect with other users. In addition, while the messaging system as part of a workflow will tend to focus on passing information between decentralised (non-technical) users and centralised (technical) admins, an important principle behind much Web 2.0 social networking is to use messaging systems in a decentralised fashion, allowing users to build networks between each other outside admin management. As this encourages a sense of ownership on the part of users, it is therefore important to allow them to take control of their own communication (for example by being able to block persistent abusers of a system).

Finally, the simple author/edit/publish workflow outlined above must be capable of handling and (if necessary) automating two further stages of content management, which is tracking multiple versions of content and archiving.

One common workflow used is that of authoring, editing and publishing, which defines different roles for users who contribute to or manage the various parts of a site.

SETTING UP A CMS

For the rest of this chapter we will concentrate on one CMS, Joomla! Part of the reason for this is familiarity (Joomla! is the package that runs the companion website), but also it is popular online, is well supported by a range of developers, and offers a compromise between simplicity of use and extended features. The core package, which can be downloaded from www.joomla.org, is relatively simple in terms of installation and adding documents, but it is also possible to extend the program in a number of ways, making it extremely customisable and flexible.

Joomla! developed out of Mambo when a number of developers decided to leave the Mambo project and set up their own content management system. Mambo had been sponsored by Miro International, a similar approach to that developed by Sun Microsystems which had built up StarOffice and OpenOffice, but an argument developed over how copyright would be assigned in Mambo.

Joomla! was set up as an open-source project. The initial release (version 1.0.x) was and remains completely compatible with Mambo, but the latest version (1.5.x) is a rewrite of the core elements of the program. It has been designed for a variety of purposes, such as creating online magazines, corporate websites, or community based portals, and the basic package is generally simple to install and use even for non-technical users. For a single-user site, it can be a little overwhelming, and web producers who wish to get content online as quickly as possible will be better off with a program such as WordPress considered in chapter 5. If you need to handle content from a number of users, however, and wish to produce something more adventurous, Joomla! is an extremely powerful application.

Content is handled via the browser, requiring no additional software to be downloaded onto a computer. The program is divided into two parts. The front end is where content is displayed and can be added, while a back end allows an administrator to manage such things as document organisation and users. Unlike some other CMSs, most users never need to see the admin panel, which helps to simplify the entire process of adding

> **Joomla! is a popular example of an open-source and free CMS that has built up a wide community with a huge number of plug-ins and modifications for a variety of tasks.**

material to a website. In addition, an extensive developer community means that there is a large number of add-ons for Joomla! which allow a website to be extended in interesting and innovative ways.

To run Joomla!, whether on a remote server or a local host, you will need the following software:

- PHP 4.2 or above,
- MySQL 3.23 or above, and
- Apache 1.3 or above.

If you are testing Joomla! on a local computer as a test site rather than a server, the simplest way to install these applications is to use XAMPP (see page 39). Throughout this chapter, we will refer to elements that deal with Joomla! 1.5.x, unless there are significant differences between this and version 1.0.x. Some extensions have not been rewritten to run natively on the latest release, and although the majority will run without problem using what is called a legacy mode, this cannot be guaranteed in all cases. For this reason, some users may wish to use the older version for the time being.

Although the rest of this chapter will concentrate on Joomla! as a sample CMS, the principles of content management that will be introduced apply to a much wider range of packages, and so core skills and principles are addressed rather than which particular button or link to use in every case.

Joomla! first encounters

Once Joomla! is installed on your remote server or the test site, opening a browser and typing in your domain name (http://localhost for a test site) will display the default version of the application.

WALKTHROUGH▶

Installing Joomla!

1   To run, Joomla! requires Apache web server, PHP and MySQL. The files from www.joomla.org must be uploaded to your site and then the executable file run through the browser. This first launches a pre-installation check which will ensure that your server is ready to run the package.

2   If everything checks out correctly, click the Next button to see the Joomla! licence, and then proceed to the first stage of installation. This requires a name for the server (usually localhost), as well as a user name and password for the MySQL database and names for the database itself and prefixes attached to tables. It is recommended that you install sample data as well to give you something to work with.

3 Clicking the Next button will ask you to confirm that the settings are correct. Click OK to begin actual software installation and, after this, you will see a page asking you to provide a name for your site.

4 When the site is up and running, it is important to enter admin details – name, password and email address – as these are necessary for you to access the administrative back end of your CMS and make modifications to the site. The final step is to delete the folder where you stored the installation files and refresh the page – Joomla! will not work until this final precautionary step is taken.

The Joomla! administrator

The default installation of Joomla! includes a link to the Administrator panel. Clicking this leads to the back end of the program, where the administrator will need to log in again (access to these features is restricted to a special category of users, as opposed to the public access and registration available via the front end).

The Joomla! administrator panel is divided into two main parts: on the left-hand side is a series of buttons from which you will be able to control most elements of a site, while the right-hand side displays links to various statistical elements such as online users and popular stories. While we shall cover many of the administrative features in more detail throughout this chapter, the main panel icons include the following:

> Joomla! distinguishes between the front end where content is viewed and uploaded and the back end where an administrator can control and fine tune various parts of the CMS.

- **Add New Content**   This is where material can be added by administrators, although in most cases it is advisable (and easier) for users to add content from the front end.
- **Content Items Manager/Static Items Manager**   Each of these allows the admin to see and modify all items posted to the site, whether in the MySQL database that powers Joomla! or as static HTML pages.
- **Frontpage Manager**   This feature is very simple in terms of its capabilities, but very important. When an item is identified as being published to the front page, this is where the administrator can determine the order of publication.
- **Section Manager/Category Manager**   Sections divide up types of content, such as news or reviews, and Categories allow site admins to refine where posts are stored, for example latest news.
- **Media Manager**   This is where you handle images for the CMS, although multimedia capabilities largely have to be controlled through plug-ins.

- **Trash Manager**   For recovering deleted files.
- **Menu Manager**   For handling menus as they appear in the front end.
- **Language Manager**   Joomla! supports various language packs other than English.
- **User Manager**   As noted in the introductory section to this chapter, various CMSs differentiate between users on a system, from those with minimal registration rights through authors to administrators who can control every element of front and back ends of the site.
- **Global Configuration**   This sets certain parameters that operate across an entire site, such as whether users are allowed to register or how links are handled.

While many other elements of the main configuration options will be covered throughout this chapter, it is worth making some further observations here about the Global Configuration options. Clicking this icon displays a series of tabbed panes, each of which can control how Joomla! works with content and users in a very general sense.

The first screen, Site, allows you to determine whether the site is offline (useful if you are doing development that you do not wish visitors to see), and sets whether visitors will be able to register with your site. Registration adds members to a user list, and can be useful if you wish certain types of information only to be visible to registered users. In addition, if you wish your site to contain contributions from other members, they will have to be registered and given author privileges at the very least.

Locale sets the time zone for your site, while Content governs how some elements of articles and posts are displayed. Options that can be set here include whether the time and date of when articles are posted or modified is displayed, as well as setting email or print articles next to posts. Database sets the name for the MySQL tables that are used by the CMS, but unless you are skilled at building SQL databases this is best left unchanged. The same also applies to the settings under the Server tab, although you may wish to change the Site and Admin Session Lifetimes, that is how long before the site logs out a user in the front and back ends after periods of inactivity: the default, 900 seconds, can cause problems if you are writing a long article in the editor – this will be perceived as inactivity on the site, and when you come to save your work it could be lost.

Metadata covers general tags for the site and, along with SEO (the final tag), will be covered in more detail in the last chapter under search engine optimisation. Mail covers general settings for sending mail from the site, while Cache stores temporary copies of your site in another folder on the server and may speed up performance (although it also means that regular updates may not be picked up so quickly). Finally, if you wish to collect statistics on your site, such as hits to pages and searches, enable these settings under the Statistics tag.

Customising templates

As is to be expected with the principles of modern web design, discussed in chapter 3, the look and feel of a Joomla! website is separate from the content and structure of the site, and controlled via the use of cascading style sheets (CSS).

The appearance of Joomla! is controlled via templates, a collection of HTML, CSS, JavaScript and image files into which all content added to the site is loaded. The default installation comes with a couple of sample templates, but it is also possible to locate a number of third-party templates online, for example at www.siteground.com, www.joomlashack.com and www.joomlashine.com, some of which are free to use.

To use templates, they must first be installed onto your server. Log into the administrator panel and go to the Installers, Templates menu. Browse to the zip file containing your template and then upload it. To assign it as the default, select the Site, Template Manager menu option and choose your new template before clicking on the Default icon at the top of the screen.

Templates downloaded from third-party sites will never be exactly what you require, and it is always advisable to modify them to some degree. For example, it is very likely that you will need to change the text that appears at the top of a site, as well as other elements that are displayed on pages. To do this, click the Edit HTML icon: this will load a code editor with the core elements of a page available for editing: in particular, look out for the header, left, and right modules, which will contain different parts of the page.

Factors such as colour and text size are controlled via CSS, and to change how these appear you will need to select a template and then click the Edit CSS button. A word of warning: the CSS files for the average Joomla! template can be extremely complex and rather mind-boggling for the casual web producer. One alternative is to download a copy of the CSS file and then open it in an editor such as Dreamweaver, which can provide some guidance on which elements control which parts of a site. If you are editing it by hand within Joomla!, it is always advisable to make a copy of the CSS file first because there will inevitably be some trial and error involved.

Templates generally work across an entire site: this has the advantage of allowing you to change the look and feel of all your web pages with only a few modifications to a template. It is possible, however, using the Template Manager, to assign different templates to different sections of a site. Generally, this is not recommended in that it can be confusing to

> By providing a standard for template design, Joomla! enables developers to create easily-installable templates for other users that are controlled via CSS.

WALKTHROUGH▶

Installing and customising a template

1 To install a template, go to Installers, Templates – Site. In the dialog box that appears, browse to locate the template package that you have installed on your hard drive or, alternatively, enter the URL for the directory on your server where the template has been uploaded. Click Upload File and Install/Install as appropriate.

2 Templates can be customised via the Template Manager (found under the Site menu). This provides a list of templates installed to the site with a series of buttons at the top of the screen. To change between templates, select the radio button next to the one you wish to use and click the Default button.

▶▶

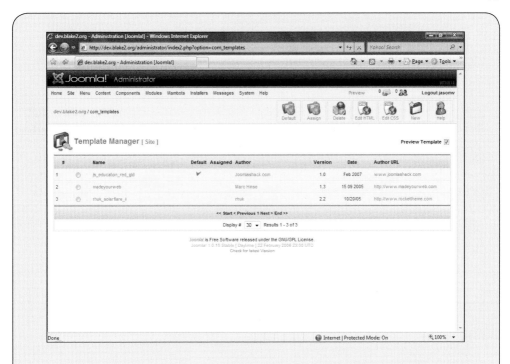

3 Customising templates requires a knowledge of HTML and CSS. In the first instance, click the Edit HTML button. This displays a very basic text editor that serves as the template for all pages on your site. Before editing, it is extremely important to make a backup of this file, so that you can restore it should anything go wrong. Click Save once you have made your changes.

4 Clicking the Edit CSS button displays a (usually extensive) style sheet that controls the appearance of all elements of your site, from text and background to such things as navigation controls and tables. As with editing HTML, click Save once you have made the necessary changes.

users if positions for common elements such as navigation links change from page to page. However, if you wish to mark radically different sections of a site, a forum, say, then selecting a template and clicking the Assign button allows you to connect that template to various menu items: when a visitor chooses that menu item, he or she will be shown pages with a different look and feel.

A final point to be aware of with templates is that they use what are referred to as modules. These are place-holders within the template for dynamic pieces of code that can be loaded into different positions within a page. All menus within Joomla!, for example, are modules, and other common modules include the header, a navigation bar at the top of the page, and most popular or latest post links. It is also possible to

define modules: to do this, go to Site, Template Manager, Module Positions and enter a new module name, for example MyModule01. We shall cover working with modules in the next section, but a handy piece of code to learn is the instruction {mosloadposition}. Used in conjunction with a module name, this will load dynamic content into any part of a page where you employ it, so that the instruction {mosloadposition MyModule01} would display whatever module was attached to your new module position.

Although we have spent a considerable amount of time considering the specifics of working with templates in Joomla!, it is worth pointing out that this is a principle that applies to most other CMSs, such as Drupal or Moodle. By uploading CSS, image and HTML files to a server and assigning them to pages, as well as linking dynamic elements of content to the template, such applications speed up the means by which you can build a sophisticated site.

CMS PLUG-INS

The core installation of Joomla! provides tools for managing content and users, but additional features are controlled via various plug-ins. These range from a page of PHP script that is added to the site to full-blown applets that allow administrators to control a number of elements on the site. It is this ability to extend the CMS that makes it so flexible.

Installation of these plug-ins has been considerably simplified with version 1.5.x, so that the various types are all installed by going to the menu Installation. For Joomla! 1.1.x, you will have to know whether the plug-in you are installing is a component, module or a bot. In addition, for both releases of Joomla! there are some plug-ins that work with specific components and have to be installed from within that piece of software.

The different types of plug-in are as follows:

- **Component**   A component is effectively a mini-program that has been designed to run in Joomla! Some of these, such as Exposé (a Flash image and video gallery) or MamboWiki, are based on standalone applications that have been modified so that they will also work in the CMS: they can be extremely sophisticated in terms of their capabilities. Others, such as the Contacts and Polls components that are part of the default installation of Joomla!, are not designed to work outside the CMS and are much more specific in terms of achieving particular tasks.
- **Module**   A module is a piece of code, whether a single file or a collection of scripts, that extends the capabilities of

Joomla! They are small content files that can be displayed in different parts of the page. Menus are modules that will be displayed on the top, left or right of a page according to your choice and the templates you are using, and other modules include the search engine and login elements that are part of the default installation. The last two also demonstrate that while modules are generally used to display information, they may also accept some interaction from visitors to your site.

- **Bot**   A Bot/Plug-in, also known as a mambot (reflecting the fact that the original specification for these was developed for use with Mambo), automatically modifies content before it is displayed. For example, bots can be used to hide email addresses to prevent them being harvested by spammers, or highlight specific words such as those used in a search.
- **Component-specific plug-in**   These are modules or bots that are designed to work with a specific component. Some of the more complex add-ons for Joomla! such as Community Builder or FireBoard can have a fairly extensive collection of plug-ins which usually have to be installed from within the component.

When components are installed into Joomla!, they may require some configuration but in general are ready to run and are usually controlled from the back end. Both modules and bots, however, will need to be published before they can display content in the front end. To do this, go to either the Modules or Mambots menu and locate the feature that you have just installed. Underneath the Published column, click on the red cross so that it changes to a green tick.

Bots change content across an entire site, but modules are used to display content in a particular position on the page. They must therefore be ascribed to a particular position.

> There are hundreds of plug-ins for Joomla! which makes this CMS incredibly flexible for your requirements.

WALKTHROUGH ▶

Setting up a poll in Joomla!

1 As one example of using components and modules, this exercise will set up a poll (which is part of the standard installation of the CMS). From the administrative back end, go to the Components menu and select Polls. This will display a list of up and running polls (the default is one on installing Joomla!).

2 Click the New button to create another poll: in the page that is displayed, enter the questions you wish to be included in the poll, as well as a title and time delay allowed between votes. To the right of your questions is a list of pages/sections where the poll will be displayed – either on every page or just certain ones such as the home page. Click Save once you have finished.

▶▶

3 Check the radio button next to your poll (as well as any others) you wish to have displayed, and click the Publish button. The final step is to determine where the poll will appear on the page. To do this, go to the Modules, Site Modules menu and click the link for Polls.

4 The module for a poll is quite simple (some modules have a much larger number of parameters that can be modified). The important ones here are to decide if the title of your poll should be displayed, as well as where it will appear on the page (top, right, left or in a user-defined position). Click Save once you have made your changes.

To do this, go to the Module menu and select the item that is to publish content on a page: on the left-hand side of the screen, select one of the options under Position (for example, left, top, or user1) and also a Module Order (to determine its rank when multiple modules are published together). The Menu Item Link(s) list on the right determines whether the module is displayed on all or selected pages.

Bots and modules may also have specific settings, known as parameters, associated with them. These include common ones, such as a title for the module and whether it is displayed, as well as others that are specific to a particular plug-in, such as the width and height of a module or whether it displays text from one category on your site. These parameters are too varied to cover for the many different plug-ins

that you will encounter for Joomla!, although when setting up some of the additional features of a CMS considered in this chapter we will explore a few of the more common ones.

Finally, as with the section on customising templates, it is important to note that plug-ins are far from peculiar to Joomla! Plenty – although not all – CMSs make use of a similar platform architecture that allows features to be added to the core program. Joomla! is unusual in that it has such a large number of extensions (you can view and download many of them at extensions.joomla.org). In addition, and this is particularly true of version 1.5.x, the installation procedure is easier than with a number of other CMSs: this said, there have been a few times when fine tuning a particular module or bot has required finding the original PHP code and making alterations by hand rather than through the menu options within the administrator panel.

Working with menus

While navigation around a site can be through hyperlinks attached to text or images within articles, the central means by which visitors will find their way to different parts of your CMS will, of course, be via menu links.

As has been mentioned already, menus within Joomla! function as modules, and the application includes a menu manager that controls and creates these modules. By clicking on the Menu Manager icon in the main administrator panel, you will see a list of menu titles. These do not include the actual links to different sections of your site, but rather the general sections that will be included on a site, usually on the top, left or right of a page, although it is possible to load a menu anywhere using the {mosloadposition} command. To create a new menu module, click the Add button and give your module a name. You can also use the Menu Manager to change the relative position of menus, moving one above another.

By going to Menu on the main menu, you will see a list of available modules. Selecting one of these will display the various links that leads to various parts of your site. In turn, selecting a link will show the parameters that can be modified for each menu item. While these change depending on what is selected, some features are common to most menu links, for example whether an image is used, the order of links, whether it is published (visible) on the site, and who can view it (public, registered, or special, that is users with author status or above). The last point can be very important. If you wish to restrict access to certain parts of your site to registered users, changing the view status of a menu link means

that it will not be visible to guests. You will also need to restrict access to the actual content items, but we shall deal with this at the end of the chapter.

It is highly unlikely that the default installation of Joomla! will include every item you need – and it will almost certainly install a few links that you definitely do not require. The latter are easy enough to remove: either set them as unpublished, or click the check box next to them and select the Trash icon at the top of the screen.

Adding links is slightly more complicated. Clicking the New icon will display a set of options which divide into five main types. The first are types of links to content, whether individual items or what Joomla! refers to as blogs, that is multiple introductory sections from articles posted to the site. Miscellaneous covers separators or wrappers (allowing you to embed an external page on the site), and Submit is useful for adding links that will allow authors to add content to your CMS. Links, as the name suggests, deals with URLs for content that is internal or external to your domain name. Components is a useful feature, that allows you to access software that you have added to Joomla!

Once you select the type of link you wish to create, depending on what it is, you will need to choose whether to type in a URL, add a menu item for a piece of software, or decide which content section, category or item is to be displayed. When a link is created, it is automatically placed at the end of a list: you can then move it up or down from the list of links for that module.

In addition, selecting the link will allow you to change parameters for that particular item.

A useful example of some of the specific parameters that can be modified is seen by selecting the Home link that is standard to the site. This will appear on just about every website, so is a good one to explore in a little depth.

> **Menus, an important means of navigating around any site, are handled in Joomla! as modules that are loaded onto templates and so can be changed across the entire site extremely quickly and easily.**

The parameters section to the right of the screen includes a slightly daunting array of options. The top ones are common to most links (whether you should use a menu image and show or hide a page title), but beneath this are four text boxes: Leading (how many articles will be displayed running across the front page), Intro (the number of stories that appear in columns beneath leading stories), Columns (how many columns are shown on the front page), and Links (the number of links to stories beneath Intro stories). Stories themselves can be ordered via a number of means, such as title or date, or through the Frontpage Manager. There are also options to determine whether such things as the author, dates and various icons should be displayed next to stories.

User management

As well as managing content, an important function played by a CMS is to manage users. A general outline of the types of users that have a role to play on such a site was presented earlier in this chapter. Here we shall consider the more specific roles that are available with a default installation of Joomla!, as well as looking at a component, Community Builder, that provides more extensive social networking features.

Joomla! distinguishes between two main types of registered user, those who can access the public front end only, and those with access to the back end of the system (that is, administrators). A list of users can be accessed via the User Manager in the main Administrator panel. As well as being able to view those members who have registered with a site, it is also possible to add members by clicking the New button, remove them by clicking the Delete button, or edit their details.

Of the user types available to Joomla!, the front end categories are Registered, Author, Editor and Publisher. Authors are able to post content to a site so that it may be moderated by admins, and edit their own material; Editors are able to edit the content of other authors, as can Publishers, with the difference that the latter user group may also publish material so

that it is publicly available without requiring administrator intervention.

Back end categories include the following: Manager, who is able to view users and content, but has no access to components or modules; Administrator, who can view all elements of the back end, but is not able to install new software; and Super Administrator, a user type that has no restrictions imposed at all.

By default, when a user registers with a site via the login module on the site, their category will be Registered. To change this, an administrator (that is someone with Manager privileges or above), will need to click on the link for a user name and change their status in the Group section of the User: Edit page. This is also the page where admins can block users if necessary, as well as change details such as user names, passwords, and the default editor (something considered in Working with Content later in this chapter).

With different user types in place, the content of your site can be customised so that it will only be available to particular users. As mentioned previously when discussing setting up menus, although this is something that also applies to content, pages can be modified so that they are only visible to registered users or those with special privileges (that is anyone with author status or above).

Social networking with Community Builder

While this immediately begins to offer a considerable degree of customisation for a site, the capabilities of Joomla! can be extended greatly through the use of Community Builder (CB), available at www.joomlapolis.com. At the time of writing, the stable release, Community Builder 1.1, is native only for version 1.1.x of Joomla!, although it runs in legacy mode on version 1.5.x. A new release, 1.2, is currently being developed for both 1.1.x and 1.5.x, although not all plug-ins for the old version of CB will automatically work with the new one.

At its simplest, CB is a replacement user manager for Joomla!, although as a component that can itself be extended and configured in a number of ways it also provides the means to add social networking features rather like a simplified version of Facebook. The extensions page at Joomla.org (extensions.joomla.org) lists 121 plug-ins for CB, which allow members to do such things as share photos, videos, Google maps and comments on boards or walls.

The walkthrough for installing and configuring Community Builder 1.1 (below) will take you through the basics of getting CB up and running on your website. This is the most complex component considered so far in this chapter, and mastering how to use this software is good practice for dealing with just about any application you may wish to use to extend Joomla's capabilities.

Once you have installed and performed a base configuration for CB so that it handles registrations and provides links to a member's profile and list of users, there are numerous ways in which the program can be modified and tweaked. Two of its most important features are providing easy access to any articles or posts that a user makes, and enabling members of a site to communicate with each other, either via email (the default mode with a standalone version of CB), or using a private messaging system that will be considered in the following section. In addition, knowing how to add CB plug-ins will allow you to enhance social networking features considerably.

In some respects, Community Builder is almost as complex as Joomla! itself and could easily fill a chapter. However, here we shall limit ourselves to some of the main elements, with further information being available on the producingforweb2.com website.

> Community Builder is an extremely popular and powerful extension to Joomla! that enables web developers to produce their own social networking sites.

- **Configuration Panel** If you have installed CB, you should already have used this to allow user registration, and it is accessed from Components, Community Builder, Configuration. A great many, but by no means all, options within CB are set here, from something as simple as determining whether user names or real names are displayed, to setting different templates for the User Profile pages and integrating with a private messaging system.

- **Plugin Management** This is where you can install and manage plug-ins by going to Components, Community Builder, Plugin Management.

- **Field Manager** When users register, they will need at the very least to enter a user name and password. However, it is possible to collect other information depending on the nature of your site (such as web pages or hobbies) by creating fields that are then completed at registration. Go to Components, Community Builder, Field Management and click the New Field button. From here you can select a variety of types of field, such as text areas or check boxes, assign each one a name and optional description, and determine whether it will be required at registration and shown on the member's profile page.

- **Tab Manager** User profiles can be used to display a variety of information, including member photos, links to articles and posts and instant message forms. Go to Components, Community Builder, Tab Management to see a list of plug-ins (some of them core, such as the Portrait option). Clicking each of these links will display various options and parameters: common to them all is a title, description and option to publish the tab (important if you wish it to be displayed). Also important, and located at the bottom of each page, is a set of options governing the position of a tab: tabs can be published in various locations on the page – top, left, right or the main part of the page – and in various formats. If you wish to display multiple plug-ins in the same section of the profile, usually on

WALKTHROUGH ▶

Installing and configuring Community Builder 1.1

1 The Community Builder zip file that is downloaded from Joomlapolis has two essential parts that must be installed: comprofiler.zip that is installed in Joomla! as a component, and mod_cblogin.zip, which replaces the default Joomla! login module. Other elements, such as mod_comprofilerModerator.zip, are optional.

2 Once the CB essentials are in place, the first step is to synchronise users with the main Joomla! user database. To do this, go to Components, Community Builder, Tools, Synchronize Users. Next, go to Components, Community Builder, Configuration and click on the Registration tab.

3 The program must be set up so that CB handles all registrations instead of Joomla! On the Registration tab, set 'Allow User Registration' to 'Yes, independently of global site setting'. After this, in the Global Configuration panel set 'Allow User Registration' to 'No'.

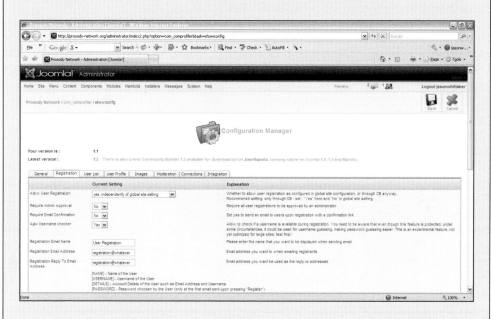

4 Now the CB login module has to be enabled. Go to the Modules menu and click on the mod_CBlogin link, then change its name to Login and publish it. The default login module has to be disabled (otherwise users will see two login forms), so click the mod_login link and unpublish it.

5 CB allows registered members to search and connect with other users. First, create and publish a user list (Components, Community Builder, List Management, New), then add a new menu item as a Link – URL with the address index.php?option=com_comprofiler&task=usersList and call it Search Users.

6 Finally, provide a link for registered users to view their profile. Add a new menu link, this time by selecting Component, Community Builder, and publish this with a name such as My Profile. It is advisable that both this link and that for the user list is accessible only by registered members.

the main part of the page, you will need to select Tabbed pane from the Display type drop-down menu.

This only scratches the surface of Community Builder's capabilities, but it is one of the most significant components that you can add to your site, changing the nature of the CMS. Whereas the standard installation of Joomla! focuses on publishing content, a CB add-on can make a site function more as a meeting place for different users, allowing them to communicate and connect in ways that are much more decentralised and closer to the principles of Web 2.0 sites outlined in chapter 1.

CB itself has been developed exclusively for Joomla! and Mambo, but other CMSs, such as Drupal have their own versions of social networking tools, such as Buddy List and Organic Groups, although none in my opinion are as developed as Community Builder.

Adding a messaging system

If you are keen to create your site as a social networking environment, then some form of messaging system is an extremely useful plug-in. While Joomla! allows users to contact other members via email by default, a private messaging system – similar to that used in social networking sites such as Facebook or LinkedIn – serves several functions. First of all it provides a more immediate means of connecting to other members, in that messages can be accessed immediately by other users online. Second, for regular users of a site, it may provide a more convenient way of collating their messages, rather than receiving them mixed up with the large amounts of email and spam that may fill up their inboxes. Finally, for web developers instant messaging is a way of building social cohesion and 'stickiness' into a site: content such as articles may not be added daily, but if members log into a site to check their messages this will encourage them to return more regularly.

Joomla! does not have a built-in private messaging system (PMS), but there are plenty of available plug-ins at extensions.joomla.org in the section for PMS, including Joomla Advanced Message, PMS Pro and uddeIM. As a sample messaging system, we shall look at uddeIM, version 1.1 of which is available in native format for both 1.5.x and 1.1.x.

The uddeIM zip file, like Community Builder, contains several elements which have to be unzipped before you can install them onto your website: a component, com_uddeim.zip, a plug-in, plug_pms_uddeim.zip, and a folder containing templates. The main component must be installed first and, once this is in place, it can be accessed via Components, uddeIM. This control panel allows the administrator to determine such things as message length, how messages are displayed, if and when they are deleted, and whether users of a site can block messages from other members.

The plug-in must be installed by going to Components, Community Builder, Plugin Management and clicking the install link on that page. Once in place, it must be published on the Plugin Management page and a tab allocated to it by going to Components, Community Builder, Tab Management. Once these are in place, members will be able to send quick messages to someone else directly from their profile page.

> An important addition to CMSs that wish to include social networking features is to add a messaging component so that users can keep in touch with each other more easily.

Using groups

Another way to extend the social networking features of Joomla! is groups, that is community pages through which messages can be posted for other members of the site.

GroupJive (www.groupjive.org) allows all registered members of a site to create their own community groups. The default installation integrates within Joomla! to allow users to post bulletin messages using the built-in editor; it can also be used to provide shared forums (through FireBoard, see below), calendars (through EventList) and comments on other postings (with JomComment).

The back end component (Components, GroupJive) allows you to control and configure general group settings. Under Settings the administrator can integrate GroupJive with other programs, as well as determine such things as whether groups have to be approved by admins or messages are sent out when a new user joins. The Categories, Groups and Members Managers control the general headings under which groups appear, as well as the actual groups and members themselves (it is possible, for example, to assign registered members of a site to a particular group from here rather than waiting for them to register).

In the front end of a Joomla! site, GroupJive creates an automatic menu link and, if you have Community Builder installed, also creates a tabbed pane in user profiles. To join an already existing group, members of a site simply select it and then click the Join this Group link that is at the top of the main page.

To create a new group, registered members click the Create your OWN Group link at the top of the main page just underneath the search box. This displays dialog boxes for: Group Category: Group Type (Open, Requiring Approval from the group administrator, or Invite Only, private groups which users cannot join until invited); Group Name and About Group, the latter an optional description; Group Logo (set by browsing to an image on a computer hard drive).

Once a group is joined or created, the main page gives options for displaying all members of a group, any bulletins, a forum (which is created automatically for a group if FireBoard is installed), and links to invite people to join or leave the group. The administrator of a group also has links allowing him or her the ability to edit the settings listed above, as well to contact all group members.

The virtue of an application such as GroupJive is that it allows registered members of a site to create content outside the central control of the site administrators – an important Web 2.0 principle. It is one of those programs, like Community Builder, that can completely transform a site from simply a display for content such as articles into a meeting place for individuals with similar interests.

Adding a forum

Creating a forum is one of the simplest ways to add interactivity to a site, and in many respects one of the oldest, predating the web in the form of bulletin boards (bbs) and Usenet newsgroups.

A forum allows members of a site to post comments and interact with each other, and while the default installation of Joomla! does not include a forum there are plenty of extensions available such as Joo!BB, Simpleboard and FireBoard Forum.

We shall concentrate on FireBoard Forum (www.bestofjoomla.com) here because it is the most developed and allows considerable scope for integrating with other parts of a site, particularly Community Builder. The walkthrough on installing FireBoard and setting up a forum (below) will show the essential steps for creating discussion boards using FireBoard, but it is also worth pointing out that the CB plug-in will create a tabbed pane in a user profile that displays all the posts made by various users. Other applications that FireBoard integrates with include GroupJive (allowing it to

> One of the oldest forms of enabling users to interact together is to include a forum or bulletin board where visitors can leave posts for each other. Extensions such as FireBoard provide a large number of options to customise the appearance and operations of your forum.

WALKTHROUGH▶

Installing FireBoard and setting up a forum

1 The stable release of FireBoard (1.0.4 at the time of writing) has several main parts. FireBoard_1.0.4.zip is the main application that has to be installed as a component, while bot_fbsearchbot.zip is a bot that integrates with the main search engine; cb.fireboard.zip is a Community Builder plug-in that shows posts on a profile.

2 As with other bots and plug-ins for CB, the last two elements listed above have to be published before they will become available. This is done through the Mambots menu option and Components, Community Builder, Plugin Manager, as well as the Tab Manager to assign a tab for FireBoard posts in CB.

3 The FireBoard Control Panel is where you configure your forum and set up new boards (Components, FireBoard Forum). There are many options to change here: Basics governs such things as the name of your board; Frontend controls such things as access; Integration is useful for linking user names to a CB profile.

4 To set up a forum, click on Forum Administration in the Control Panel. Click the New button and choose Top Level Category as your first Parent category (you will not be able to post anything here, but it serves as a placeholder for subsequent boards). Provide a name and description for this first category.

5 Once a Parent category has been established, this time you can create the boards where users will actually be able to post. Click New again, but this time select your previous category as the parent. When the forum is saved, you must click on the cross in the Published column to make it publicly available.

▶▶

6 Boards can be made available to different types of member. The Security and Access section of each forum determines whether a board is locked (no posts possible) or restricted to a particular user group. In addition, the security settings in the main settings panel are where you allow/disallow anonymous posts.

provide group forums) and various messaging programs such as uddeIM.

FireBoard also provides a wide range of statistics and additional features, some aimed at administrators (such as the ability to moderate boards or log users' **IP** addresses) and others which can be useful for developing interactivity. At a simple level, this may consist of no more than tagging the number of posts a member makes, but slightly more advanced is the use of what FireBoard refers to as 'karma', effectively points allocated based on the number of posts made. Higher levels of karma allows a web developer to change the status of posters, giving them extra privileges (such as access to special group boards) and displaying them more prominently on the site.

Using DOCman

As well as handling content such as articles and users, a CMS can also be employed as a document manager, dealing with a wide range of files such as Microsoft Office documents, PDFs, image files and exe or zip files, some of which are not necessarily easily displayed within a browser.

Some very basic file handling can be provided through FireBoard Forum, but a much better option for Joomla! is DOCman (www. joomlatools.org). Version 1.4.0 at the time of writing is available in native mode for both Joomla! 1.1.x and 1.5.x, being a document and file/download manager that provides management of a range of files such as PDF, Word .doc and image files, with the possibility to assign licences to files to control who can download. It installs in Joomla! as a component, and there is also a search bot from the same address that integrates DOCman searches with the main Joomla! search module. The front end can also be modified via a number of templates to change the look and feel of a downloads section of your site.

The program is configured from the back end of a Joomla! website by going to Components, DOCman, which displays a number of icons for groups, files and categories. The Configuration icon shows a screen from which you can change settings in the program, including a path for storing files on the server and also permissions for who can view or download files.

The core features of handling documents come from setting up categories to organise them on the site (click on the Categories icon or go to Components, DOCman, Categories, then click Add to create a new category), along with adding files (stored on the server) and documents (that is files in categories with added information such as permissions and licences). From the administrator panel for DOCman, it is also possible to set up groups, allocating specific permissions to different members on a site so that some documents visible to one group will not be available to others.

When a link is added for downloads which connects to the DOCman component, downloading is very simple: users browse or search for the file they are looking for and, depending on user group permissions and various licences, then click the download link for that document.

Uploading is slightly more complex. After clicking the Submit file button, DOCman prompts a user to select a file from your computer (there are other options, such as transferring from another server, but these tend to be used much more rarely). Once a file is selected, clicking the upload button will load the file onto the server. The next stage is to set information for the document, such as a description of a file, as well as permissions as to who can view the file, as well as any licensing details such as copyright restrictions.

Once these details are entered, the document is now ready to be published. The approve and publish icons appear in the menu

> Another useful add-on is DOCman which provides file-sharing capabilities for users on the site with options to tag and catalogue documents as well as distribute them.

beneath the document, although these are only available to those with publisher and admin status.

Using JoomlaWiki

For web developers who wish to incorporate a wiki in their site but also wish to integrate it more fully with their CMS, JoomlaWiki (formerly MamboWiki, www.joomlawiki.org) is an extremely useful component. Available in native versions for Joomla! 1.1.x and 1.5.x, it is not perfect: there are numerous complaints about the fact it runs in an iframe (that is the software is loaded into a separate frame on the main site) in particular, but while this can create some problems for users coming to a site from a search engine it does mean that you can deploy a wiki on your Joomla!-powered site that has the same format as your other pages.

> JoomlaWiki is based on the same software (MediaWiki) that is used for Wikipedia, but integrates within a site run on Joomla!

Because MediaWiki, the software on which JoomlaWiki is based on, was covered much more extensively in chapter 5, in this section we shall deal only with how to install and configure JoomlaWiki rather than how to use it.

JoomlaWiki is installed as a component, and once up and running it can be accessed by going to Components, JoomlaWiki (or Components, MamboWiki for users of Joomla! 1.1.x). The first step is to click on the Install database tables and initialise MediaWiki, after which the program will be ready to use.

The other important part to configure is found at the bottom of the main screen. Here you can determine relatively minor things, such as whether the MediaWiki logo is displayed on your site. More important are the drop-down menus for determining who can read and edit pages (Nobody, Users – that is registered users on a site, or Both, allowing guests to read and/or make changes as well), as well as that for allowing or disallowing direct access to pages. If this is set to Yes, visitors from a search engine will be taken directly to the relevant MediaWiki page even if they have not come from the front page of your Joomla! website.

Also available from the JoomlaWiki site are a number of bots and modules that allow such things as searching the wiki from the main search module, linking to wiki content from within a main Joomla! article, and a module that displays latests posts in JoomlaWiki and the Joomla CMS.

For more information and updates on content management systems, visit www. producingforweb2.com/cms.

CHAPTER 8

Writing, ethics and regulation

While multimedia and coding skills are essential for the modern web producer, the fact remains that the vast majority of content online consists of text. For this reason, the ability to write well to attract your audience's attention cannot be underestimated. As well as considering some of the key elements that will enable your writing to shine on the web, this chapter will also look at some of the regulatory and ethical issues affecting web producers today.

CONTENT CREATION

Setting the style

As well as becoming a content provider, successful web development also depends on developing an appropriate style for the presentation of material. Such a style depends on establishing an audience and cultivating a distinctive voice, and the basics of developing a good style cannot be repeated enough: revise and edit your work and master the basics of accurate writing, including good grammar and punctuation. Demonstrating programming skills and multimedia proficiency may count for very little if public perception of your pages is based on an inability to spell.

In many cases, the best style is often that which is clearest and plainest (though these are not synonymous). There is no reason why you should stick to such a style – after all, many world-famous writers are florid, metaphorical and elaborate – but if your desire is to appeal to as wide an audience as possible, you should write appropriately. As Matthew Arnold commented, 'Have something to say, and say it as clearly as you can. That is the only secret of style.'

Expanding on Arnold's advice, in most cases it is advisable to write as you speak but more precisely, paying attention to rules of grammar and avoiding colloquialisms unless they are relevant. Note, however, that simplicity in good writing is often more apparent than real, concealing painstaking art behind its artlessness. Indeed, clarity is often not the same as plainness: it can elaborate a subject but does so by avoiding jargon as much as possible.

For the web, where readers may be scanning articles very quickly before clicking on hyperlinks that take them to the next page, the principles of news writing often provide an extremely useful foundation for creating stories. Disciplining your writing so that important facts are included in the opening sentence, and building an inverted pyramid so that a story is front-loaded with information, will help readers decide whether they wish to continue reading.

Style must be appropriate to the subject: it should not rise above content, but is the means of expressing your ideas in as lively, clear and vivid a manner as possible. Sometimes a provocative and opinionated writing style may be the best way to attract readers. If you are writing a news story or for an online catalogue, however, you should be as self-effacing as possible, offering information clearly and succinctly to visitors.

Selecting an audience

All this leads on to the question of establishing an audience. For example, when publishing news (which has been very successful on the web) there must be facts to report but, equally important, these must appeal to readers. One useful tip is to look at what is being published to see what is on offer on other sites. Remember also that a story is something that is crafted and has an angle.

How do you determine a market on the web? The first step should be to look at what is available across other sites. There are plenty that offer editorial. Some are based on traditional print media such as *Guardian Unlimited* (www.guardian.co.uk) or *Time* magazine (www.time.com), although the best of these will develop content in new and innovative ways. Others, such as MSN (www.msn.com) or Salon (www.salon.com) develop editorial material specifically for an internet audience, sometimes including features and news as part of a range of other services.

Many blogs or personal sites offer factual information, or a provocative stance on certain issues, or locate other people who share similar enthusiasms. One of the virtues of the web is that 'professionals' have not always staked out the relevant territory in advance; see, for example, Mario Lavandeira's gossipy celebrity site, Perezhilton.com, and Pim Techamuanvivit's food reviews site, chezpim. typepad.com.

Crafting stories

News stories have been one particularly successful form of content on the web. There

are several reasons for this, such as the ability to update information on a regular basis and to search through stories and also the fact that news writing tends to pack a considerable amount of information into a relative short space. While sites such as Project Gutenberg (www.gutenberg.org) and Bartleby (www. bartleby.com) perform an admirable task of transferring classic texts to the net, few people want to read *War and Peace* on their screens.

Such journalistic writing also offers some useful tips for developing a style appropriate to the web. Introductions to stories should be short and punchy, containing relevant information in the first 20 or 30 words. The inverted 'news pyramid' developed for papers traditionally enabled editors to cut stories from the bottom up so that important information would not be omitted if new items had to be added to the page. While the web appears to offer unlimited space, in practice few readers will make it to the end of an article but will click a hyperlink once they have read enough.

When developing such a pyramid, it is common to provide a brief statement that summarises the story, followed by a more extensive repetition of the introduction (often called the pivot paragraph, which explains what the story is about) before finally expanding details in the main body of the text. This is not the only way to develop an article, especially as a good story should have a dramatic ending.

The physical experience of reading from a screen, as well as the various publishing systems used to get information online, may impose other considerations. For example, it is useful to extend a feature over several pages rather than have one long page which readers must scroll through before they can assess its value. A general rule of thumb is that text that spans more than two screens will be tiring to read. In addition, many content management systems will divide text into introductory and main parts, the former being

> Before producing content for your site, be sure to study similar sites elsewhere to determine the appropriate market and material that is suitable for the readers you wish to attract.

posted to a front page or section, with a read more link leading onto the body copy.

As Nicholas Bagnall has remarked in his book, *Newspaper Language* (1993: 15): 'Everyone knows the old saying: if you can't get their attention in the first sentence (or the first eight seconds) they won't bother with the rest.' At the same time, a website should offer the opportunity to explore, to allow the reader to determine their own pathways through the stories they find interesting. A person who has bought a newspaper or magazine has, in some sense, already committed him or herself to looking through it, however cursorily; the same is not true of a website user.

> For longer articles, graphical devices such as boxes, bullet points and panels can be an extremely effective technique for getting information across to a reader quickly.

Storytelling techniques

Introductions to stories may consist of a narrative or anecdote, descriptive scene-setting, provocative statements or a quote or question. Endings tend to restate or refer to the beginning. The classic example is the detective story where the gun on a table in the opening paragraph is used to shoot someone in the final scene. It is not always practical to have a story that is so tightly plotted, but a good conclusion to a piece will progress ideas in the text as well as restating them.

A common technique is to include single line headings or descriptions with a link to the relevant story: if the reader is curious, he or she will follow that link. While it may seem unfair for your hours, days or weeks of work to be dismissed with a single click, an important technique for maximising a site is to create as many internal links as possible. Visitors will generally make their mind up about a page within a few seconds before hitting the back button or another link: if those links lead to attractive-sounding pages on your own site, you may be able to build up a wider readership than by insisting that visitors trudge through every page before deciding whether to stay.

Use boxes, bullet points, panels, sidebars and tables to offer information at a glance. Frequently readers will skim through an article looking at such things as pull-quotes (where a line of text is displayed in larger type), captions and boxes to see if the story is interesting before returning to the main body text. These various panels and boxes can summarise the information contained in an article or expand on additional details not dealt with in the body copy.

Prepare for an audience, but don't slavishly follow a formula – allow for surprises. There is no single technique that can cover every story, every article and review, every feature. Bear in mind that some of the most interesting articles will include information that the reader does not already know. Regarding writing style, the flow of content is important, especially if the text is fact-heavy, and one of the best ways of establishing copy flows is to reread material on a regular basis – to stop being a writer and *become a reader*.

TIPS FOR WRITTEN CONTENT

- **Select an audience** While not necessary in the sense that you may wish to create a website entirely for your own benefit and to express your own interests, having a clear idea of the audience you wish your site to appeal to can be helpful in terms of producing appropriate text and other content.
- **Write as you speak** Or, to be more accurate, write as you would speak but more precisely. In most cases, this is the best way to produce clear, readable copy. Avoid jargon and aim for clarity.
- **Use the pyramid** A technique from news journalism: offer a summary of your story at the beginning and expand from there. While this was originally useful for

subeditors who needed to cut stories from the bottom up, it is useful on the web not to save space but for readers who may wish to move onto other pages.

- **Use links**   A good way to keep visitors on your site is to give them lots of things to visit. You can't guarantee to provide everything for everyone on one page, so include plenty of links to other parts of your site.
- **Become a reader**   Read and revise your copy on a regular basis.

ETHICS AND REGULATION

The rapid growth of the internet since the mid-1990s has brought its own range of challenges for web producers, users and regulators. This section will concentrate on those issues that tend to affect web designers.

Copyright

Although we are concentrating on ethics and regulation as they affect web producers, it must be said that it is perhaps for regulators and content providers from other media that copyright creates the biggest headaches. Computers are eminently suitable for making perfect copies of information, whether text, images, audio or data. (Note: this is not the same as saying that, in contrast to analog media, digital reproduction encodes data perfectly – rather that once a digital version is made it can be reproduced exactly.) What is more, the ability to copy such data and transmit it around the world is open to anyone with a computer and internet connection, and the rise of fast broadband connections means that illegally copying huge files, such as movies, once too cumbersome for online piracy, is now more prevalent than ever.

> The ease with which material can be copied and distributed online has made piracy a matter of major concern for content providers using the web or other digital formats to publish new material.

Previous international legislation, such as the Berne Convention of 1886 (revised 1971) and the Universal Copyright Convention (1952, 1971), has always approached copyright from the standpoint that significant infractions would be centralised in some way, and that copying via media such as video or audio tape would always involve some deterioration of the original source material.

Concerns over copyright infringements across the internet prompted the European Parliament in 1999 to propose the Copyright in the Information Society Bill, followed by the EU Copyright Directive of 2001. This legislation placed heavy restrictions across the EU, taking into account the ease with which data can now be copied. It was seen as highly restrictive at the time, although member states of the EU have considerable freedom in implementing certain aspects of the directive. In the UK, current law is enforced according to the Copyright, Designs and Patents Act (1988), with various amendments to the original statute, most of these to bring it into line with EU directives. Once in physical form (including digital variants), an original work is automatically protected under UK law, with a 1996 amendment extending that protection for 70 years after the author's death (although this can vary for some media such as sound and video recordings).

While copyright law in the United States was relatively static throughout most of the twentieth century, the turn of the final decade saw more legislation passed in ten years than for the whole of the preceding ninety years. Some of this, such as the Copyright Term Extension Act (1998), increasing terms of copyright to 95/120 years, or life plus 70 years, had little to do with new media per se. However, the Digital Millennium Copyright Act (1998) and the Family Entertainment and Copyright Act (2005) were aimed particularly at digital media. The DMCA implemented a 1996

World Intellectual Property Organisation (WIPO) treaty, criminalising any attempt to circumvent measures used to control access to copyright work, usually known as digital rights management (DRM). It also exempted ISPs from direct or indirect liabilities for copyright infringements (something introduced later in the EU by the Electronic Commerce Directive in 2002). The Family Entertainment and Copyright Act consisted of two parts: the Family Home Movie Act which permitted the sanitisation of potentially offensive DVDs, and the Artist's Rights and Theft Prevention Act which targeted movie and software piracy with increased penalties.

The early years of both the internet generally and the web in particular gave rise to the assumption that a great deal of content consisted of a free lunch. In part, this was because much of the content produced was intended to be freely distributed, and developments such as Open Source concentrated on producing software which could be circulated and modified as widely as possible. However, a side effect has been that content providers with a more traditional interest in protecting their intellectual property are often adversely affected by the assumption that the ability to download something makes it freely available for copying to others. Many people may break the law inadvertently, for example by posting someone else's photos for which they do not own the copyright to a website, and if no commercial use is intended many original artists will turn a blind eye – although not always. Indeed, in many countries producers concerned about protecting copyright have to be aware of the 'use it or lose it' status of the law: ignoring minor infringements may lead to losing a case against larger ones.

In the late 1990s, the first major acts of internet piracy that came to the attention of authorities involved illegally distributed music. The **peer-to-peer** (p2p) service Napster, established in 1999, enabled a wide range of users to share music stored digitally on their hard drive. Indeed, one of the problems for Napster was that because it provided a centralised search utility it was not a truly p2p system such as BitTorrent and so was easier to target by the authorities. Similarly, in 2007 police shut down a music file sharing website, Oink, which had an estimated 180,000 users, while throughout 2007 and 2008 the RIAA (Recording Industry Association of America) and EMI began prosecuting personal users who shared thousands of MP3s illegally online. How effective such actions are in terms of preventing such activity is hard to determine.

While MP3 files, which can reduce a track to a few megabytes in size, was a growing problem for content providers at the beginning of the decade, until very recently the problems of transmitting movies digitally across the internet meant that this was perceived as much less of a problem. However, the popularity of YouTube, established in 2004 and bought by Google for $1.6 billion in 2006, led companies such as Time Warner to threaten legal action for the wide number of illegally uploaded clips on the site. The simplicity of YouTube's system for uploading video for a mass audience to see, combined with the growth of broadband, meant that large amounts of copyrighted material was now available to millions of users. While YouTube explicitly points out that copyright belongs to the original authors, and content cannot be shared without the express permission of the copyright owners, a considerable amount of illegal material does make it online. This said, in some cases Google has done advertising deals with original providers, who also – in some instances – have seen the Web 2.0 phenomenon as a means of marketing and promoting other content.

> Napster was probably the first major site to attract the interest of the authorities when it made it easier for online users to share music at the end of the 1990s. More recently, video sharing via sites such as YouTube have caused more concern for producers and distributors.

While there are laws about fair use when citing or referencing text, in most countries this applies only to text. It does not matter how long or short a clip is, it cannot be distributed without the original owner's express permission. Simply crediting a clip does not transfer permission, nor does it matter if such material is not being distributed commercially. Editing together a series of sounds or images does not transfer copyright, as the intellectual property of the originals still belongs to their authors. Minor cases of using other people's material on your website are not likely to be prosecuted, but it is still not worth the risk of having a site closed, particularly if you wish to use it for professional or commercial purposes.

Alternative approaches to copyright, in some cases much better suited to online media, have begun to be developed. The GNU Public License (now in version 3, www.gnu.org/licenses/gpl.html) was initially implemented to support the open-source software GNU (GNU's Not Unix), an operating system that end users can freely modify so long as they make their own altered code available. More suitable for content creators in a variety of media is the Creative Commons licence (creativecommons.org), which allows producers to specify the rights they wish to retain, and those they wish others to have. This extends from full rights to reserved (as with traditional copyright), to no rights reserved (as with material in the public domain). More interesting is the fact that authors can specify some rights reserved using the licences available on the site – for example if you wish your work to be freely distributable for non-commercial use only, or to allow others to modify it. You can specify what rights you wish to make available by going to the Creative Commons website and clicking on the License Your Work icon.

> In recent years, courts and lawyers have taken a much greater interest in the issue of defamation online, where the ease of communication and sense of anonymity sometimes encourages contributors to make potentially libellous statements.

Libel

As well as copyright issues, web producers need to beware of defamation. Writers and critics are not immune to libel laws, and simply because you publish a website without making a profit does not mean that you may not be taken to court. There is, however, a defence against libel in the form of 'fair comment'. This allows someone to be as harsh in their criticism as they like as long as it is their honest opinion, is true and is not motivated by malice. In the US, the constitutional protection of free speech under the First Amendment has generally made for a much less harsh regime than in Europe (particularly the UK). The writer's right to free speech about public affairs was established in the 1964 case *New York Times* v. *Sullivan*, which set out that where the injured party is a public figure he or she must prove 'actual malice'.

Until the end of the 1990s, a relative lack of prosecutions or settlements meant that there was a perception of the web as something of a free for all. Two earlier cases in the US, *Cubby* v. *CompuServe* (1991) and *Oakmont* v. *Prodigy* (1995) provided apparently contradictory evidence as to the status of ISPs. The first acknowledged the instantaneous nature of internet postings and treated CompuServe as a free carrier (rather like a telephone company). The family-oriented nature of Prodigy, specifically its claims to regulate its bulletin boards, led to a judgment that treated it as a publisher. The 1998 DMCA established clearer lines as to the nature of ISPs as free carriers, a position reinforced by *Lunney* v. *Prodigy* (2000), where the US Supreme Court ruled that ISPs have full protection against libellous or abusive postings over the web, after a former boy scout served Prodigy with a lawsuit following postings of threatening messages by an impostor using his name.

In the UK, the 1996 Defamation Act attempted to clarify the position of ISPs as secondary carriers, although their status was not fully settled until the 2002 Electronic Commerce Directive. A consequence of legislation is that, rather than encouraging a hands-off approach (concerns about legal action in the 1990s led many companies not to monitor their sites at all), the law attempts to encourage ISPs to watch what is held on their servers while accepting the impossibility of checking everything.

> **One of the inadvertent consequences of online communications has been the rise of 'libel tourism', where a plaintiff in one country pursues a lawsuit in another which has stricter rules regarding defamation.**

Until 1999, there had been little significant legal action against ISPs and web producers in the UK, although things have changed radically since then – so much so that some authorities claim that the much stricter libel laws in the UK are threatening free speech. In 2008, the New York State Legislature passed the Libel Terrorism Protection Act, whereby libel judgments from other countries would not be recognised in New York. In addition, the proposed Free Speech Protection Act would extend such protection across the United States. The growth of web publishing has also seen a rise in what is referred to as 'libel tourism': because the burden of proof under British law lies with the defendant rather than (as in the US) with the plaintiff, the UK has been seen as extremely attractive to those who wish to silence their critics. Libel tourism is by no means new (and has often been pursued against book, magazine and newspaper publishers even if only a few copies were sold in the UK), but the fact that media from other countries can be viewed so easily across the web has made the UK, in the words of some commentators, the 'libel capital' of the world.

Although in many cases plaintiffs target ISPs as being more willing to threaten sites with closure than fight, libel remains a particularly thorny issue for publishers who do not have the defence of being a free carrier. In many examples, web publishing can follow the straightforward rules governing defamation for print, but where a forum, for example, is included on a website it is the producer's responsibility to manage this as much as possible, meaning that postings must be monitored and, more importantly, a complaint-handling procedure must be in place. Should a complaint be received, a posting should be suspended until it is assessed and a response made as quickly as possible. It is also advisable to make clear the limits of acceptable behaviour on a website, something that will be dealt with under moderation below.

When using the defence of fair comment for information placed on a website by a producer rather than a third party, it is doubly important to get the facts right: opinion is not the same as facts, so saying that an item is too expensive and then quoting the wrong price will not be helpful if you are later sued. Second, and this is often the most difficult part of defending against libel, an opinion that is judged excessive – such as calling a person obese who has put on a little weight – may not be held to be honest opinion. The last test for fair comment is whether a piece of work is in the public interest. If you are writing about something that has been published or distributed, such as a book or a film, this is usually less of a problem than reciting gossip about a figure who may not be in the public eye.

Obscenity and censorship

For most web producers, copyright will be the largest problem when creating content. However, part of the excitement of the internet revolves around its status as the largest uncensored mass medium in history. Scare stories of paedophilia, terrorism and racism abound on the internet, as well as in other media discussing it. There are unsavoury, and even criminal, sites on the web, but not necessarily to the saturation point indicated by such stories.

In 1996, responding to the prevalence of such material online, the US government attempted to control the publication of obscene material on the net by means of the Communications Decency Act, part of a wider telecommunications bill. This proved to be a rather draconian and heavy-handed regulatory tool in that the letter of the law applied more excessive regulation to the web than to other media, and the Act was declared unconstitutional within months. More recently, another act passed in the same year, the Child Pornography Prevention Act, was tested in *Ashcroft* v. *Free Speech Coalition* (2002), particularly with regard to virtual child pornography (that is computer-generated images and video); the Supreme Court decreed that two parts of the original Act were overbroad in relation to the First Amendment protecting free speech, and a revised Act was passed in 2003.

In the UK, the 1990 Computer Misuse Act and notoriously slippery 1959 Obscene Publications Act (OPA) have been used to deal with online obscenity. Various ISPs use services such as Cleanfeed and Webminder to identify pages containing child pornography, with the possibility that other types of content could also be blocked in the future. In 2003, following the murder of Jane Longhurst by a man who claimed to be obsessed with internet pornography, the government began work on legislation to ban possession of extreme forms of content depicting such things as rape and torture, although this has proved to be more controversial.

While the argument in the USA has often been polarised between those advocating free speech whatever the cost and those advocating censorship whatever the cost, attempts to introduce such things as the Communications Decency Act and Child Pornography Prevention Act have demonstrated some of the difficulties (but not the impossibility) for a national government to legislate for this particular international medium.

The other side of proliferation of obscene materials is the way in which some governments actively control access to the internet. At its most extreme, as in Burma or North Korea, this is generally implemented in terms of denying access to parts or the majority of the population, but a more sophisticated and interesting form of censorship is practised by China. The Golden Shield Project, also referred to as the Great Firewall of China outside that country, was begun in 1998 and was decreed effective for use in 2006. This is a firewall and proxy server that blocks certain IP addresses from being viewed within China. In addition, over 60 regulations have been passed restricting access, and an estimated 30,000 so-called 'internet police' work to monitor and censor content, often removing critical comments within minutes.

Relations between new media companies and Chinese officials have often resulted in controversy. In 2006, for example, Google agreed to censor content (information on Tibet, or the banned Falun Gong movement, for example) in order to gain access to the fast-growing Chinese market. In 2005 Yahoo! was accused of passing on personal information to the authorities that led to the arrest of a dissident, and Microsoft has been criticised for censoring blogs. As the number of Chinese users has already passed that of users in the US (hitting

> Censorship of a political and ideological nature has often struggled with the ease of online communications, but dedicated efforts such as those in China can still have a definite effect in restricting access to parts of the internet for millions of users.

220 million in early 2008, compared to 216 million in the US), major technology companies simply cannot afford to ignore the world's largest online market. Around the same time as it overtook the US in its number of users, the Chinese government decided to ease some of its restrictions on which sites were blocked as part of an agreement with the International Olympic Committee in preparation for the Beijing Olympics.

Spam and privacy

While copyright infringement has tended to concern producers and regulators more than users, the problem of junk-mail, or spam, is one appreciated by just about everyone. Spamming occurs when an individual or company sends out a message (often anonymously) to a list of recipients. Such messages may be illegal or unsuitable for the recipient, such as pornographic links or phishing mails which attempt to lure visitors into providing personal details such as credit card or banking information. Even if this is not the case, spam is ultimately paid for by the person who downloads the information and can be a major irritation, with accounts becoming unusable because of the large number of unsolicited emails.

For web producers, there is the added problem that areas of a site that are open to user contributions, such as forums, can be flooded with spam messages. This unwanted noise will deter legitimate users from reading or posting to a site, although bulletin board software such as FireBoard usually can be configured to prevent spamming, for example by restricting the time between posts or by rejecting anonymous messages to multiple users. While such restrictions can have an adverse effect on other site members who may wish to post on a regular basis, this is a necessary evil to prevent a forum becoming unusable (the inevitable

consequence for a lot of older newsgroups which are full of unwanted and unwelcome postings).

The Spamhaus Project (www.spamhaus.org) estimates that up to 80 per cent of spam generated in the US and Europe is generated by around 200 professional spam gangs, mostly based in the Russian Federation but with many others to be found elsewhere in Europe and the US, as well as China and India. One of the world's most prolific spammers, Robert Soloway, who advertised that he could send up to 20 million emails a day, was arrested in 2007 and charged by the US federal authorities with fraud and identity theft. Major spammers such as Soloway use so-called 'zombie' computers to circulate large amounts of mail, infecting PCs with a virus or Trojan that can be used to forward messages to other users with users being unaware that their computer has been compromised.

Because of the scale of the problem, various countries have introduced anti-spam legislation. In the US, the CAN-SPAM Act of 2003 (updated in 2008) sought to control unsolicited email, requiring legal mass-mailings to include opt-out instructions and forbidding the use of misleading headings. In the EU, regulations have tended to be much stricter, as with the E-Privacy Directive (2002): although the original directive, which imposed a £5,000 fine on spammers in the UK, was branded ineffective, it has at least meant that most junk-email received by European users originates outside EU borders.

> One of the scourges of modern day life, most spam messages are produced by a small number of professionals based in Russia and a few other countries.

Protection of privacy generally is one area where European legislation is probably more advanced than in the US, although this is not the case with freedom of information. The original 1998 Data Protection Act in the UK was criticised for its failure to address the problem of spam, emphasising as it did the responsibility of users for their own data. Nonetheless, the UK and EU governments have sought to address this issue, particularly as more and more companies collect greater amounts of information about customers online, and the individual is not entirely helpless in the face of spamming. Rather than simply deleting a message or replying to it, users can often work out where an email came from and complain to the ISP that delivered it.

For more information and updates on content and regulation, visit www.producingforweb2.com/content.

CHAPTER 9

Post-production

Once your site is up and running, the final stage is to test that it works as expected before promoting it. In this chapter we shall look in detail at how such testing takes place, as well as looking at ways to drive traffic to your site, for example through search engine optimisation (SEO) and by using various tools to analyse how your site is being used by visitors.

SITE TESTING AND MAINTENANCE

While having great ideas for a site is immensely important, these will count for very little if your site does not work properly. So when you are producing a site it is important to get into the mindset of testing everything you do on a regular basis.

Testing is something that should be done throughout the production process: when you create a section or implement a feature, it should be checked to see what impact it has on the rest of the site and, if necessary, amended and modified. So, although we are dealing with site testing in the final chapter of this book, it should actually be taking place fairly early on during your design as a means of providing feedback on what you do.

What is more – and this becomes a crucial issue with usability, which we shall consider later in this section – there are limits as to what the web producer can do him- or herself. Proper testing requires real users, people who do not approach a site with your outlook and expectations but instead want to use the site their own way. They are likely to spot bugs or unexpected occurrences much more quickly than a producer working on his or her own, precisely because those bugs were unexpected to the original designer.

During the beta stage of a site, before you publicise it, try and get as many people to use it who you know will provide feedback and help you iron out any glitches before it goes public.

Using FTP

File transfer protocol (FTP) is one of the core internet technologies that, as its name indicates, governs downloading and uploading files. Most users encounter it via such things as music and game sharing, and for web designers it is often an essential part of producing and maintaining a site.

For many of the technologies and approaches outlined in this book, raw FTP – that is using a client to upload files to a web server – may appear redundant: blogs, many content management systems and other forms

> **FTP is a core internet technology used to download and upload files to sites and between users.**

of web design run through the browser and require no knowledge of FTP (although it often handles many transactions in the background).

A dedicated FTP site uses the convention ftp:// rather than http:// in its URL, and often (although not always) will be run on an FTP server that handles only this type of connection. As with a filing cabinet, FTP sites contain different folders for different users to store their documents, requiring a user ID and password to access it – although sometimes transfer is anonymous and either no password is needed or a visitor simply enters his or her email address. It is because of this possibility of anonymous transfer that many users of the web do not even realise that they are transferring files from an FTP site rather than **HTTP** web server.

FTP connections may be made via the browser or a dedicated client. The latter is usually preferable for web producers in that it is easier to handle transfers of a large number of files. Indeed, if you are doing your web design from within an editor such as Dreamweaver, the chances are that it has FTP capabilities built in: once you have entered the address of your server, along with a user name and password, files can be uploaded automatically from within the editor.

Using an FTP client is usually very simple – most come with two panes (one showing the local hard drive, the other the remote server) and uploading is simply a question of dragging and dropping files from one pane to the other.

Quality and reliability

When it comes to testing a site, this can be broken down into two main areas: issues of quality, and issues of usability.

The quality of a website is typically tied up with (but by no means limited to) its reliability. A website that cannot be accessed because of hardware or software issues is useless, and while it is impossible to guarantee access to a

server 100 per cent of the time the server needs to be available more or less constantly (check the terms and conditions of pretty much any contract you sign with an ISP – in the small print there will almost certainly be a clause guaranteeing up-times of somewhere over 99, even 99.9, per cent, but less than 100).

Along with reliability, a website's performance is also crucial – how fast it loads pages and delivers files to users. The time taken to respond is a server's latency, and performance may vary at different times and should be tested regularly to see if bottlenecks occur. Quality, however, covers much more than the factors of reliability and performance – although these are the ones that are most easily automated in that they do not require much in the way of subjective opinion. A website is available or it is not, and page load times can be measured in milliseconds. Some of the other elements that you should consider, however, will often call upon other considerations on the part of the audience to be taken into account.

> The quality of a site depends on its reliability and performance as well as the value of any material stored there.

For example, an important element to the perception of your website will be its timeliness and the relevance of information that you provide. The importance of this will vary from site to site: a guide to the classical verities of Roman literature may look as though it will not need as much updating as a rolling news site, but it will still need to take into account recent scholarship if it is to be at all authoritative. For all sites, regular updates and maintenance become important to the audience's perception that this will remain a site worth visiting again and again.

Likewise, accuracy is an important feature for a site, and covers a variety of aspects. First of all, there is the very simple (but often neglected) fact that inaccurate writing that is full of errors in spelling, grammar and punctuation will affect how visitors view the value of your content. In addition, factual errors will undermine your credibility, and where possible sources for information should always be indicated. Tim Berners-Lee has recently commented on the unfortunate role of the web as a source of disinformation, and while his proposals for some kind of credibility rating system are unlikely to catch on, there is no reason why your site should contribute to the general confusion online.

In addition, you need to test the 'architecture' of your website, how it performs in different browsers and how the whole thing hangs together. Different browsers, such as Safari, Firefox and Internet Explorer, can display elements of a page differently. Although this is not as much a problem as it was in the days of Internet Explorer versus Netscape Navigator, when each company introduced proprietary tags into their code, it is an unfortunate fact that the most popular browser on the planet, Microsoft's IE, is not always as compliant with various standards as others (and this is particularly true of version 6.0, which although superseded by 7.0 at the time of writing still remains in place on plenty of systems).

In addition, what happens if a crucial part of your site relies on Flash? And which release of the Flash Player is needed to view it? While Adobe claims well over 95 per cent (indeed, according to some of their comments, over 98 per cent) of computers have Flash installed, this drops to around 50 per cent with the latest version. If you rely on Flash for navigation, for example, you could be denying plenty of visitors the ability to use your site, so a non-Flash version should also be available. Similarly, depending on a scripting language such as JavaScript can also cause problems if a visitor has scripting turned off.

Finally, to end on a basic but often overlooked point, at regular intervals you need to go back and check all the links on your site. Few things are more frustrating than clicking a link only to be brought to a dead end: in particular, if you are using some form of dynamic CMS to upload content, URLs may change as pages are modified, and you should make sure that all hand-coded links point to the page you intended.

Usability testing

Although it is separated out from quality and reliability testing, a website's usability is frequently intimately tied to these other qualities. At its simplest, a website that is too slow to load will frustrate users and be judged by them as unworkable.

Usability refers to the experience of a visitor to a site, and in general deals with how easily and quickly that visitor can achieve his or her aims. If a visitor wishes to find a contact, or post a message or find information on fixing a computer, usability testing should take into account how effectively that is achieved. On a more advanced level, usability may also consider cost-effectiveness and usefulness – some of the factors that have already been discussed under quality and reliability. The ISO definition of usability indicates that it is judged acceptable when specified (that is not random or general) visitors can achieve specific goals effectively, efficiently and to their own satisfaction.

A key phrase that is often referred to in this regard is user-centred design, which emphasises the feedback nature of web production: a designer should plan, construct, test and then use the information that he or she gains from testing to refine and restructure a design.

To re-iterate some of the key concepts of user-centred design stated, a website has to be useful to visitors, and so the first step is defining who these visitors are and their objectives, followed by how those goals tie into your own aims. For example, if your site is aimed at gaining feedback from visitors (say you have

> **User-centred design emphasises the importance of feedback as part of the production process, using the information gained from testers to refine and restructure a site.**

been commissioned to construct a site that gathers information on products or services for a company), then what you should do is determine the kinds of feedback customers may wish to provide, and then what mechanisms will best serve this end. A simple mail form may be the most suitable for this particular site, although you should also consider that plenty of customers really want a phone number when they need to complain about something. A forum might be too dangerous for your organisation's needs, but in other circumstances (and with careful moderation) could be perfect for stimulating wider discussion by allowing visitors to see beyond their own immediate interests. Likewise, for articles and stories, it might be that some form of comments system could be the best way of getting information quickly and easily.

User-centred design focuses on trying to put yourself in the place of your users – what functions they expect and how they anticipate the site will work. Proper testing for this can't really be simulated – you need real users to try out your design – but the steps involved are as follows:

1   Speak to users to find out what they want (sometimes quite a difficult task, as many people will be relatively unclear).
2   Use this information to inform the planning process. This will determine what the aims of a site should be and what mechanisms will best achieve them.
3   Develop a prototype of the site, including content.
4   Test that prototype with users, again using any data collected to inform redevelopment work.

Usability.gov provides some extremely helpful information on usability testing, and there are some general observations that are indicative of the things to look for when testing your site with users:

■   How easy is the site to learn? A common problem for technically minded web producers is that they will understand a

technology inside out, but visitors have other things to do with their lives.
■   How efficient is a site once a visitor has learnt how to use it? How quickly can they achieve their aims?
■   Is the site memorable? Once a visitor has learnt its operation, can he or she return to it even after some time or must they learn how to do everything again?
■   How often do users make errors, and how severe are they? Can visitors recover from errors and find their way back to a useful starting point?
■   What is the level of subjective satisfaction? How do visitors feel about using your site?

Lauren Kirby (http://www.sitepoint.com/article/website-usability/) makes a pertinent observation about usability: treat it as a 'pay now or pay later' option. You do not have to engage in usability testing, but if you don't and visitors to your site do not find it easy to navigate and locate what they want, they won't bookmark it and return later.

Testing for disabled users

Another important consideration for web design is to take into account the needs of users who have a disability, particularly visual or aural impairment, but also motor-impairment. In the UK, the Disability Discrimination Act (1995, the DDA), makes it unlawful for a service provider to make available to the public information or services, including websites, that cannot be accessed by disabled visitors – something which was clarified by a Code of Practice published in 2002.

Considerations about accessibility and web design are usually restricted to visually impaired users, but while this is obviously important (perhaps the most important factor of testing a site), these users are not the only ones whose needs must be addressed. The Code of Practice for the DDA defines a disabled person as someone with a physical or mental impairment that affects their daily activity. Sites that use audio obviously have to think of deaf or partially deaf visitors, and people with motor difficulties will often find it difficult to navigate a site with a mouse. Likewise, for visitors with learning difficulties, such as those caused by dyslexia, many sites can simply be confusing.

Accessibility software and utilities used by disabled visitors will include screen readers and screen magnifiers which, as the names suggest, read out text on a web page or make it larger; anything which interferes with this will immediately make a site less accessible. For example, images without ALT tags will simply be omitted and if those images provide navigation for a site it will become impossible for a blind user to move around from page to page. In the case of deaf users, Windows can be set up to employ SoundSentry which generates visual warnings when the operating system creates a sound, but for websites such things as podcasts will require an alternative transcript that can be read rather than listened to.

> **Ensuring that your site can be accessed by users with disabilities (such as visual impairment) is not just a question of etiquette but also a legal obligation in countries such as the UK.**

The World Wide Web Consortium (W3C) has drawn up a Web Accessibility Initiative (www.w3.org/WAI/) which, at the time of writing, is currently being revised as version 2.0. Key elements include providing text alternatives for images and time-based media (audio and video), as well as making content consistent and flexible enough to be presented in different formats. As the W3C points out, many of the features that will make web content more accessible for disabled users are also of benefit to visitors without disabilities.

It is worth noting some of the specific difficulties created by Web 2.0 techniques and technologies. For example, Ajax as a collection of web technologies to improve interactivity and presentation can cause problems with screen readers: because Ajax can be used only to update part of a page, a reader may not realise that the page has changed or, alternatively, may start reading the entire page again rather than simply the section which has been modified. In addition, may Web 2.0 features require a mouse to work and cannot be used with a keyboard alone, for example to drag and drop files into a browser window.

A more serious issue, however, is raised by the proliferation of sites that rely on user-generated content (UGC). While organisations may spend a great deal of time training web managers and content producers to pay particular attention to making their sites accessible, when the number of potential authors increases both inside and outside a company then it becomes harder than ever to test for accessibility. In particular, external contributors tend to add rich media without additional text and so fail to provide non-visual information for blind or partially sighted visitors. This last point leads to the fact that with the explosion of such UGC, there may be a return to alternative versions of sites. Quite rightly this had become frowned on in recent years, with text-only versions of sites being replaced by single sites that paid more attention to accessibility issues, but UGC sites have generally been rather poor when it comes to paying attention to the needs of disabled visitors.

When testing a site for accessibility, the following elements should be borne in mind:

- Always implement the ALT text attribute for rich media such as pictures, but there is no need to be verbose (a common mistake made by many developers). If you feel the need to include an extensive description, use the longdesc attribute.
- Text should be at a decent font size, and you should never set absolute font sizes using CSS.
- Do not insert empty text into a form field for the sake of it, because this can be confusing for someone using a screen reader.
- Links should be descriptive rather than simply 'click here'.

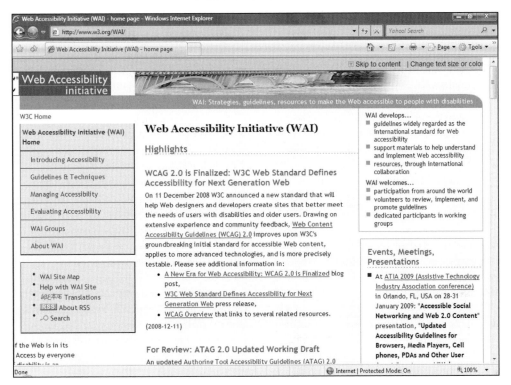

The Web Accessibility Initiative is concerned to make as much of the web open to as many people as possible.

- All functions should be accessible from a keyboard as well as a mouse, which will help users with visual and motor disabilities.
- Visitors with motor disabilities need the largest possible area for links: while this can be achieved by replacing text with images, this can create problems for visually impaired users. It is better to use CSS attributes to increase the padding around text links. Likewise, drop-down menus can create a problem for disabled visitors.
- Be aware of colour blindness, whereby certain combinations of colours will not display clearly on screen. Likewise, dyslexic visitors will find text difficult to read against a white background.
- Accessibility is not just about the structure of a page (such as where navigation is located), but also its content which needs to be as clear and as usable as possible.

Visitors with learning difficulties in particular need to be able to find their way back to simpler content, and pages work best when they are broken into smaller chunks of information that are clearly signposted. This is actually one area where usability guidelines benefit more than disabled users, as many visitors may wish to access the relevant information they need as quickly as possible.

Testing checklist

Performance and quality testing is one element that can be automated with various software tools such as the following:

- If all you need is a simple tool to test data transfers (effectively by pinging the site – that is sending a request for data and then timing the response), www.websitepulse. com allows you to do this, as well as check links in pages and how long it takes to download complete web pages.

- For validating your site's XHTML code, enter the URL for pages at validator.w3.org. Similarly, online validators for RSS feeds, cascading style sheets and links can be found at validator.w3.org/feed/, jigsaw. w3.org/css-validator/ and validator.w3.org/ checklink/.
- Remember to make use of any spellcheckers/grammar checkers included in your web editor or content management system.

Usability and accessibility need to be tested in conjunction with other users, and below is a sample questionnaire that could be completed with those testers.

- What sort of information do you think the site contains?
- Who is it intended for and why?
- Who manages the site and how would you contact them if necessary?
- What is your overall impression of the site?
- What do you think of its search facility?
- What do you like best about the site?
- What do you like least about the site?
- If you needed to find a specific piece of information, how would you go about finding it? (To evaluate this, both the number of participants successfully finding information and the time it took them to locate it would need to be evaluated.)
- In what ways would you wish to use this site? (This also allows the tester to evaluate ways in which visitors may employ a site in ways not considered by the original designers.)
- Is it accessible for disabled users (for example those suffering from visual or motor impairments)?
- Can the site be navigated and used with the keyboard alone?
- Are images and other rich media described with alternative text?
- Have you tested your site with a screen reader?

- Are sections of content clearly labelled?
- If you had to describe the site in a sentence, how would you do so?
- If you were the web developer, what feature would you change immediately?

SECURITY

With your website constructed and online, anyone with an internet connection will be able to view your content. Obviously this is a good thing. However, you will not want all your data to be on view to all users. Casual visitors should not be able to access the back end of your site and so (inadvertently or otherwise) break carefully constructed pages. Some areas may be protected, and only accessible to certain registered users. Worse still, hackers may seek to make malicious attacks on your site. Paying attention to the security of your web server is therefore an important consideration as part of the testing process.

Encryption and secured networks

No one wants their website to be hacked, but where particularly sensitive data is stored online (for example credit card details for an e-commerce site), then encryption becomes doubly important. Login details and transactions that are secured with encryption will be indicated via a padlock icon next to the browser address bar or in the lower toolbar.

The standard for secure communications across the internet is Secure Socket Layer (SSL), with an upgraded version, Transport Layer Security (TLS), due to replace it. Although TLS has officially replaced SSL 3.0, most of the following comments will apply to SSL as this is still the most widely used process.

There are several ways in which SSL can be deployed to protect the transfer of data to and from a website, but the essential steps are as follows: the client (a visitor's browser) connects to the host site and performs what is known as a 'handshake', the initial connection that requests the server to send its identification details. This is provided in the form of a digital certificate that includes the server's public encryption key. From this, the client creates a 'session key', a random number that can only be encrypted by means of the server's private key (which, as the name suggests, is not publicly available). The random number is sent back to the client to authenticate the server's status and start the secured connection.

The reference to private and public keys draws attention to one way in which encryption can work. A site makes use of two keys, one which is publicly available and is used to generate a large random number. That number can only then be decrypted using a secret private key – the two keys are related, but the private

> **Encryption is a common technique to prevent sites being hacked into and is particularly important for the transfer of sensitive information such as commercial transactions.**

key cannot (easily) be derived from the public key. A potential problem for public key use is proving in the first place that it derives from an appropriate source, and to this end digital certificates are used: these usually work via a public-key infrastructure (PKI), in which a certificate authority verifies ownership of the public key. If a server certificate does not match the domain name, then a warning will appear in the browser.

There are different types of certificates, which are usually provided by hosting services or can be applied for via a third party such as Network Solutions. The highest level is an organisationally validated certificate, which verifies that the business behind the

OpenPGP Alliance is one of several organisations concerned with encryption and protection of data online.

website is a legitimate company. This is the most rigorously tested of the three (and consequently the most time-consuming and expensive), but is important for organisations that are setting up business online. A domain validated certificate simply checks that the applicant's information matches their WHOIS details for the website being registered. Finally, extended validation, introduced in 2007, is limited to corporations and government bodies: the most restricted in terms of availability, it provides easy colour-coded information to the visitor in that the browser address bar turns green when validated.

> **If your web host provides backup software, be sure to use it regularly. If such software is not available, there are plenty of alternatives available to keep copies of your data.**

For small-scale developers, it is most common that a shared SSL certificate will be provided at a low cost by the hosting company. This is either an organisation or domain validation that is then used to verify the domain names hosted on the ISP's servers.

On another level, it is also worth bearing in mind that when working on website development the security of the network you are using is important. If you are connecting to the internet via a wireless network, for example, this should have some form of encryption in place – uploading your personal details via an open-access network in a coffee shop, for example, is not really the best of ideas.

Backing up

While web producers will hope for the best with any site that they produce, they should also prepare for the worst. Hardware failure, software glitches, malicious attacks on a server, all these and other problems can result in the loss of data on a carefully prepared site. Ensuring that your site is regularly backed up is extremely important.

Many web hosting providers will automatically back up files loaded onto their servers and it is important to locate where such files will be stored. If your host uses cPanel, then creating a backup is extremely simple. The Backup Wizard included as part of the software creates a single zip file that includes the home directory and SQL databases on the server, as well as any email configurations and as many elements as you wish to include. Once completed, this can be downloaded to another PC, and the same Wizard also allows you to restore it at a later date.

An alternative route to backing up your site is to use separate software such as SiteVault (www.site-vault.com) or Handy Backup (www.handybackup.net), which use wizards to create copies of all files and databases in a fashion similar to the wizard in cPanel.

If you do not have backup software to hand and do not wish to invest in software, it is also possible to back up a site manually, by using FTP to download files to your computer and a utility, MySQLDump, that is included as part of MySQL.

FTP works in exactly the same way as when uploading files to the remote server – although obviously in the opposite direction. MySQLDump is slightly more complicated to use, and is usually run from the console as a command with a series of instructions that specify which database is to be backed up as follows:

```
mysqldump —-user [user name]
    —-password=[password] [database
    name] > [dump file]
```

In the above command, obviously the elements in square brackets must be replaced with an actual user, password and database to be downloaded, while [dump file] refers to the file that is created by the utility, for example:

```
mysqldump —-user admin
    —-password=mypassword mydatabase >
    mynewfile.dmp
```

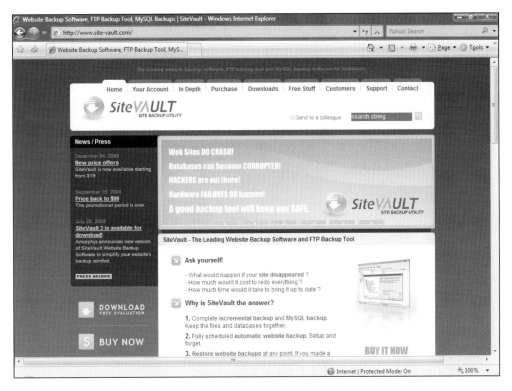

SiteVault is an example of a dedicated application that can back up a website.

The dump file that is created can then be downloaded via FTP. To restore the file, use the following command (noting the way the arrow points):

```
mysql --u [user name] --p [password]
    [database name] < [dump file]
```

Website vulnerabilities

A major concern for web producers is the vulnerability of their site in the face of hackers, whether concerted or casual attempts to exploit flaws in software running on a server. These are often referred to as common vulnerabilities and errors (CVE) and a comprehensive database of such flaws (not limited to server applications) is maintained on the US government's National Vulnerability Database (nvd.nist.gov). There is also a dictionary of CVEs available at cve.mitre. org. Here we shall concentrate only on the

general scope of these vulnerabilities as well as a few of the most commonly found.

CVEs may take several forms. Many are due to poor configuration, where default settings allow hackers access to private information, for example by leaving the admin name as 'root' or failing to set a password. There are also known bugs in software or operating systems which, if not kept up to date with patches and new releases, may leave a site exposed. Finally, there are patterns of attack which, when linked to poor configuration of software bugs, may bring down a server or allow a hacker to take over the site. In some cases, the latter may not even be due to failings in the actual server itself, but to a concerted effort to knock out a site. Most notorious is a distributed denial of service attack (DDoS): this can work in several ways, but the general concept is that a server is flooded with requests that prevent it from communicating with its intended audience, usually by installing a virus, or Trojan, on multiple machines that then target the same site – with the owners of these computers blissfully unaware that their PC has been infected.

Serious attacks like this will, in a small number of cases, be ideologically motivated (as when Russian hackers attacked Lithuanian sites in July 2008 following the banning of communist symbols) or, more commonly, be an attempt to extort money. The vast majority of sites are unlikely to be affected by large-scale attacks, but there will still be everyday, mundane attempts to compromise security on a server. Sometimes this will not even be because the site itself is particularly valuable to a hacker in terms of its content (although, of course, anything that deals with e-commerce will always be tempting), but as a means of hosting malware to attack other sites. And of course, the egotism of a hacker – attempting to penetrate security to show that it can be done – should never be underestimated.

It pays to be realistic about security, therefore. Most sites are not the targets of the worst attacks online, but even small breaches may compromise your data and cause embarrassment. A fairly common technique is for an unscrupulous company or individual to look out for domain names that are close to expiry and then buy them up if they are not renewed. In such instances, you could be forced to pay out a considerable amount of money to prevent your company name or personal site being associated with, for example, pornography or cheap Viagra substitutes. It pays to be vigilant and keep your registrations up to date.

Here we shall just concentrate on three common vulnerabilities, and how best to rectify them:

SQL injection

This is where malicious code is inserted into a query made against a SQL database-driven site in order to make it perform more actions. It works by terminating a string of text prematurely and adding a new command at the end, for example to draw up a list of user names or passwords or to stop the database

working altogether. The procedures to prevent SQL injection are fairly complex, but essentially require all input to be validated, for example by ensuring that an entry asking for a visitor's post code is limited to a few characters – and therefore cannot be compromised by adding a 5 megabyte MP3 file instead.

Cross-site scripting

Often referred to as XSS to differentiate it from cascading style sheets, cross-site scripting allows code to be injected into web pages viewed by other visitors using client-side scripts or even HTML. This is often employed in phishing attacks, whereby sensitive information is taken from a visitor's computer. It can work by inserting malicious code into a hyperlink, so that when someone clicks the link for a page it loads a malicious site instead. For web services, techniques to prevent this taking place include substituting < and > to the HTML code < and > which will render scripts ineffective.

Session hijacking

When users connect to a website that requires a login, this is often authenticated by means of what is known as a session key, validated by a cookie stored on the server and the visitor's personal computer. If an attacker is able to steal the remote cookie (that is the one stored on the server), they will be able to access personal data. Techniques to prevent this include the use of random numbers for session keys (so that they cannot simply be guessed), encryption and changing the session key after each login. This last may cause its own problems, such as the back button on the browser not working properly, or forcing users to log in every time they visit a site, but these are generally preferable to allowing false users access to private information.

There is much more that could be written on the technical complexities of maintaining security on your server. In general, however, always ensure that the most up-to-date version of any software is running on your server and any patches are in place, and monitor in particular areas where visitors can have input. If you can put anti-spam measures in place, do so, and watch out in particular for potential malicious links that could steal personal information from visitors and ruin the credentials of your own site.

PROMOTING AND ANALYSING YOUR SITE

After constructing and testing your site, the final stage is to try and increase the traffic it generates by letting as many people as possible know about it. In recent years, search engines have become the main means by which visitors find what they are looking for, so optimising pages for search engines has become a major industry in its own right. In this section, we shall consider some tips to make your site as helpful as possible to the automatic robots, or bots – software applications that crawl through the web following links to content, sometimes known as spiders or crawlers – and look at ways to analyse important information that is collected when anyone clicks a link onto your pages.

> Promoting a site is important to build up traffic which, in turn, can be analysed with special software to monitor which pages are the most popular.

Meta tags

The oldest way to promote your site to increase rankings in search engines is to use HTML meta tags. This is not necessarily the most effective means any more (we shall look at other strategies as part of search engine optimisation and using sitemaps), but as part of the web production arsenal it should not be overlooked.

Meta tags are metadata about a page or site that is inserted into the <head> element of a page. This information is not visible to visitors and not necessarily of concern to them; rather, it is used to provide data to automatic search bots that can interpret this information when returning links on search engines.

The <meta> element follows on from the <title> element in the head section of a page:

although not strictly a meta tag, the title element is important in providing some information to a search engine. Typical meta tags as they would be included in an HTML file are as follows:

```
<title>Biography of William Blake</title>
<meta name="description"
    content="Everything you need to know
    about the life of William Blake">
<meta name="keywords" content="William
    Blake, biography, life, eighteenth-
    century, nineteenth-century, art,
    poetry">
```

The description tag provides some control over how a page is described in a search engine listing (although Google is one that ignores this). The keywords tag is useful in that it is sometimes employed by crawlers to locate pages – although if you do not use the terms elsewhere on the page, it is likely to be ignored, and plenty of major bots do not reference it any more because of misuse in the past.

Previously, web producers would try to boost rankings by inserting plenty of keywords that had nothing to do with relevant content on the page. Meta tags are much less significant now, but they are worth knowing for those few bots that still employ them. However, there are much better ways to optimise your site for search engines.

Search engine optimisation (SEO)

Because of the importance of search engines for generating traffic to a site, a great deal of time and effort is devoted by professional web producers to search engine optimisation (SEO). If a site's ranking can be improved – that is, it is made to appear higher up the listings when a visitor to a search engine types in a key word or phrase – then it is more likely that a person will click its hyperlink.

SEO techniques generally concentrate on the content of a site and its HTML coding. Although we are covering SEO as part of the post-production process, in practice it is much better to engage with such optimisation as part of the development of pages rather than add it on after the event. Making sites as search-engine-friendly as possible is one way to increase rankings, but it is also worth bearing in mind that some techniques previously employed (such as spurious meta tags) are now largely ignored by search bots.

The earliest form of making sites search-friendly consisted of submitting a URL to a search engine in order to prompt it to crawl through related links and create an index. A few directories, such as Yahoo! and the Open Directory Project, still require submissions to be made manually before they are reviewed by editors. More often, however, the process is automatic as search bots crawl the web following link after link. By the late 1990s, it became clear that plenty of web producers were stuffing pages with irrelevant metadata which resulted in irrelevant and misleading page rankings on different search engines, and so those search sites adjusted the way they indexed and ranked pages to try and overcome these effects.

Search engines themselves provide guidelines as to how to improve ranking, and in general this consists of ensuring that your content is clearly designed for visitors to your page and then made accessible to search bots without any element of deception. The latter (involving techniques such as hiding text off the screen that is not relevant to the main content, making it invisible to users by changing its colour to the same as the background, or providing false alternative text for images) is frowned upon and may even be penalised by search engines.

Because so many visitors follow initial search links, quite an industry has grown up

> **Search engine optimisation has become a major industry in its own right, reflecting the importance of search engines such as Google in directing visitors to different parts of the web.**

around this kind of optimisation, but companies that offer to guarantee top results for a huge number of search sites are at best offering something that is too good to be true and, at worst, may even be out to scam web producers.

Unfortunately, in many cases there are no shortcuts as sites such as Google and Yahoo! have attempted to weed out manipulation of their search algorithms.

The root of a successful SEO strategy has to lie with content: techniques to enhance HTML coding and site structure will bear little success if the correlating content on a page cannot be found. Because well-produced content is more likely to attract returning visitors, these visitors are more likely to link to your site which, in turn, affects such things as Google's PageRank algorithm. As well as making that content as effective as possible, refreshing and updating it will also encourage not only visitors but also search bots to return to re-index a site.

The following are a few pointers to creating successful content that will be helpful in terms of SEO:

- **Spelling is important** Misspelt content is liable to miss out in that it will not show up in searches. However, if optimisation is important for an international audience, then American spellings of English (such as color instead of colour, or optimization instead of optimisation) are likely to get better rankings.
- **Provide descriptive titles** The significance of the <title> element has already been mentioned in the section on meta tags, but it is also worth bearing in mind that the more descriptive a title is, the more likely it is to be returned in a keyword search. 'Welcome to the Gadget X Manufacturer's Home Page' is much better than simply 'Home Page'. In addition, it is vital that you

do not provide the same title for each page on your site.

- **Include keywords in your opening paragraph** Important text that you hope will be rated highly on a search engine should appear as early as possible in the text on your page. This is where news writing skills come into their own, and indeed as most visitors will be scanning text before moving on (or staying to read the page), this is important for people as well as bots.

- **Use headings instead of graphics for sections of your page** Using the <h1> to <h6> elements in a page instead of images will indicate to a search engine that something structurally important is happening at this point in the page.

- **Use search engine friendly URLs** Dynamic sites often generate URLs automatically from a string of characters that do not convey much useful information about a page. Packages such as Joomla!, however, have settings (as well as third-party plug-ins) that allow you to create human- (and bot-) readable web addresses.

- **Use clean markup** While a browser can usually make sense of the tangled code that is often produced by visual web editors in particular, this will slow down results for a search bot, especially if presentation markup (such as font formatting) is mixed up with structural HTML such as that which indicates paragraphs and headings. Use CSS for presentation, and also concentrate on accessibility, which makes your pages more readable for search bots as well as human visitors.

- **Use simple navigation** Complex navigation techniques such as JavaScript or Flash menus will make links harder to find and should be avoided. Likewise, graphical buttons for links instead of text could be overlooked.

- **Don't use frames** Websites with frames are so 1990s, and for one simple reason: they can be very difficult for search engines to navigate. Because of this, creating a website with frames has not been covered at all in this book.

Much of this is common sense for web writers, and it is worth noting that much of the section in this book on content creation is important when thinking of improving your site's page rankings. In the end, the aim of search engine optimisation is to try and improve how many people visit, read and thus link to your site.

Sitemaps

One way to improve the performance of your website with search engines is to generate a sitemap. A sitemap is a document which includes links to most if not all of the pages contained on your site. At its simplest, a sitemap can be constructed by the web master as an individual page for smaller sites and is an HTML file with hyperlinks; more complex ones can be generated by programs such as Dreamweaver. Such files are really designed to help human visitors navigate your site more easily rather than provide information to automated search engine robots.

When a search engine compiles a list of information to display against keyword searches, a crawler will follow each link and so compile an index of the site: it is this index that is searched when a visitor to the search engine types in a word or phrase, making for much faster searches. To speed up this process even further – and to ensure that all relevant pages are indexed – this kind of sitemap is an XML file that lists URLs for the site as well as additional information such as when pages were updated or how important it is in relation to other URLs.

This kind of metadata does not guarantee

> **A sitemap provides an index of the pages on your site. As an XML file, it makes it easier for search engines to index pages and so is an important part of SEO techniques.**

that pages will be indexed, but it does make it more likely that the most important pages will not be missed if a crawler fails to pick up on a URL (for a regularly updated page, for example).

It is possible to hand code an XML file for your site and, at its most basic, requires only three XML instructions – the <urlset> or container element, the <url> that holds all the information about your URL (for more complex sitemaps, this will include information about when and how often the page was modified, as well as its priority), and the <loc> or location, specifying where the page is actually found. As such, a simple sitemap file would look like the following:

```
<?xml version="1.0" encoding="UTF-8"?>
<urlset xmlns="http://www.sitemaps.org/
    schemas/sitemap/0.9">
    <url>
        <loc>http://www.mysite.com/pages/
changedpage.html</loc>
    </url>
</urlset>
```

In this example, the <urlset> element defines it against an established XML schema for generating sitemaps, the widely available and supported sitemap 0.9 schema. However, creating this file by hand for anything but the smallest site would become incredibly tedious and I recommend that you use software such as InSpyder (www.inspyder.com) or sites such as xml-sitemaps.com. The latter is more useful than many sitemap generators you will find online because it can output to different formats that are useful to search engines other than just Google.

Logs and analysis

Once a site is up and running, there will be various times when you may wish or even need to analyse how the site is operating, for example in terms of bandwidth, visitors and which pages are particularly popular. Such statistics may be important for keeping track of visitors for advertising purposes, or to check on how much traffic is being passed through your site.

A server will maintain a log of different types of activity that take place based on the page requests made by client connections to the server. Included in this log will be the client IP address (which can be tracked back to individual visitors), date and time, the user agent (typically a browser, but also search engine spiders), and the referrer, that is the web page that linked to the particular page requested. These and other elements are encoded according to standards maintained by the W3C.

A log is stored on the server as a text file which is not available to general visitors, only the web master. In its raw form, this is hard to decipher, but it is typically imported into web analysis software such as Analog, WebTrends or AWStats so that it can be converted into a graphical and/or tabular format.

When using this software, it is possible to see at a glance factors such as how much traffic has passed through the site, how many individual users visit over a given time period (whether a day or month or longer), where they come from, which operating system and browser they use, which pages were viewed and for how long, and any error messages. Such information can be extremely exhaustive, usually being provided in the form of a summary with links that drill down to much more detailed charts and tables.

One application that has started to gain a considerable following is Google Analytics, a free service available from www.google.com/analytics. There is a difference between Analytics and the other software mentioned above in that it is primarily aimed

> Analysing traffic of a site revolves around log files that are generated by and stored on the web server. This raw data is imported into software to generate visual reports of activity that takes place when visitors open pages and download files.

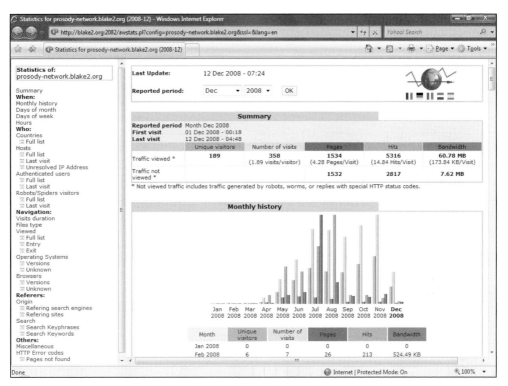

An example of the sort of information collected by web statistics software.

at advertisers and marketers rather than web masters, concentrating on tracking referrers in particular to note where visitors are coming from – particularly useful in such things as pay-per-click advertising.

Web advertising and marketing

The commercialisation of the web followed its deregulation in the early 1990s when commercial business began to take over the role of providing the infrastructure that had previously been handled by governmental organisations. By the mid-1990s, business had begun to move online either in the form of electronic retailers (notably Amazon, founded by Jeff Bezos in 1994, and eBay, started in 1995

> Online advertising has become the mainstay for the commercial operations of many sites, beginning with banner advertising in the 1990s and now incorporating such things as Google AdWords.

by Pierre Omidyar) or as content providers that, in the well-established formula established by other media formats, began to use advertising to generate revenues.

In the dotcom boom that began to take off at the end of the 1990s, banner advertising, now extremely familiar as the most common form of advertising online, became extremely lucrative. Borrowing the model provided by magazines, the most popular sites could charge an amount such as $30 per thousand impressions – that is, simply loading the page in the browser would generate a hit, and with millions of visitors to pages each month this quickly looked as though it would provide substantial sums of money to successful ventures.

As websites proliferated, however, so advertisers came to the opinion that the model that worked well for magazines was not so effective online. It became increasingly clear that the majority of visitors to a site would not follow through the advertisement (let alone make a purchase). In addition, for all but the largest sites it became clear that increasing competition was driving down costs as more and more commercial enterprises sought advertising to provide revenues for their websites, especially after the dotcom crash. Costs for banner impressions have now tumbled to a few cents per thousand for most contemporary sites.

The function of advertising can be to enhance branding for a product, service or manufacturer or, more commonly on the web, to promote direct sales. Ideally for advertisers, this means that a small percentage of visitors to a site will click on an advert and follow through to a site where they can buy goods or services.

Standard banner advertising is typically 728 pixels wide and 90 pixels high (a format established when most computer screens, and thus most sites, were capable of a resolution 800 pixels wide). Because of its familiarity, and thus the ease with which such advertising is ignored by most visitors, advertisers are frequently willing to pay more for alternative formats such as the following:

- **Sidebar ads**   Vertical rather than horizontal, these can be up to 600 pixels high and 120 pixels wide, offering more space than a traditional horizontal banner ad as well as remaining on the page longer as a user scrolls down to further content.
- **Different sizes and positions**   While standard banner ads tended to appear at the top or bottom of a page, square or irregularly sized ads will often occupy positions within content, making them harder to avoid.
- **Pop-ups and pop-unders**   The bane of many web surfers, as the names suggests these ads appear in a separate window above or (more recently) below the main content. They are liked by advertisers,

however, because they are much more effective in terms of click-through rates and, because more is paid for them, they are increasingly common even though browsers and other programs can be set to prevent them loading.

- **Floating ads**   A relatively recent occurrence employing technologies such as Ajax, these ads fly or hover over the page, blocking content for a few seconds before disappearing or a close button appears. Because of their intrusive nature, they are hard to ignore (especially as many are animated) and have a much higher click-through rate – although their annoyance factor is also much higher.
- **AdWords**   Perhaps the most successful online advertising format, Google AdWords operate by providing relatively innocuous text ads that advertisers pay for on a click-through basis, and which can be hosted on a range of websites, not simply those owned by Google (for example, Blogger).

Advertising may be one option for web producers who wish to promote their sites. AdWords (adwords.google.com) is an extremely flexible option that allows producers to place ads next to Google keyword searches. Once signed up, a budget can be set with no minimum amount (the site offers the example of a daily budget of five dollars a day and a maximum of ten cents per click-through, which would of course limit you to less popular keyword searches). More extensive (and, for small-scale advertising at least, more expensive) services are offered by specialist providers such as Doubleclick (www.doubleclick.com) and Netklix (www.netklix.com), while it is also possible to sign up for advertising on Facebook at www.facebook.com/ads.

In addition to providing advertising services to those wishing to sell online, companies such as Google, Netklix and Doubleclick also make it possible for websites to earn revenue by hosting advertising. To make use of these, a producer must sign up and provide information about the website where advertising is to be hosted as well as banking details where money is paid (usually monthly) for any click-throughs on a site.

WEB 2.0 GO

Throughout this book we have covered the essentials of web design for the contemporary environment, from initial concepts and planning to testing and analysis of traffic on your site.

The options open to web producers are more varied than ever before, and over the past five years these have become ever simpler to use. Mastering them, however, has returned attention to the core principles and technologies of the web. This book has paid a great deal of attention to the skills that students require to succeed in the modern multimedia world. To these skills must be added your own ideas and creativity, but the virtue of today's platforms is that there is always the tool for you, whether a fast and easy blog to get those ideas before a wider audience or a complete content management system to handle resources from multiple users.

For more information and updates on post-production, visit www.producingforweb2.com/post-production.

XHTML reference

STANDARD ATTRIBUTES

The following attributes are common across nearly all XHTML elements:

- **class** indicates a particular class that an element belongs to,
- **dir** sets text direction,
- **id** specifies a unique identifier for an element,
- **lang** specifies the language of an element,
- **style** specifies an inline style for an element, and
- **title** provides a title for an element that is sometimes displayed as a tooltip.

Element	Attributes*	Example	Description
<!DOCTYPE>	none	<!DOCTYPE html PUBLIC "-//W3C// DTD XHTML 1.0 Strict//EN" "http:// www.w3.org/TR/xhtml1/DTD/xhtml1-strict.dtd">	This declaration (rather than true element) must appear at the very top of an XHTML document and indicates which specification the document conforms to.
<a>	standard charset coords href rel shape type	<a title="Producing for Web 2.0" class="producing" href="http://www. producingforweb2.com">Producing for Web 2.0</a>	Specifies an anchor within a document, either as a shortcut within the same page or as a link to another document.
<area>	standard alt* coords href shape (circle, poly, rect)	<area shape ="rect" coords ="0,0,20,35" href ="start.htm" alt="start page" />	Defines a region in a client-side image map. Must be used with the <img> and <map> elements. It has no end tag, so must be properly closed in XHTML.

Element	Attributes*	Example	Description
`<base>`	href*	`<base href="http://www.mysite.com/images/" />`	Used to define a base URL for relative URLs in a document. It is used in the `<head>` section.
`<blockquote>`	standard	`<blockquote><p>Long quotation here</p> </blockquote>`	Defines a long quotation. In XHTML, should include a block element (such as `<p>`) as well as plain text.
`<body>`	standard	`<body>...</body>`	This defines the document's body and contains all content for the document.
` `	class id style title	` `	Inserts a line break. It has no end tag, so must be properly closed in XHTML.
`<button>`	standard disabled name type value	`<button type="button">Submit </button>`	Creates a push button that can contain text or images.
`<caption>`	standard	`<caption>The table's contents</caption>`	Inserts a caption above a table that is not placed in a row or cell.
`<col>`	standard align char charoff span valign width	`<col span="2" width="20"></col>`	Used to define the attributes for one or more columns in a table. It does not create columns (the td element does this) and is used inside a `<colgroup>` element.
`<colgroup>`	standard align char charoff span valign width	`<colgroup span="3" style="color:#00FF00;">`	Must be used inside a `<table>` element and is used to define a group of col elements.

Element	Attributes*	Example	Description
\<dd\>	standard	\<dl\> \<dt\>Water\</dt\> \<dd\>A liquid\</dd\> \</dl\>	Must be used inside a \<dl\> element and marks the definition of a term.
\<del\>	standard cite datetime	Updated on \<del\>Monday\</del\> Tuesday	Indicates where text has been deleted, usually as strikethrough text.
\<div\>	standard	\<div\>Content here... \</div\>	Defines a section within a document.
\<dl\>	standard	\<dl\> \<dt\>Water\</dt\> \<dd\>A liquid\</dd\> \</dl\>	Marks the start of a definition list.
\<dt\>	standard	\<dl\> \<dt\>Water\</dt\> \<dd\>A liquid\</dd\> \</dl\>	Marks the start of a term in a definition list. Must be used inside a \<dl\> tag.
\<fieldset\>	standard	\<fieldset\> Name \<input type="text" size="20" /\> Address \<input type="text" size="30" /\> \</fieldset\>	Groups elements within a form and applies a box around them.
\<form\>	standard action* accept enctype method	\<form\>Form inputs here... \</form\>	Required to contain the other elements that make up a form such as text fields and buttons.
\<h1\>–\<h6\>	standard	\<h2\>A level 2 heading\</h2\>	Defines headers within a document from the largest (\<h1\>) to the smallest (\<h6\>).
\<head\>	dir lang profile	\<head\> \<title\>My web page\</title\> \</head\>	Contains information about the document. Nothing (other than the title) is displayed in the browser.
\<hr\>	standard	\<hr /\>	Inserts a horizontal line in the document. It has no end tag, so must be properly closed in XHTML.

Element	Attributes*	Example	Description
<html>	dir id lang	<html> <head></head> <body></body> </html>	Tells the browser that the file is an HTML document and is the parent of other elements. First element after <!DOCTYPE>
<img>	standard alt* src* height ismpa longdesc usemap width	<img id="landscape" src="landscape.jpg" alt="picture of a landscape" />	Specifies an image within a document. It has no end tag, so must be properly closed in XHTML.
<input>	standard accept alt checked disabled maxlength name readonly size src type value	<label for="fullname">Name </label> <input type="text" name="fullname" value="enter name" />	Specifies various types of input (text, radio buttons, buttons, etc.) and must be used in a <form> element. It has no end tag, so must be properly closed in XHTML.
<ins>	standard cite datetime	Updated on <del>Monday</del> <ins>Tuesday</ins>	Indicates where text has been inserted, usually as underlined text.
<label>	standard for	<label for="fullname">Name </label> <input type="text" name="fullname" value="enter name" />	Defines a label for an input element in a form.
<legend>	standard	<legend>Caption for a fieldset</legend>	Defines a caption and must be used within the <fieldset> element.
<li>	standard	<ol> <li>First item</li> <li>Second item</li> </ol>	Indicates each item displayed in a numbered (<ol>) or bullet-point (<ul>) list.

Element	Attributes*	Example	Description
<link>	standard charset href media rel rev type	<link rel="stylesheet" type="text/css" href="mystyle.css" />	Defines the relationship between two documents (most commonly a style sheet and the current HTML document). It has no end tag, so must be properly closed in XHTML.
<map>	standard id* name	<map id ="MyImageMap" name="MyImageMap">Image map here...</map>	Specifies a client-side image map, and is used with <img> and <area> elements.
<meta>	dir lang content* http-equiv name scheme	<meta name="keywords" content="web design routledge" />	Provides information about the document (*meta*data), as keywords or descriptions. Can also be used to refresh content automatically. It has no end tag, so must be properly closed in XHTML.
<noscript>	standard	<noscript>Your browser does not support JavaScript.</noscript>	Specifies alternative content if scripting is not allowed in the browser.
<object>	standard archive classid codebase codetype data declare height name standby type usemap width	<object data="myPDF.pdf" type="application/pdf" width="300" height="200"> alt : <a href="myPDF.pdf">myPDF.pdf</a></object>	Used to embed other objects to be embedded in the document. If these are multimedia objects (audio or video files), this can be used with the <param> element to pass along any required values.
<ol>	standard	<ol> <li>First item</li> <li>Second item</li> </ol>	Specifies an ordered, or numbered, list.

Element	Attributes*	Example	Description
<optgroup>	standard label* disabled	<optgroup label="vehicles"> <option value ="car">Car</option> <option value ="van">Van</option> </optgroup>	Creates an option group (where options are combined together). Is used with the <option> element and must be used inside the <select> element.
<option>	standard disabled label selected value	<option value ="car">Car</option>	Specifies an option in the drop-down list. Must be used inside the <optgroup> element.
<p>	standard	<p class="standard"> Paragraph text here </p>	Defines a paragraph within a document.
<param>	id type value valuetype	<param name="Min" value="0" /> <param name="Max" value="10" />	Is used inside the <object> element to set values for multimedia objects. It has no end tag, so must be properly closed in XHTML.
<pre>	standard	<pre>Preformatted content here...</pre>	Preserves spaces and line breaks in preformatted text.
<script>	type* charset defer src	<script type="text/javascript"> document.write("Hello World!") </script>	Indicates dynamic content such as JavaScript.
<select>	standard disabled multiple name size	<select> <option value ="car">Car</option> <option value ="van">Van</option> </select>	Creates a drop-down list and is used with the <option> element.
<span>	standard	<span style="color:#0FED45;"> Content to go here... </span>	Groups inline elements within a document.
<style>	dir lang title type* media	<style type="text/css"> h1 {color: red} </style>	Sets up inline styles within a document (as opposed to external styles linked to via the <link> element).
<sub>	standard	_{subscript text}	Defines subscript text.

Element	Attributes*	Example	Description
<sup>	standard	^{superscript text}	Defines superscript text.
<table>	standard border cellpadding cellspacing frame rules summary width	<table border = "1"> <tr> <td>First cell</td> <td>Second cell</td> </tr> </table>	Used to define where a table begins and ends in a document.
<td>	standard abbr align axis char charoff colspan rowspan valign	<table border = "1"> <tr> <td>First cell</td> <td>Second cell</td> </tr> </table>	Defines a cell within a row in a table. Must appear between the <tr> elements.
<textarea>	standard cols* rows* disabled name readonly	<textarea rows="3" cols="20"> Text to go in here… </textarea>	Allows multiple lines of text input in a form.
<title>	dir id lang style	<title>My web page</title>	Defines a title that is displayed in the title bar of the browser. Must be used in the <head> element.
<ul>	standard	<ol> <li>First item</li> <li>Second item</li> </ol>	Specifies an unordered, or bullet-point, list.

* Indicates a required attribute

CSS reference

Property	Values	Example	Description
Font			
font-family	any font family name	p {font-family: sans-serif, Arial, Helvetica}	Sets the typeface for the font.
font-size	number xx-small x-small small medium large x-large xx-large	h1 {font-size: x-large} p {font-size: 12pt} strong {font-size: larger}	Sets the size of a font either as point size or relative to general body text.
font-style	normal italic oblique	h1 {font-style: oblique}	Sets three style types: normal, italic or oblique (slanted).
font-variant	normal small-caps	h2 {font-variant: small-caps}	Allows the font to be set to small caps.
font-weight	normal bold bolder lighter 100-900	h1 {font-weight: 800} h2 {font-weight: lighter}	Sets the boldness of a font (note: not all font-families have nine weights).
font	font-style font-variant font-weight font-size line-height font-family	p {font: italic bold 12pt Times, serif}	Short hand for the various font declarations.

Property	Values	Example	Description
Text			
letter-spacing	normal number	h1 {letter spacing: 0.2em}	Sets additional spacing between words in either absolute (pt, cm, etc.) or relative (em, px) values.
line-height	normal number	p {line-height: 150%}	Controls baseline spacing between lines of text as percentages, absolute (pt, cm, etc.) or relative (em, px) values.
text-align	center justify left right	h1 {text-align: center} p {text-align: justify}	Aligns text in a block element.
text-decoration	none blink line-through overline underline	a:link {text-decoration: none} .deltext {text-decoration: line-through}	Applies a number of modified styles to text.
text-indentation	number	p {text-indentation: 5em}	Sets an indent to text as percentages, absolute (pt, cm, etc.) or relative (em, px) values.
text-transform	none capitalise lowercase uppercase	h2 {text-transform: uppercase}	Capitalises (or removes capitalisation) from text.
vertical-align	baseline bottom middle sub super text-bottom text-top top	.exponent {vertical-align: super} img.topalign {vertical-align: top}	Aligns text to other elements, such as neighbouring text or images.
word-spacing	normal number	p {word-spacing: 0.5em}	Sets additional spacing between words in either absolute (pt, cm, etc.) or relative (em, px) values.

Property	Values	Example	Description
Colour and background			
color	any colour	h1 {color: red} h2 {color: #ef3232}	Sets colour for elements as either a named colour or hexadecimal values for red, green and blue.
background-attachment	fixed scroll	body {background-image: url(/images/pic.gif); background-attachment: fixed }	Determines whether a background image scrolls or is fixed in position relative to the page.
background-color	any colour transparent	body {background-colour: blue}	Sets colour for background of element such as the page or a table.
background-image	none url	body {background-image: url(/images/pic.gif)}	Sets a background image for an element.
background-position	number bottom center left right top	body {background-image: url(/images/pic.gif); background-position: bottom right}	Sets the initial position for a background image as percentages, absolute (pt, cm, etc.) or relative (em, px) values.
background-repeat	no-repeat repeat repeat-x repeat-y	body {background-image: url(/images/pic.gif); background-repeat: repeat-y}	Defines whether a background image is repeated, either across the entire page or just the x or y axes.
background	background-color background-image background-attachment background-position background-repeat	body {background: url(/images/pic.gif) #f0f8ff fixed }	Shorthand for the various background declarations.
Border			
border-color	any colour	table {border-color: #34e5f5}	Sets the colour of a border as a named or hexadecimal value.
border-style	dashed dotted double groove inset none outset ridge solid	table {border-style: groove}	Sets a style for a border and must be specified if a visible border is to appear around an element.

Property	Values	Example	Description
border-width	medium number thick thin	table {border-width: thin medium thick}	Sets the width for a border using between 1 and 4 values (for top, right, bottom and left borders).
bottom-border	border-bottom-width border-style color	table {bottom-border: thin dashed red}	Shorthand for the various bottom border declarations.
left-border	border-left-width border-style color	table {border-left: thick inset blue}	Shorthand for the various left border declarations.
right-border	border-right-width border-style color	table {border-right: thin solid black}	Shorthand for the various right border declarations.
top-border	border-top-width border-style color	table {top-border: thin dashed red}	Shorthand for the various top border declarations.
bottom-border-width	medium number thick thin	table {bottom-border-width: thick}	Sets the width of the bottom border only.
left-border-width	medium number thick thin	table {left-border-width: medium}	Sets the width of the left border only.
right-border-width	medium number thick thin	table {right-border-width: 10px}	Sets the width of the right border only.
top-border-width	medium number thick thin	table {top-border-width: medium}	Sets the width of the top border only.
border	border-style border-width color	table {border: thick double red}	Shorthand for the various border declarations.

Property	Values	Example	Description
Margin			
margin-bottom	auto number	table {margin-bottom: 2em}	Sets the width of the margin at the bottom of an element.
margin-left	auto number	table {margin-left: 5px}	Sets the width of the margin at the left of an element.
margin-right	auto number	table {margin-right: 3cm}	Sets the width of the margin at the right of an element.
margin-top	auto number	table {margin-top: 10%}	Sets the width of the margin at the top of an element.
margin	auto number	body {margin: 10% 5% 20% 7%}	Shorthand for the various margin widths using between 1 and 4 values (for top, right, bottom and left margins).
Padding			
padding-bottom	number	table {padding-bottom: 2em}	Sets the width of padding at the bottom of an element.
padding-left	number	table {padding-left: 5px}	Sets the width of padding at the left of an element.
padding-right	number	table {padding-bottom: 3cm}	Sets the width of padding at the right of an element.
padding-top	number	table {padding-bottom: 10%}	Sets the width of padding at the top of an element.
padding	number	body {padding: 10% 5% 20% 7%}	Sets padding for all sides of an element using between 1 and 4 values (for top, right, bottom and left sides).

Glossary

ActionScript   The programming language used in Flash to add interactivity.

ActiveX   A set of instructions devised by Microsoft that describe how objects interact with the browser and operating system.

Ajax   Asynchronous JavaScript and XML, a term used to refer to web development technologies (that may, ironically, involve neither JavaScript nor XML) to create interactive and media rich websites.

Apache   A popular web server used on a wide range of operating systems.

API   Application programming interface, a set of tools including libraries of code, functions and methods, that are used to provide access to data and build plug-ins for websites.

applet   A program designed to be launched from within another program, typically a browser.

AVI   Audio visual interleave, a video encoding format developed by Microsoft and commonly found online.

bitmap   A photographic image.

blog   Contraction of weblog, originally an online diary but now a means of rapid online publishing.

CGI   Common gateway interface, a protocol enabling web pages to transfer instructions to a server.

client-server   A means of connecting computers whereby the server provides information that is accessed via the remote machine (client).

CMS   Content management system, a piece of software designed to handle multiple users and allow them to publish information online.

cookie   A text message sent from a server to a browser and then returned to the server when a user revisits the site. Cookies are generally used to identify users and store information between visits or generate statistics.

CSS   Cascading style sheets, the main means by which design elements such as text formatting, colour and positioning of elements is controlled on a web page.

DAM   Digital asset management, a blanket term referring to the processes involved in cataloguing, restoring and retrieving files such as images, video and music.

DHTML   Dynamic HTML, sometimes used to refer to the ways in which CSS and scripting are employed to create more interactive pages.

DOM   Document object model, an API for HTML and XML documents which defines the logical structure of a page and how different elements interact with each other.

DRM   Digital rights management, a range of technologies used to control access to content and media, detailing what can and cannot be done with such content.

DTD   Document type declaration, an instruction at the beginning of an SGML document (such as XML or HTML) that describes the rules for such things as its syntax and well-formed structure.

ECMAscript   A standard scripting language that forms the basis for JavaScript and ActionScript among others.

EOT   Embedded OpenType, a format for downloadable fonts that can be included in web pages.

FAQ   Frequently asked questions, a document designed to answer common queries and help new users.

firewall   Hardware or software designed to prevent unauthorised access to a network.

FLV   Flash video, a video compression format commonly found online.

folksonomy or social tagging   A means of organising information that is bottom-up rather than top-down, as in more traditional taxonomies such as directories.

FTP   File transfer protocol, one of the main sets of rules governing the transfer of information across the internet.

GIF   Graphic interchange format, an image format that uses 'lossless' compression to make files shorter without losing information. Is restricted to 256 colours, but can also employ animation and transparency.

HTML   Hypertext markup language, the set of formatting commands interpreted by a browser to determine how pages are displayed on the web.

HTTP   Hypertext transfer protocol, the communications protocol used to define how documents link to each other and information is transmitted across the web.

hypertext   The presentation of documents that connect to other files or parts of the same document. Hypermedia is another term for such documents that also make use of images and multimedia elements to create links.

IP   Internet protocol, a series of numbers between 0 and 255 that create a unique address for each device connected to the internet.

ISP   Internet service provider, an intermediary between the internet and end users that provides IP addresses and other services to subscribers.

Java   An object-oriented programming language that has the advantage of running across multiple operating systems by using a 'virtual machine' to interpret the original code on a particular platform.

JavaScript   A scripting language, originally called LiveScript, that adds interactivity to web pages and is run in the client browser.

JPEG   Joint Photographic Experts Group, a standard used to compress images that is 'lossy', meaning that extraneous information is discarded. Can display up to 16.7 million colours and is the most common image format on the web.

LAN   Local area network, a network of computers in a relatively small area, such as an office or building, in contrast to a WAN, or wide area network such as bank networks or the internet.

Linux   A free version of UNIX incorporating software designed to run on the UNIX clone GNU (GNU's not UNIX).

mashup   A web application that combines data from more than one source, for example map data or images from other parts of the web, into one end product.

MIME   Multipurpose internet email extensions, a series of instructions telling clients such as browsers how to interpret different types of file.

MP3 or MPEG3   A highly compressed format for sound that can deliver near CD-quality audio.

MPEG   Motion Pictures Expert Group, a standard for video compression commonly used on the web.

MySQL   Popular database format that is open-source and free.

PDF   Portable document format, a cross-platform file format that allows documents to be exchanged and viewed with their original formatting.

peer-to-peer   In contrast to a client–server network, one that is peer-to-peer (or P2P) has no central server when computers are linked together.

Perl Practical extraction and reporting language, a scripting language commonly used to provide interactivity to web pages.

permalink A link used to refer to a blog or forum entry once it has passed from a front page to an archive.

PHP Originally Personal Home Page tools, now PHP: Hypertext Preprocessor, a programming language run from the server for dynamic websites.

plug-in Software used to extend the capabilities of the browser or another application.

PNG Portable network graphics, a file format for images that combines elements of JPEG and GIF formats, such as support for both high colour definition and transparency.

protocol A rule or set of rules governing how computers and applications connect and communicate with each other.

QuickTime A video format developed by Apple and commonly found online.

RM RealMedia, a video and audio format developed by Real Networks and commonly used for online multimedia.

RSS Really Simple Syndication, a method for distributing updates from websites to readers and other web pages.

scripting A means of extending the interactive capabilities of HTML by processing a series of instructions via scripts.

SGML Standard generalised markup language, the set of formatting instructions from which HTML was developed.

social networking With reference to online sites, a method of connecting users to share messages, files and other data in a decentralised fashion.

social tagging A bottom-up method of organising data. See also folksonomy.

SQL Structured query language, programming language for databases.

SVG Scalable vector graphics, an open-source specification for vector graphics, similar to Flash.

TCP Transfer control protocol, along with IP the standard governing communication between all computers on the internet.

TLD Top level domain, the part of the URL that identifies its type such as .com, .org or .net.

UGC User-generated content, that is material that is uploaded by end users rather than the producer of a website.

URL Uniform resource locator, the address of a web page or document.

Usenet Newsgroup archives which are now incorporated into internet services but were originally text bulletin boards running alongside the original ARPANET.

vector Used to refer to computer-generated drawings (a vector being a line between two points in a particular direction).

W3C The World Wide Web Consortium, a non-governmental organisation responsible for governing standards across the web.

WAN A wide area network distributed over a large geographical area, such as the internet.

Web 2.0 A broad term used to refer to a range of practices, technologies and techniques to simplify publishing by end users.

WEFT web embedding font tool, allows visitors to download and view unusual fonts in web pages.

wiki Named after the rapid bus service at Honolulu International Airport, a wiki is a content management system that allows quick and easy editing of content.

WYSIWYG What you see is what you get, describes editors that provide a visual representation of documents as they are modified.

XHTML An extended version of HTML 4.0 that includes stricter implementations of HTML rules.

XML Extensible markup language, a means of making web documents self-describing so that they can pass data more easily to other sites.

XMLHttpRequest An architecture used to transfer XML and other text data between a web server and a browser.

XSLT Extensible stylesheet language transformations, transforms XML documents into formats that can be read by people.

Resources

WEB 2.0 CONCEPTS AND THEORY

Anderson, C. *The Long Tail: How Endless Choice is Creating Unlimited Demand*. New York: Random House, 2006.

Beck, T. *Web 2.0: User-Generated Content in Online Communities*. Hamburg: Diplomica, 2008.

Cesarez, V., Cripe, B., Sini, J., and Weckerle, P. *Reshaping Your Business with Web 2.0: Using New Social Technologies to Lead Business Transformation*. New York: McGraw-Hill Osborne, 2008.

Coleman, D., and Levine, S. *Collaboration 2.0: Technology and Best Practices for Successful Collaboration in a Web 2.0 World*. Cupertino, CA: Happy About, 2008.

Jones, B. L. *Web 2.0 Heroes: Interviews with 20 Web 2.0 Influencers*. Indianapolis, IN: Wiley Publishing, 2008.

Leadbeater, C. *We-Think: The Power of Mass Creativity*. London: Profile Books, 2008.

Vickery, G., and Wunsch-Vincent, S. *Participative Web and User-Created Content: Web 2.0, Wikis and Social Networking*. Zurich: OECD, 2007.

Vossen, G. *Unleashing Web 2.0: From Concepts to Creativity*. San Francisco: Morgan Kaufmann, 2007.

Weinberger, D. *Everything Is Miscellaneous: The Power of the New Digital Disorder*. New York: Henry Holt, 2008.

Attwell, G., and Elferink, R. *Developing an Architecture of Participation*, project.bazaar.org/wp-content/stall_project_uploads//2007/09/111_final_paper.pdf.

Barnett, A. *The Unifying Theory of Web 2.0*. http://blogs.msdn.com/alexbarn/archive/2006/04/18/578078.aspx.

Bradshaw, P. *A Model for the 21st Century Newsroom*. http://onlinejournalismblog.com/2007/09/17/a-model-for-the-21st-century-newsroom-pt1-the-news-diamond/.

Cohen, M. *Separation: The Web Designer's Dilemma*. http://www.alistapart.com/articles/separationdilemma.

Garrett, J. *Ajax: A New Approach to Web Applications*. http://www.adaptivepath.com/ideas/essays/archives/000385.php.

Helmond, Anne. *How Many Blogs Are There? Is Someone Still Counting?* http://www.blogherald.com/2008/02/11/how-many-blogs-are-there-is-someone-still-counting/

Langley, N. *Web 2.0: What Does It Constitute?* http://blogs.zdnet.com/web2explorer/?p=5

McManus, R. *What Is Web 2.0?* http://blogs.zdnet.com/web2explorer/?p=5

O'Reilly, T. *What Is Web 2.0?* http://www.oreillynet.com/pub/a/oreilly/tim/news/2005/09/30/what-is-web-20.html

Patton, T. *Sifting Through Different Versions of the Web*. http://articles.techrepublic.com.com/5100-10878_11-6142748.html

Web 2.0 Rights Project, www.web2rights.org.uk

Web 2.0 Workgroup, www.web20workgroup.com

WEB DESIGN (GENERAL)

Beaird, J. *The Principles of Beautiful Web Design*. Sebastopol, CA: Sitepoint, 2007.

Chapman, N., and Chapman, J. *Web Design: A Complete Introduction*. Hoboken, NJ: John Wiley and Sons, 2006.

Cooper, A., Reimann, R., and Cronin, D. *About Face 3: The Essentials of Interaction Design*. Indianapolis, IN: Wiley Publishing, 2007.

Grannel, C. *Web Designer's Reference*. Berkeley, CA: Friends of ED, 2004.

McNeil, P. *The Web Designer's Idea Book: The Ultimate Guide to Themes, Trends and Styles in Website Design*. Cincinnati, OH: How, 2008.

Niederst, J., Gustafson, A., Celik, T., and Featherstone, D. *Web Design in a Nutshell*, 3rd edition. Sebastopol, CA: O'Reilly, 2006.

Nielsen, J. *Designing Web Usability: The Practice of Simplicity*. Berkeley, CA: Peachpit Press, 2000.

Nielsen, J., and Loranger, H. *Prioritizing Web Usability*. New York: New Riders, 2006.

Nielsen, J., and Tahir, M. *Homepage Usability: 50 Websites Deconstructed*. New York: New Riders, 2001.

Robbins, J. N., Yvelik, T., Featherstone, D., and Gustafson, A. *Web Design in a Nutshell: A Desktop Quick Reference*. Sebastopol, CA: O'Reilly, 2007.

Rosenfeld, L., and Morville, P. *Information Architecture for the World Wide Web: Designing Large-Scale Web Sites*, 3rd edition. Sebastopol, CA: O'Reilly, 2006.

Sklar, J. *Principles of Web Design*, 4th edition. Florence, KY: Course Technology, 2008.

Tidwell, J. *Designing Interfaces: Patterns for Effective Interaction Design*. Sebastopol, CA: O'Reilly, 2005.

van Duyne, D. K., Landay, J. A., and Hong, J. I. *The Design of Sites: Patterns for Creating Winning Web Sites*. 2nd edition. Upper Saddle River, NJ: Prentice Hall, 2006.

321Webmaster, www.321webmaster.com

Big Webmaster, www.bigwebmaster.com

First Principles of Interaction Design, www.asktog.com/basics/firstPrinciples.html

Google Webmaster Central, www.google.com/webmasters

Jakob Nielson on Usability and Web Design, www.useit.com

The Principles of Design, www.digital-web.com/articles/principles_of_design/

W3Schools, www.w3schools.com

Web Design Library, www.webdesign.org

WebKnowHow, www.webknowhow.net

Webmaster Directory, www.wmdirectory.com

Webmaster Toolkit, www.webmaster-toolkit.com

Webmonkey, www.webmonkey.com

WEB DESIGN (HTML AND CSS)

Andrew, R. *The CSS Anthology: 101 Essential Tips, Tricks and Hacks*. Sebastopol, CA: Sitepoint, 2007.

Bowers, M. *Pro CSS and HTML Design Patterns*. Berkeley, CA: Apress, 2007.

Budd, A., Collison, S., and Moll, C. *CSS Master: Advanced Web Standards Solutions*. Berkeley, CA: Friends of ED, 2006.

Castro, E. *HTML, XHTML, and CSS*. 6th edition. Berkeley, CA: Peachpit Press, 2006.

Collison, S. *Beginning CSS Web Development: From Novice to Professional*. Berkeley, CA: Apress, 2006.

Grannell, C. *The Essential Guide to CSS and HTML Web Design*. Berkeley, CA: Friends of ED, 2007.

Lane, J., Moscovitz, M., and Lewis, J. *Foundation Website Creation with CSS, XHTML, and JavaScript*. Berkeley, CA: Friends of ED, 2008.

Lloyd, I. *Build Your Own Website: The Right Way Using HTML and CSS*. Sebastopol, CA: Sitepoint, 2008.

Lloyd, I. *The Ultimate HTML Reference*. Sebastopol, CA: Sitepoint, 2008.

McFarland, D. *CSS: The Missing Manual*. Sebastopol, CA: Pogue Press, 2006.

Meyer, E. *CSS: The Definitive Guide*. Sebastopol, CA: O'Reilly, 2006.

Musciano, C., and Kennedy, B. *HTML and XHTML: The Definitive Guide*. 6th edition. Sebastopol, CA: O'Reilly, 2006.

Robbins, J. N., and Gustafson, A. *Learning Web Design: A Beginner's Guide to (X)HTML, StyleSheets, and Web Graphics*. Sebastopol, CA: O'Reilly, 2007.

Schultz, D., and Cook, C. *Beginning HTML with CSS and XHTML: Modern Guide and Reference*. Berkeley, CA: Apress, 2007.

Shea, D., and Holzschlag, M. E. *The ZEN of CSS Design: Visual Enlightenment for the Web*. Berkeley, CA: Peachpit Press, 2005.

HTML Source, www.yourhtmlsource.com

HTML Writers Guild, www.hwg.org

Markup Validation Service, validator.w3.org

W3C HTML 4.01 specification, www.w3.org/TR/html4/

W3C XHTML 1.0 specification, /www.w3.org/TR/xhtml1/

W3Schools learn CSS, www.w3schools.com/css/

W3Schools learn XHTML, www.w3schools.com/xhtml/

W3Schools learn XML, www.w3schools.com/xml/
Zen Garden, www.csszengarden.com

PHP, MySQL AND SCRIPTING

Davis, M., and Philips, J. *Learning PHP and MySQL: Step-by-Step Guide to Creating Database-Driven Web Sites*. Sebastopol, CA: O'Reilly, 2007.
DuBois, P. *MySQL Cookbook*. Sebastopol, CA: O'Reilly, 2006.
Flanagan, D. *JavaScript: The Definitive Guide*. Sebastopol, CA: O'Reilly, 2006.
Gilmore, W. J. *Beginning PHP and MySQL: From Novice to Professional*. 3rd edition. Berkeley, CA: Apress, 2008.
Resiq, J. *Pro JavaScript Techniques*. Berkeley, CA: Apress, 2006.
Trachtenberg, A., and Sklar, J. *PHP Cookbook*. Sebastopol, CA: O'Reilly, 2006.
Ullman, L. *PHP 6 and MySQL 5 for Dynamic Web Sites*. Berkeley, CA: Peachpit Press, 2008.
Vaswani, V. *How to Do Everything with PHP and MySQL*. New York: McGraw-Hill Osborne, 2005.
Yank, K. *Build Your Own Database Driven Website Using PHP and MySQL*. Sebastopol, CA: Sitepoint, 2004.

JavaScript Mall, www.javascriptmall.com
JavaScript tutorials, www.yourhtmlsource.com/javascript/
LearnPHP.org, www.learnphp.org
MySQL reference manual, dev.mysql.com/doc/refman/5.0/en/index.html
MySQL tutorial, www.mysqltutorial.org
PHPBuddy, www.phpbuddy.com
PHP beginner tutorial, uk3.php.net/tut.php
Tizag MySQL tutorial, www.tizag.com/mysqlTutorial/
Tizag PHP tutorial, www.tizag.com/phpT/
W3Schools JavaScript tutorial, www.w3schools.com/JS/default.asp
W3Schools PHP tutorial, www.w3schools.com/PHP/

MASHUPS AND APPLICATIONS

Cesar, J. *Building Web 2.0 Business Websites: Business Process Innovation with Web 2.0 Tools, and Joomla!* Levittown, NY: Verticalbit, 2008.
Chow, S. *PHP Web 2.0 Mashup Projects: Practical PHP Mashups with Google Maps, Flickr, Amazon, YouTube, MSN Search, Yahoo!* Birmingham: Packt Publishing, 2007.
Feiler, J. *How to Do Everything with Web 2.0 Mashups*. New York: McGraw-Hill Osborne, 2007.

Hoekman, R. *Designing the Obvious: A Commonsense Approach to Web Application Design*. New York: New Riders, 2006.

Powers, D. *The Essential Guide to Dreamweaver CS4 with CSS, Ajax, and PHP*. Berkeley, CA: Friends of ED, 2008.

Zervaas, Q. *Practical Web 2.0 Applications with PHP*. Berkeley, CA: Apress, 2007.

AlchemyPoint, www.orch8.net/ap/index.html

Dapper, www.dapper.net

Google apps and APIs, code.google.com

KickApps, www.kickapps.com

LiquidApps, liquidappsworld.com

Mashup Station, www.mashupstation.com

Microsoft Popfly, www.popfly.com

Openkapow, www.openkapow.com

Open Mashups Studio, www.open-mashups.org

SpringWidgets, www.springwidgets.com

Widgetbox, www.widgetbox.com

Widgipedia, www.widgipedia.com

Yahoo Pipes, pipes.yahoo.com

MULTIMEDIA

Aaland, M. *Photoshop for the Web*. Sebastopol, CA: O'Reilly, 2002.

Bourne, J., and Burstein, D. *Web Video: Making It Great, Getting It Noticed*. Berkeley, CA: Peachpit Press, 2008.

Cope, P. *Web Photoshop*. Lewes: Ilex, 2003.

Curtis, H. *Hillman Curtis on Creating Short Films for the Web*. Berkeley, CA: New Riders, 2005.

Farkas, B. G. *Secrets of Podcasting: Audio Blogging for the Masses*. Berkeley, CA: Peachpit Press, 2006.

Golbeck, J. *Art Theory for Web Design*. London: Addison Wesley, 2008.

Grover, C., and Vander Veer, E. *Flash CS3: The Missing Manual*. Sebastopol, CA: Pogue Press, 2007.

Haffly, C. *The Photoshop Anthology: 101 Web Design Tips, Tricks and Technology*. Sebastopol, CA: Sitepoint, 2006.

Kentie, P. *Web Graphics Tools and Techniques*. Berkeley, CA: Peachpit Press, 2001.

McIntyre, P. *Visual Design for the Modern Web*. Berkeley, CA: New Riders, 2007.

Reinhardt, R., and Dowd, S. *Adobe Flash CS3 Professional Bible*. Hoboken, NJ: Wiley Publishing, 2007.

Shupe, R., and Rosser, Z. *Learning ActionScript 3.0*. San José, CA: Adobe, 2007.

Verdi, M., Hodson, R., Weynand, D., and Craig, S. *Secrets of Video Blogging*. Berkeley, CA: Peachpit Press, 2006.

Wells, P. *Digital Video Editing: A User's Guide*. Marlborough: Crowood Press, 2007.

Audacity, audacity.sourceforge.net
FotoFlexer, fotoflexer.com
Media Convert, media-convert.com
Online image editor, www.imageeditor.net
Onlinephototool, www.onlinephototool.com
Pixlr, www.pixlr.com
Sound editor software, sound-editor.qarchive.org
Splashup, www.splashup.com
Zamzar, www.zamzar.com

Index

Related titles from Routledge

Broadcast Journalism

Edited by Jane Chapman and Marie Kinsey

Broadcast Journalism offers a critical analysis of the key skills required to work in the modern studio, on location, or online, with chapters written by industry professionals from the BBC, ITV, CNN and independent production companies in the UK and US. Areas highlighted include:

- interviewing,
- researching,
- editing,
- writing, and
- reporting.

The practical tips are balanced with chapters on representation, ethics, law, economics and history, as well as specialist areas such as documentary and the reporting of politics, business, sport and celebrity.

Broadcast Journalism concludes with a vital chapter on career planning to act as a springboard for your future work in the broadcast industry.

Contributors: Jim Beaman, Jane Chapman, Fiona Chesterton, Tim Crook, Anne Dawson, Tony Harcup, Jackie Harrison, Ansgard Heinrich, Emma Hemmingway, Patricia Holland, David Holmes, Gary Hudson, Nicholas Jones, Marie Kinsey, Roger Laughton, Leslie Mitchell, Jeremy Orlebar, Claire Simmons, Katie Stewart, Ingrid Volkmer, Mike Ward, Deborah Wilson

ISBN13: 978-0-415-44154-4 (hbk)
ISBN13: 978-0-415-44155-1 (pbk)
ISBN13: 978-0-203-88645-8 (ebk)

Available at all good bookshops
For ordering and further information please visit:
www.routledge.com

Related titles from Routledge

Writing for Journalists
2nd edition

Wynford Hicks with Sally Adams, Harriet Gilbert and Tim Holmes

Writing for Journalists is about the craft of journalistic writing: how to put one word after another so that the reader gets the message – or the joke – goes on reading and comes back for more. It is a practical guide for all those who write for newspapers, periodicals and websites, whether students, trainees or professionals.

Writing for Journalists introduces the reader to the essentials of good writing. Based on critical analysis of news stories, features and reviews from daily and weekly papers, consumer magazines, specialist trade journals and a variety of websites, *Writing for Journalists* includes:

- advice on how to start writing and how to improve and develop your style,
- how to write a news story which is informative, concise and readable,
- tips on feature writing, from researching profiles to writing product round-ups,
- how to structure and write reviews,
- a new chapter on writing online copy, and
- a glossary of journalistic terms and suggestions for further reading.

ISBN13: 978-0-415-46020-0 (hbk)
ISBN13: 978-0-415-46021-7 (pbk)
ISBN13: 978-0-203-92710-6 (ebk)

Available at all good bookshops
For ordering and further information please visit:
www.routledge.com

Related titles from Routledge

The New Media Handbook

Andrew Dewdney and Peter Ride

The New Media Handbook deals with the essential diversity of new media by combining critical commentary and descriptive and historical accounts with a series of edited interviews with new media practitioners, including young web developers, programmers, artists, writers and producers.

The book provides an understanding of the historical and theoretical development of new media, emphasising the complex continuities in the technological developments associated with particular cultural uses of media, rather than understanding new media as replacing or breaking what has gone before.

Also, there is a focus upon the key concerns of practitioners and how they create their work and develop their projects – from artists to industry professionals, web designers to computer programmers. It includes a discussion of key concepts such as digital code, information, convergence, interactivity and interface and, finally, identifies key debates and locates the place of new media practice within contemporary culture.

The New Media Handbook includes:

- interviews with new media practitioners,
- case studies, examples and illustrations,
- a glossary of technical acronyms and key terms, and
- a bibliography and list of web resources.

ISBN13: 978-0-415-30711-6 (hbk)
ISBN13: 978-0-415-30712-3 (pbk)
ISBN13: 978-0-203-64578-9 (ebk)

Available at all good bookshops
For ordering and further information please visit:
www.routledge.com